RICHARD III
The Great Debate

RICHARD III
The Great Debate

Sir Thomas More's
HISTORY OF KING RICHARD III

Horace Walpole's
HISTORIC DOUBTS ON THE LIFE
AND REIGN OF KING RICHARD III

Edited with Introductions by Paul Murray Kendall

W · W · NORTON & COMPANY

New York · London

First published as a Norton paperback 1965; reissued 1992

ISBN 0–393–00310–8

W. W. Norton & Company, Inc.
500 Fifth Avenue, New York, N. Y. 10110
W. W. Norton & Company Ltd
10 Coptic Street, London WC1A 1PU

PRINTED IN THE UNITED STATES OF AMERICA

CONTENTS

GENERAL INTRODUCTION

Was Richard the Third as black as Shakespeare painted him? Did he drive a dagger into hapless Henry VI and into Henry's young son Prince Edward, do down his brother Clarence even as he pretended to plead for him, murder the two sons of his brother Edward IV, poison his wife Anne, and commit numerous other villainies? Or was he a goodly king who became a tragic victim of history when his reputation fell into the hands of his enemies?

For three-and-a-half centuries the Great Debate has raged, while larger issues and bloodier questions fell into oblivion. Religious change, civil strife, the Industrial Revolution, and two world wars have thrust the fifteenth century into a remote antiquity; yet passions flare and people rush into print at the mere mention of 'the little princes in the Tower'.

Beefeaters continue to point out the very spot where Richard's minions smothered the princes, but on August 22, the anniversary of Bosworth Field, obituary notices in *The Times*, of London and New York, memorialize a 'much defamed King'. From Land's End to Berwick-on-Tweed, the Fellowship of the White Boar propagate Richard's cause, while in the United States—which, along with the language, the common law, and freedom of speech, inherited the Great Debate—the Friends of Richard III, Inc., tend the flame.

Saint Thomas More began it, with a *History* which became the meat on which Shakespeare's *Richard the Third* fed. Two-and-a-half centuries later, Horace Walpole resoundingly challenged the high authority of Thomas More. This first publication of More's *History of King Richard the Third* in modern English and first reprinting of Walpole's *Historic Doubts* since the early nineteenth century bring together the original antagonists of the Great Debate.

Why has so much ink been shed, such a wealth of feeling expended, over the disappearance of the princes and the character of King Richard? For one thing, since precisely what happened to the sons of Edward IV will probably never be known and since no human being could be as villainous as Richard has been portrayed, the 'mystery' offers a tempting prospect for lovers of puzzles and of unpopular causes. For another, the refusal of historians, over the centuries, to admit obvious weaknesses in the Tudor tradition has stimulated the romantically inclined to take arms against a 'conspiracy' of falsification.

The cast of characters has no doubt also contributed to the longevity of the Great Debate:

Richard himself, the only monster (or the noblest victim) to wear the English crown, the only King to die in battle (if we except Richard Lionheart, mortally wounded in a small siege operation), the last of the fierce, valiant, and, on the whole, remarkably able Plantagenet line;

The 'little princes'—winningly portrayed by Shakespeare as quick-witted precocious lads, affectingly painted by Victorian artists as delicate highborn lambs—done to death, as in a fairytale, by the Wicked Uncle;

A pair of arch-plotters, Margaret, Countess of Richmond, mother of Henry Tudor, the bluestocking who after weaving the ladder by which her son climbed to a kingdom did much for the advancement of learning in the realm, and John Morton, Bishop of Ely, the indefatigable intriguer who duped Buckingham, prompted conspiracies against Richard, and ended as Cardinal, Archbishop of Canterbury, and Chancellor, much hated;

And finally Henry Tudor, an enigma in himself, master of devious stratagems and dark manoeuvres, a Welsh Louis XI marvellously preserved for us in his portrait, where, with tough and quizzical gaze, he seemingly dares the artist to catch him on canvas if he can.

The fight to rescue Richard from Shakespeare and the Tudor historians offers, furthermore, the appeals of supporting the underdog, standing by a lost cause, realizing oneself to be a vessel of esoteric truth, and cocking a snook at Authority. Like the King over the Water, the King under a Cloud has stirred romantic sentiments and genuine, if sometimes uncritical, devotion.

On the other side, the traditional view is hallowed by two of the three greatest figures of the English Renaissance, Saint Thomas More and William Shakespeare, while the third, Francis Bacon, composed an admiring biography of the Tudor who defeated Richard III at Bosworth; and from the seventeenth century to the end of the First World War, the most eminent historians of the English Middle Ages firmly repeated the tale of usurping Richard's villainy.

What has been variously called by recent scholars this Tudor verdict, or tradition, or myth, sprang from two historical works which were composed in the second decade of the sixteenth century: More's *History of King Richard III*, first appearing in 1543 as a continuation of Hardyng's *Chronicle*, and Polydore Vergil's *Anglica Historia*, published in 1543 (in the version ending at 1485). While More supplied the substance and tone of Richard's portrait, Vergil created a moral-theological pattern to explain the Wars of the Roses. The portrait and the pattern were fused in the *Chronicle* of Edward Hall (1548), M.P., judge, and ardently loyal subject of Henry VIII.

Following Vergil, the history of England from 1399 to 1485 is invested with a portentous significance: the deposition and murder of Richard II (1399), fracturing the divinely appointed order of society, generates a bitter civil strife, the wars of Lancaster and York, from which emerges the epitome of evil, Richard, Duke of Gloucester, who, after he has served as God's scourge, is cut down by God's knight, Henry Tudor; and the marriage of Henry and Edward IV's daughter Elizabeth unites the Red Rose and the White and restores divine concord to England. The atmosphere is heavy with the beating wings of chickens coming home to roost; and More's creation of the arch-villain Richard, deformed

[7]

of body and of soul, is matched by Hall's portrait of the all-white Henry VII—his marriage to Elizabeth is compared to the union of godhead and manhood in Christ.

It is Hall's fervid work, via Holinshed's *Chronicle* (in the second edition of 1587), that William Shakespeare exuberantly dramatized in his *Richard the Third* (about 1593). The youthful playwright zestfully exploited ironic nemesis by curses, prophecies, and dreams, and seized on Marlowe's technique of shaping a play around a superman of evil—*Tamburlaine, The Jew of Malta*—to create the world's most popular melodramatic tragedy. While the Tudor chroniclers made up the minds of subsequent historians about Richard III, Shakespeare has made up the imagination of everybody else.

Yet, by the time Elizabeth I died in 1603, a short rebuttal of this view, probably written by Sir William Cornwallis the Younger, was already circulating in manuscript: *A Brief Discourse in Praise of King Richard the Third: or an Apology against the Malicious Slanders and Accusations of his Detracting Adversaries.* When published (1616), however, the work was prudently issued in a collection of *Essays of Certain Paradoxes*, which include the praises of French Pocks, debt, and Julian the Apostate, and ends its defence with the phrase, 'Yet, for all this, know I hold this but as a Paradox.'

A few years later, Sir George Buc, Master of the Revels to James I, composed the first full-scale attack on the Tudor tradition, a *History of the Life and Reign of Richard the Third*, published in 1646 and reprinted in White Kennett's *Complete History of England*, 1719. For all his Yorkist partisanship—his great-grandfather had fought for King Richard at Bosworth and was executed by Henry VII— Buc was a friend of the best antiquaries of the day, John Stow, William Camden, and Sir Robert Cotton; he conscientiously searched old records, and was the first to make use of the late fifteenth-century 'Second Continuation' of the *Croyland Chronicle*, a source of great importance, in attempting to discredit More's *History*. Sir George writes, however, in the most tiresome of seventeenth-century styles, at once cumbersome and capricious, and he is driven, like Cornwallis, to dispose of the Tudor tradition by dismissing its charges as improbabilities or justifying them on the basis of *raison d'État*.

But the rehabilitation of Richard III had been set in motion. A generation after, in *England's Worthies* (1684), William Winstanley declared, 'But as Honour is always attended on by Envy, so hath this worthy Prince's fame been blasted by malicious traducers, who like Shakespeare in his Play of him, render him dreadfully black in his actions, a monster of nature, rather than a man of admirable parts. . . .'

Almost a century later, that prince of dilettantes, Horace Walpole, stimulated by the discovery of what he took to be new evidence of Richard's victimization, published *Historic Doubts on the Life and Reign of Richard III* (1768). Replies by scholars and Walpole's rejoinders further stirred public interest. *Historic Doubts* has obvious weaknesses, as we shall see, but it mounts the first really telling attack upon the picture of Richard III created by More and dramatized by Shakespeare; and thus, in drawing the fire of the 'traditionalists' and providing support for subsequent 'revisionists', establishes the battle-line of the Great Debate.

In the nineteenth century, while historians, generation unto generation, reaffirmed the traditional view, the defence of King Richard achieved something of the dimensions of a Cause.

Caroline Halstead's *Life of Richard III*, 2 vols, 1844, written in the vein of the Victorian gift-book, presents a figure resembling one of the nobler characters in the *Idylls of the King*, though it must be added that Miss Halstead industriously dug into, and printed selections from, important documentary materials like Harleian MS. 433, Richard's docket-book of grants and official correspondence. It is pleasant to report that the romance of her hero's life touched her own: she married the rector of the church of Middleham, Yorkshire, once the collegiate establishment of Richard III. A generation later, Alfred O. Legge composed *The Unpopular King*,

2 vols, 1885, which elaborates Walpole's arguments and suggests that Buckingham, Catesby, and Ratcliffe made away with the princes without Richard's knowledge.

Finally, traditionalist and revisionist collided head-on in the scholarly pages of the *English Historical Review*, VI (1891). Sir Clements R. Markham's 'Richard III: A Doubtful Verdict Reviewed', an ardent defence of Richard, was attacked by James Gairdner, most eminent of fifteenth-century scholars, in his equally ardent 'Did Henry VII Murder the Princes?'; Markham produced a rejoinder, 'Richard III and Henry VII', to which Gairdner made a brief final reply.

In 1906 Sir Clements Markham elaborated his arguments in *Richard III: His Life and Character*, a book which has little to do with either subject: it is almost entirely devoted to clearing Richard of all crimes and fastening the guilt for the death of the princes on Henry VII. Markham's white and black are as intense as those of the Tudor tradition, only reversed. The Lancastrians are a pack of rascals; John Morton, who, Markham insists, wrote More's work, is a 'treble-dyed traitor and falsifier of history', while Richard emerges as a sterling symbol of 'English pluck'. The case which Markham builds against a villainous Henry VII as murderer of the princes, unconvincing in itself, became outmoded with the exhumation of the skeletons in Westminster Abbey in 1933.

Meanwhile Gairdner, issuing in 1898 a revised edition of his *History of the Life and Reign of Richard III* (1878), was forced to modify parts of the Tudor verdict no longer tenable but clung fiercely to the substance of the tradition, buttressing his arguments by Victorian moralizing.

In our own century Philip Lindsay continued the revisionist attack in *King Richard III* (1933), mainly an emphatic restatement of Markham's arguments; a few years ago Josephine Tey created an ingenious detective story, *The Daughter of Time*, which likewise unravels the mystery of the princes' death in Markham's terms; and historical fiction and forensic tract have also kept warm the cause (for example, V. B. Lamb, *The Betrayal of Richard III*, 1959).

It is perhaps well to note here that the Great Debate has always been waged between amateurs and professionals—scholars imperturbably holding ranks against the irregular sallies of guerillas. However, if, on the one hand, the revisionists have been much too ready to build on flimsy evidence or flat assertion, the traditionalists proved less than willing to acknowledge undoubted errors and violent distortions in More and Shakespeare. Furthermore, controversy over the 'mystery' was concentrated on pushing back and forth all-white and all-black counters labelled *Richard*, instead of attempting to uncover the lineaments of the man and to explore the accomplishments of the ruler.

Meanwhile, beginning with the 1930s the Great Debate took a new turn, in consequence of two important discoveries and of the increasingly rigorous objectivity of historical writing.

In 1933 a medical and a dental authority examined two skeletons which had come to light in 1674 during the excavation of a staircase outside the White Tower and which, by command of Charles II, had been inurned in Westminster Abbey. According to the physiological evidence, the skeletons appear to be the remains of two boys about the ages of Edward V (12) and his brother Richard (10) in the summer of 1483; and if the bones are indeed relics of the fifteenth century, as seems likely, rather than of an earlier age, there remains little question that the princes were killed between Richard's coronation on July 6 and the outbreak of Buckingham's Rebellion in October.

Three years after this exhumation there was published Dominic Mancini's *Usurpation of Richard III*, translated from the Latin and edited by C. A. J. Armstrong, who had discovered the manuscript on the Continent. This exciting document, composed in December of 1483 by an Italian humanist who had witnessed in London the critical events of May–June and left England a few days before Richard's coronation, supplies invaluable fresh details of fact and characterization, though it throws but little light on the disappearance of the princes and is by no means free of error.

Since the Second World War scholars have withdrawn from the Great Debate. Discarding once for all the Tudor tradition and basing their researches on fifteenth-century sources, they have worked to illuminate the complex character and the strangely flawed career of a man who was successively a loyal brother, usurping uncle, and able King.

The distance which historians have travelled in this century can be measured in contrasting quotations from James Gairdner's *Life*, and E. F. Jacob's *The Fifteenth Century*, Oxford History of England Series, 1961.

Gairdner: '. . . a minute study of the facts of Richard's life has tended more and more to convince me of the general fidelity of the portrait with which we have been made familiar by Shakespeare and Sir Thomas More'. (What is amazing is that Gairdner could regard Shakespeare's magnificent monster as the portrait of a human being.)

Jacob: 'That there was a sound constructive side to Richard III is undoubted. He was very far from being the distorted villain of tradition.'

As for the murder of the princes, whether Richard himself appointed agents to commit the deed, or whether, even, the Duke of Buckingham perpetrated the crime to embarrass the King and further his own chances, the usurpation of the throne inevitably led to the extinction of the dethroned Edward V and his brother— as deposition had led to the violent deaths of Edward II, Richard II, and Henry VI—and for this, Richard III must be held responsible.

But if scholars have reached general agreement, the Wicked Uncle still lives in guide-books and school texts, while the Faultless King and Martyr is still revered by devotees of the White Boar.

In order that the reader may compare More's *History* and Walpole's refutation with the established facts, the following is a brief outline of the chief events of Richard's life.

On March 4, 1461, the Earl of March, handsome 19-year-old heir of Richard, Duke of York, recently killed in battle, was proclaimed King Edward the Fourth in the city of London. Within a month, he and his mentor, Richard, Earl of Warwick, 'the Kingmaker', had crushed the House of Lancaster at the Battle of Towton (March 29) and forced King Henry VI and Queen Margaret and their son, Prince Edward, to flee into Scotland.

Thus was concluded, for a decade, the civil strife which had begun with the marriage, in 1445, of pious ineffectual King Henry and passionately imperious Margaret of Anjou, niece of Charles VII of France, and which had moved to open warfare ten years later when at St Albans the lords supporting Richard, Duke of York, in his campaign for reform of the government and suppression of baronial turbulence had defeated and killed several great nobles supporting the crown, the Lancastrians. The quarrel between York and Lancaster was exacerbated by the fact that the Duke of York, descended on his mother's side from Lionel of Clarence, second son of Edward III, could be considered to have a better claim to the throne than Henry VI, great-grandson of John of Gaunt, Duke of Lancaster, the fourth son.

For a few years Edward IV, intelligent but pleasure-loving, seemed content to let the Earl of Warwick dominate his government; but in September of 1464, even as the Kingmaker was preparing to cross the Channel and meet King Louis XI of France in order to secure a peace-treaty for England and a bride—Bona of Savoy—for his master, Edward suddenly announced that he was already married: on May 1 he had secretly wedded Elizabeth Woodville, beautiful widowed daughter of Lord Rivers and the mother of two sons.

This marriage was the beginning, but not the final cause, as More writes, of the rupture between the King and the Kingmaker.

For several years more Warwick struggled to maintain his preeminence, continuing to advocate an alliance with Louis XI who had artfully won his confidence. As the numerous and ambitious Woodvilles gobbled up offices, honours, and lands, the embittered Earl, in turn, though he failed to suborn the King's youngest brother Richard, Duke of Gloucester (born 1452), succeeded in 'drawing over' George, Duke of Clarence, three years older.

Marrying Clarence to his elder daughter Isabel, Warwick, in the summer of 1469, provoked a rising against his erstwhile *protégé* and ended by capturing the King; but with the realm falling into anarchy, Edward adroitly succeeded in regaining his freedom and his power. There followed in the next two years a violent and bizarre welter of events.

In the spring of 1470 Warwick and Clarence were driven from the realm, only to ally themselves in France with Margaret of Anjou and, with aid furnished by Louis XI, to return to England in September, force Edward IV to flee to his brother-in-law the Duke of Burgundy, and set upon the throne dim-witted Henry VI (captured in the North in 1465 and since imprisoned in the Tower).

In his turn, Edward IV recrossed the Channel in mid-March of 1471. Within three months, he had defeated and killed Warwick at the Battle of Barnet (April 14)—the very day on which Margaret of Anjou and her son, Prince Edward, now married to Warwick's younger daughter Anne, landed in England —and crushed Queen Margaret's Lancastrians at Tewkesbury (May 4), Prince Edward perishing in the battle. George, Duke of Clarence, had deserted Warwick to rejoin his brother Edward before Barnet was fought; Richard, Duke of Gloucester, aged 19, who had accompanied King Edward on his flight to the Low Countries, so distinguished himself in commanding the right wing at Barnet and the left wing at Tewkesbury that Edward made him Constable of England.

On May 21 the victorious Yorkists returned to London. A few

[14]

hours later Henry VI was put to death in the Tower, to which he had been consigned when Edward entered the city just before Barnet. There is no reason to doubt that the killing was ordered by the King and his council, and supervised, under royal command, by the Constable, Richard of Gloucester. Apparently, the House of Lancaster was wiped out.

For the remaining twelve years of his reign Edward IV, beloved by most of his subjects, kept a sure grip upon his kingdom. The Duke of Clarence, feckless and perpetually discontented, hated by Queen Elizabeth and her kin, was, in 1478, condemned to death on a charge of treason by the peers of Parliament and, though his brother Richard pleaded for his life, executed privately in the Tower. Unlikely though his demise in a butt of Malmsey seems, all contemporary reports which specify the mode of death describe it in such terms.

While Richard of Gloucester, now chief prop of his brother's throne, kept himself far from the intrigues of court, the Queen, her eldest brother Anthony, Earl Rivers, and her two sons by her first marriage, the Marquess Dorset and Lord Richard Grey, engaged in a bitter feud with the King's closest intimate and Lord Chamberlain, William, Lord Hastings. Just before he died (April 9, 1483), Edward IV, fearful for the future, succeeded in securing a hollow show of reconciliation between Hastings and the Woodvilles.

It is at this point that More's *History* begins. Shakespeare's *Henry VI*, Parts I, II, and III, cover the years from the death of Henry V, 1422, to the murder of Henry VI, 1471. *Richard the Third* compresses in a single play events between 1471 and Bosworth Field, 1485. *Henry VI*, Part III depicts Richard, Duke of Gloucester, taking a fearsome part in battles which were fought when, in fact, he had not reached the age of 9, and soliloquizing on his determination to 'set the murderous Machiavel to school' in order to win the crown, in 1464, when he was 12.

The grasping Queen and her kindred, unpopular with nobles

[15]

and commons alike, manoeuvred to crown young Edward V immediately in order to forestall the protectorship Edward IV had designed for his brother Richard, Duke of Gloucester. However, the Duke, then in Yorkshire, was able, with the support of Henry, Duke of Buckingham, and Lord Hastings, to intercept Edward's journey to London. Arresting the Queen's brother Anthony, Earl Rivers, her younger son Richard, Lord Grey, and Sir Thomas Vaughan, the Dukes of Gloucester and Buckingham assumed charge of the King at Stony Stratford, as More recounts, and brought him on May 4 to London. Richard was at once acknowledged as Protector and Defensor of the realm and organized a government.

The intricate interplay of forces—including counter-moves by the Woodvilles, in sanctuary—which then pushed the Protector to reach for the throne is still by no means clear, but the outward stages can be easily tabulated:

After May 4: Plans are set on foot for the crowning of the King in late June.

June 10: Richard dispatches to the city of York an appeal for aid against the Woodvilles, who, he declares, are conspiring to destroy the Duke of Buckingham and himself.

June 13: At a council meeting in the Tower the Protector seizes and immediately executes Lord Hastings, who, discontented with his share of authority, was probably plotting with the Woodvilles to gain control of the King.

June 16: Under pressure, Queen Elizabeth permits the King's brother Richard, Duke of York, to be removed from sanctuary and quartered with the King in the Tower, then a royal dwelling.

Probably mid-June: John Stillington, Bishop of Bath and Wells, declares to the Protector that Edward IV had been precontracted to Lady Eleanor Butler and that, under the laws of the Church, his marriage to Elizabeth Woodville is invalid and his issue are illegitimate.

June 22: In a sermon at Paul's Cross, Dr Ralph Shaa announces the invalidity of Edward IV's marriage and proclaims the true title of the Protector to the throne.

June 25: A quasi-Parliament of Lords and Commons petitions the Protector, on the basis of Edward V's illegitimacy, to assume the crown as rightful King.

June 26: In response to the petition, Richard seats himself upon the King's Bench of Justice in Westminster Hall and from this day dates his reign.

Following his coronation on July 6, notable for its splendour and the number of peers present, King Richard went a progress into Yorkshire; while his chief adherent, the Duke of Buckingham, returned to his castle at Brecon in Wales. Here Buckingham fell under the spell of John Morton, Bishop of Ely, arrested during the *coup* of June 13 and sent prisoner to Brecon. It is at this moment that More's *History* abruptly breaks off.

At the same time, rumours of the princes' murder, which had been whispered even before Richard's coronation, were beginning to agitate the adherents of the Woodvilles in southern England. The Juno of the developing conspiracy, Margaret, Countess of Richmond—whose third husband Thomas, Lord Stanley, was the Steward of King Richard's household—was in touch with Buckingham and Morton, with Queen Elizabeth, still in sanctuary, and with her son by her first marriage, Henry Tudor, who had escaped to Brittany after Edward IV's return in 1471.

Henry was the last hope of Lancaster but his claim to the throne was devious and flawed: his father, Edmund Tudor, Earl of Richmond, was the issue of a liaison, perhaps a marriage, between Owen Tudor, a Welsh gentleman, and Henry V's widow, Katherine of France; on his mother's side he was descended from a son born out of wedlock to John of Gaunt, Duke of Lancaster, and Katherine Swynford, a son later legitimated by Richard II but debarred from the succession by act of Henry IV, Gaunt's legitimate son.

The Duke of Buckingham himself was derived, on his mother's

side from a younger brother of the Countess of Richmond's father and on his father's side both from Joan Beaufort, a daughter of the Gaunt-Swynford liaison, and from Thomas of Woodstock, youngest son of Edward III. There survives no record of what Buckingham had in mind as the Bishop of Ely began to play upon his shallow character: he may have toyed briefly with the idea of claiming the throne himself, having discovered how easy it was to crown a king, or, with Morton's prompting, he may have immediately decided to play kingmaker for Henry Tudor; it is unlikely that, as More has it, he quarrelled with Richard over the Bohun inheritance and thus became disaffected.

After the Countess of Richmond secured from Elizabeth Woodville a promise that she would give her eldest daughter Elizabeth to the Countess's son, Buckingham and his forces, the Woodville adherents, and Henry Tudor, aided by the Duke of Brittany, concerted their plans.

The rebellion, breaking out in early October (1483), took King Richard by surprise when he was still in the North. Showing his usual skill and energy as a commander, however, at the same time that the Duke of Buckingham's Welsh troops were deserting, the King quickly crushed the rising, captured and executed Buckingham (November 2), and forced the Woodville chiefs to flee to Brittany. Meantime, Henry Tudor had touched at Plymouth and then Poole, but finding Richard III's forces in control, sailed back to Brittany.

After a handful of executions, Richard dealt mildly with his enemies: the Countess was merely put in custody of her husband, Lord Stanley, who had remained loyal, or thought it best to appear so, and even John Morton, Bishop of Ely, prudently slipping away from Buckingham to take refuge in the Low Countries, was offered a pardon.

In the spring of 1484, King Richard's only son, Edward, died in the North; the following spring his frail wife Anne, languishing from tuberculosis, followed her son. Richard designated his nephew, the Earl of Lincoln, son of his sister Elizabeth and the Duke of Suffolk, as heir to the throne. If the King momentarily thought of marrying his niece Elizabeth in order to keep her from Henry Tudor, he quickly realized the force of opinion against the match and made a public denial of such intention.

On August 7, 1485, Henry Tudor, in French ships and with some 2,000 French troops, landed at Milford Haven, gathered some Welsh adherents as he headed for Shrewsbury, and then, covertly assured of aid by Lord Stanley and Stanley's brother Sir William, moved towards Leicester.

King Richard, who in anticipation of invasion had taken up a central position at Nottingham, marched with John Howard, Duke of Norfolk, Henry Percy, Earl of Northumberland, and an army something like double Henry's to meet his enemies at Bosworth Field.

The Stanleys, holding aloof, menaced the flanks of Richard's army, while the Earl of Northumberland, long jealous of Richard's hold upon the North, kept his forces idle in the rear. These three men decided the fate of the English crown.

After the Duke of Norfolk, leading Richard's front-line against the invaders commanded by the Earl of Oxford, had fallen in the fighting on the slopes of Ambien Hill, the King with his household charged upon Henry Tudor, who had positioned himself well to the rear. Then the Stanleys closed in; King Richard was killed 'fighting manfully in the thickest press of his enemies'—as even Vergil felt compelled to record. After Henry had been crowned on the field, Richard's naked body was hauled to the Grey Friars at Leicester. At the dissolution of the monasteries, his grave there was destroyed and the remains cast into the River Soar.

Two years after Bosworth, Henry VII defeated a Yorkist invasion from Ireland, which, though led by Richard's heir the Earl of Lincoln, was undertaken in behalf of the supposed younger brother of Edward V, who turned out to be an ignorant lad named Lambert Simnel. About five years later, however, another 'feigned boy', one Perkin Warbeck, popped up in Ireland, likewise calling himself the younger son of Edward IV. Perkin was successively supported and dropped by several European powers as their English policy veered from hostility to friendship. In 1497 a feeble invasion of Cornwall ended in Perkin Warbeck's flight and capture; two years later he was executed. There have been those, like Walpole, who believe in Perkin's claim, but modern historians are satisfied that the imposture is proved.

Though one of Richard's shoulders was slightly higher than the other, he had no withered arm nor hunched back nor game leg; he was a prince of sensitive, even intellectual mien, probably somewhat stiff and reserved; he showed himself hardy in the exercise of arms and a successful commander; he spent his happiest years when dwelling in Yorkshire as Lord of the North, and remained popular there; as King, he proved himself, though harried, an accomplished and conscientious ruler; but he could not live down—probably in his own mind as well as in the minds of his subjects—the ruthless and violent means by which he thrust himself into power. As A. R. Myers observes ('The Character of Richard III', *History Today*, IV, August 1954), 'If he could have prolonged his reign to twenty years instead of two, he might have overlaid with success and good deeds the memory of his path to the throne.'

An Introduction to
HISTORY OF RICHARD III

The *History of King Richard III* was written, not by Lord Chancellor More, soon to become a martyr for his faith and afterwards saint—the figure that the world knows best—nor yet by the knight, Sir Thomas More, high in Henry VIII's service and favour, but by the brilliant lawyer-humanist Master More, who lives in the letters of Erasmus, in his own preface to *Utopia*, and in the record of his versatile legal practice in London.

The *History* was composed about 1513 when More, then aged 35, was an Under-Sheriff (judicial adviser to the Sheriffs) of the city. In 1518, he became a member of Henry VIII's Council, and thus embarked on the career that would bring him to the block seventeen years later. It seems probable that by the time he went to Flanders as a member of a trade embassy in May of 1515, he had abandoned the *History* and conceived the idea for *Utopia*.

Published eight years after More's death by Richard Grafton as a continuation of Hardyng's *Chronicle* (1543) and again by Grafton as part of Hall's *Chronicle* (1548), the *History of King Richard III* first appeared in its own right in the magnificent black-letter edition of More's *English Works*, issued by his nephew, William Rastell, in 1557. It is Rastell who reveals the time of composition and furnishes the title of the *History* and who, annoyed by Grafton's publications, 'very much corrupt in many places', devotedly reproduces More's manuscript 'from the copy of his own hand. . . .'

After the accession of Queen Elizabeth I (1558), Rastell, a Catholic, sought refuge in the Low Countries, taking with him a Latin version of the *History* which was published in More's *Opera*, Louvain, 1565.

Though two works composed in mid-sixteenth century but not published till the seventeenth—the *Life* of More by his son-in-law, William Roper, and the *Life* of Cardinal Wolsey by his gentleman-usher, George Cavendish—must be counted superior as *biographies*, More's *Richard III* is the first great work of prose in the language; it initiates modern English historical writing—for all the glories of the Elizabethan Age, there is nothing that comes close to matching it until Bacon's *Henry VII* (1622); and as a bilingual narrative it is unique. That sprightly godson of Queen Elizabeth and inventor of the water closet, Sir John Harington, spoke for his era when he declared (1596) that 'the best written part of all our chronicles, in all men's opinions, is that of *Richard the Third*'.

The Great Debate over the 'little princes' has had its parallel, however, in a debate about the authorship of the *History* and the relationship between the English and the Latin text. Harington himself was the first, in print, to suggest that John Morton might be the author, at least of the Latin version. Sir George Buc gave publicity to the notion in his *Richard III*; and, though Walpole ignored it, the attribution to Morton has given aid and comfort to revisionists up to our day. The case for More's writing both the Latin and the English is now, however, firmly established. Similarly, literary historians have fought over whether the Latin version preceded the English or vice versa, but recent scholarship on both sides of the Atlantic concurs in the fascinating, but convincing, conclusion that witty Master More worked on both versions at the same time.

The errors in the *History* and the recurrence of phrases like 'as men say' indicate that Thomas More gathered most of his information by word-of-mouth. Some of it he undoubtedly remembered from the days (around 1489–92, only half a dozen years after Bosworth Field) when he had served as a page in the household of that John Morton who did so much to overthrow King Richard and had become Archbishop of Canterbury and Chancellor under Henry VII. In his mature years, More was acquainted with others who had worked for Henry Tudor, like Christopher Urswick,

King Henry's almoner, and the influential Bishop Fox of Winchester; he would hear a good deal from his father, a great admirer of Edward IV; and he undoubtedly talked with Robert Fabyan, the London chronicler, and with Henry VII's historian, Polydore Vergil.

What Thomas More learned about Richard III from those on the winning side at Bosworth, gave him the opportunity to shape recent events into the sort of history his humanist training and his humanist friends approved, that is, a dramatic, boldly patterned narrative, soaring beyond actualities into art and seeking psychological verisimilitude rather than factual accuracy. Horace Walpole, in declaring (see p. 170) that More wrote his *History* 'to amuse his leisure and exercise his fancy', does not score a bull's eye but comes closer to the mark than scholars who for centuries treated *Richard III* as utter fact.

Master More, however, did not merely imitate Thucydides, Suetonius, and Lucian. He was himself a born dramatist and ironist: metaphors scattered throughout his writings as well as the exuberant dramatic power unleashed in the *History*, reveal his fascination with plays and role-playing.

He concentrates one-third of his work upon dialogue, or speeches, by his principal characters. He transforms the over-ambitious and unpleasant Elizabeth Woodville into a pathetic heroine. He puts into the mouth of Buckingham an eloquent oration on sanctuaries hardly consonant with the Duke's learning and more appropriate to the author's own day when the right of sanctuary had become a political issue. He generates an opportunity for coruscating irony by substituting—unwittingly or not—Edward IV's light-of-love Elizabeth Lucy as the victim of the alleged pre-contract in place of Lady Eleanor Butler, daughter of the great Talbot, Earl of Shrewsbury, the woman named by Richard's Parliament and a far more likely choice on King Edward's part. Out of bits and pieces of hearsay he fashions a tale of the princes' murder so compelling that it has taken scholars three centuries and a half to accept its manifest unreliability—Sir James Tyrell, for example, knighted at the Battle of Tewkesbury, made Knight-Banneret by Richard during his Scots campaign, elevated after Richard's coronation to the office of Master of the Horse (and for fifteen years a high official of Henry VII), is re-created as a malcontent desperado, so little known to his sovereign that a page must point him out, who receives knighthood as a reward for villainy. Finally, deploying all his wonderful talents to anticipate Marlowe's 'one-man plays', More zestfully projects, stage centre, a monster of dissimulation whose raven wings shadow all the world. And across the stormy sky of this drama plays the incessant lightning of ironic wit.

The errors of the work—the reader will immediately notice the inaccuracies in More's account of Edward IV and Warwick the Kingmaker—are such as we would expect in a manuscript which is based on oral information gathered a generation after the event and which was neither finished nor revised. Blanks left for places and dates, careless mistakes in the first names of well-known figures (both corrected in the present text) confirm the conclusion that More abruptly broke off his history and never returned to it.

Why he abandoned this exuberant masterpiece, so obviously close to his heart and suited to his powers, is bound up with the question of why he undertook it.

Acclaimed for his skill in law but conscious of other talents, he undoubtedly set about his *History* for the same reason that, according to Falstaff (*Henry IV*, I, v, i), the Earl of Worcester undertook a rebellion—it 'lay in his way, and he found it'. Furthermore, as an avid student of the classical historians, he perhaps perceived in the materials available to him an opportunity to emulate the famous portraits of the monster-ruler Tiberius drawn by Tacitus in his *Annals* and by Suetonius in *Lives of the Twelve Caesars*.

As a humanist, on the other hand, Thomas More was impelled to try to exert a moderating influence on the power-hungry monarchs of Europe and their councillors. Hopes for a golden age of peace, coinciding with Henry VIII's accession to the throne in 1509, were now being dashed by the amoral manoeuvrings of the new statecraft. In 1513 political writing was in the air. Machiavelli had begun *The Prince*, Polydore Vergil was finding a didactic pattern for recent English history, Erasmus had probably conceived his advice to rulers, *The Institution of the Christian Prince* (1516), and the *Memoirs* of Philippe de Commynes, that 'textbook for princes', as the future Emperor Charles V called it, completed about the turn of the century, was to be published in 1524. There is little reason to doubt that the *History* is intended, in part at least, as an attack, by horrible example, on the *realpolitik*, the new power-politics of the age, which More was soon to criticize in *Utopia*.

The two versions of the *History* reflect the mixed motives of the author. The Latin text, with its fuller explanations of English institutions, is intended for the edification of a European audience; the English text—the amazing phenomenon—springs from More's joy in discovering that he can draw a golden music from the then unlikely instrument of the English tongue.

There now enters the picture, tantalizingly, that master of devious statesmanship King Henry VII. Three things must be borne in mind: (1) Master More had planned to continue his *History* to the end of Henry VII's reign (see page 103); (2) he abandoned his work at a moment when Henry was bound to enter it; (3) he gave his King Richard the dominant trait of a dark dissimulation, which, whatever one may think of Richard, was far more characteristic of the ways of Henry Tudor.

Indeed, More's attitude towards Henry does not have to be conjectured. According to Roper, young Thomas More, when M.P. in the Parliament of 1504, so imprudently spurred on the resistance to an extortionate tax proposed by the King that Henry angrily seized on a pretext to imprison More's father till he paid a fine of £100. The story may be a little exaggerated; but in Latin verses celebrating the accession of Henry VIII, Thomas boldly

[27]

proclaimed his dislike of the oppressive acts and devious dealing of Henry VII's 'gloomy reign'. Even in the *History* itself he refers, with prudent vagueness, to Henry's dissimulations: '. . . all things were in late days so covertly managed, one thing pretended and another meant, that there was nothing so plain and openly proved but that yet for the common custom of close and covert dealing men had it ever inwardly suspect. . .' (p. 103).

Now, More abruptly casts down his pen at the moment when he is zealously fashioning a scene of deliciously ironic comedy: Morton entrapping the Duke of Buckingham in his web. No doubt he was suddenly embarrassed by the realization that he must show his boyhood patron, Archbishop and Chancellor Morton, as a consummate intriguer, and that, in picturing a Duke of Buckingham conspiring to overturn a king, he was drawing a deadly parallel for that Duke's son, who already had talked too freely of his claim to the throne (and who would one day be executed by Henry VIII for that talk). However, it was probably the figure of Henry Tudor, now looming just offstage, that finally forced him to give over.

Master More, M.P. and lawyer, would know that it was impossibly dangerous for him to reveal his feelings about Henry VII, and Thomas More, historian, could perceive that he would be unable to continue his work without doing so.

Therefore, abandoning the 'middle way' of history, More expressed his political concerns more obliquely in the satiric fantasy *Utopia* (1516) and then more directly by entering the service of the King in 1518.

Irony of ironies—that the blackness of Richard III's character may spring not only from the author's information about that King's 'villainies' but also from his detestation of Henry VII's statecraft; and that the abandonment of the *History*, which was to serve so well the Tudor dynasty, was occasioned by the impossibility of writing historically about the founder of that dynasty!

In order to complete the story of King Richard's reign there is appended to the *History* a 'continuation' composed by Grafton for his edition of Hardyng's *Chronicle*. Hall's continuation (in his *Chronicle*) is much more elaborate. The reader will quickly remark 'what a falling off was there!' between Thomas More's masterwork of dramatic irony and Grafton's pedestrian chronicling, based on Vergil's *Anglica Historia*. In both texts the spelling has been modernized and the often excessively complex sentence structure brought more into line with present-day practice. Every attempt, however, has been made to keep the flavour of the original —even where this has meant the retention of redundancies and repetitions.

The modernized version of the *Continuation* is based on *The Chronicle of John Hardyng ... Together with the Continuation by Richard Grafton*, 1543 (edited by Henry Ellis, London, 1812). Rastell's original black-letter edition of the *History* is reproduced in *English Works, I* (Oxford University Press, 1931), and in the recent Yale University Press edition edited by Richard S. Sylvester.

The History of
KING RICHARD THE THIRD

King Edward, of that name the fourth, after he had lived fifty and
three years, seven months, and six days, and thereof reigned two
and twenty years, one month, and eight days, died at Westminster
the ninth day of April, the year of our redemption a thousand four
hundred four score and three, leaving much fair issue. To wit:
Edward the Prince, thirteen years of age; Richard, Duke of York,
two years younger; Elizabeth, whose fortune and grace was, after,
to be Queen, wife unto King Henry the Seventh and mother unto
the Eighth; Cecily, not so fortunate as fair; Bridget, who, representing the virtue of her whose name she bore, professed and observed a religious life in Dartford at a House of enclosed nuns;
Anne, that was afterwards honourably married unto Thomas, then
Lord Howard and after, Earl of Surrey; and Katherine, who, long
time tossed in either fortune, sometimes in wealth, often in adversity, at the last—if this be the last, for yet she lives—is by the
benignity of her nephew, King Henry the Eighth, in very prosperous estate and worthy her birth and virtue.*

This noble prince deceased at his Palace of Westminster and,
with great funeral honour and heaviness of his people from thence
conveyed, was interred at Windsor—a king of such governance and

* Edward IV was born April 28, 1442, assumed the crown March 4, 1461,
and died April 9, 1483; he thus died nineteen days before his forty-first
birthday, reigning twenty-two years, one month, six days. At the King's
death, Prince Edward, born November 2, 1470, was 12 years, 5 months old,
and his brother Richard, born August 17, 1473, was 9 years, 7 months old.
Cecily, her betrothal to the heir of James III of Scotland broken by her father,
was afterwards married to John, Viscount Welles, and then to a William
Kyme of Lincolnshire. Katherine married Lord William Courtenay, heir of
the Earl of Devonshire. There were two other daughters and a son, all of
whom died young.

behaviour in time of peace (for in war each party must needs be other's enemy) that there was never any prince of this land attaining the crown by battle so heartily beloved by the substance of the people, nor he himself so specially in any part of his life as at the time of his death. This favour and affection, even after his decease—by the cruelty, mischief, and trouble of the tempestuous world that followed increased more highly towards him. At such time as he died, the displeasure of those that bore him grudge for the sake of King Henry the Sixth, whom he deposed, was well assuaged and in effect quenched, in that many of them were dead in more than twenty years of his reign—a great part of a long life—and many of them in the mean season had grown into his favour, of which he was never strange.

He was a goodly personage and very princely to behold: of heart courageous, politic in counsel, in adversity nothing abashed, in prosperity rather joyful than proud, in peace just and merciful, in war sharp and fierce, in the field bold and hardy, and nevertheless no further than wisdom would, adventurous. Whoso well consider his wars, shall no less commend his wisdom where he withdrew than his manhood where he vanquished. He was of visage lovely; of body mighty, strong and clean made; howbeit in his latter days, with over liberal diet, somewhat corpulent and burly but nevertheless not uncomely. He was in youth greatly given to fleshly wantonness, from which health of body in great prosperity and fortune, without a special grace, hardly refrains. This fault not greatly grieved the people, for no one man's pleasure could stretch and extend to the displeasure of very many, and it was without violence; over that, in his latter days, it lessened and was well left.

In which time of his latter days this realm was in quiet and prosperous estate: no fear of outward enemies; no war in hand, nor none towards but such as no man looked for; the people towards the Prince, not in a constrained fear but in a willing and loving obedience; among themselves, the commons in good peace.

The lords whom he knew at variance, himself in his death-bed appeased. He had left off all gathering of money (which is the only thing that withdraws the hearts of Englishmen from a Prince), nor anything intended he to take in hand by which he should be driven thereto, for his tribute out of France he had before obtained, and the year foregoing his death he had obtained Berwick.* And albeit that all the time of his reign he was with his people so benign, courteous, and so familiar that no part of his virtues was more esteemed, yet that condition in the end of his days (when many princes, by a long-continued sovereignty, decline into a proud port from the debonair behaviour of their beginning) marvellously in him grew and increased. This was so far true that in the summer, the last that ever he saw, his Highness, being at Windsor hunting, sent for the Mayor and Aldermen of London for none other errand but to have them hunt and be merry with him. There he made them not so stately but so friendly and so familiar cheer, and sent venison from thence so freely into the city, that no one thing, in many days before, got him either more hearts or more hearty favour among the common people, who oftentimes more esteem and take for greater kindness a little courtesy than a great benefit.

So deceased (as I have said) this noble king in that time in which his life was most desired, whose love of his people and their entire affection towards him would have been to his noble children (having in themselves also as many gifts of nature, as many princely virtues, as much goodly promise, as their age could receive) a marvellous fortress and sure armour, if division and dissension of their friends had not unarmed them and left them destitute, and if the execrable desire of sovereignty had not provoked him to their

* Crowning a successful campaign against the Scots, Richard, Duke of Gloucester, received the surrender of Berwick on August 24, 1482.

In accordance with the Treaty of Picquigny, signed by Louis XI of France and Edward IV on August 29, 1475, Louis paid Edward 50,000 gold crowns a year, which the French called a pension and the English, tribute.

destruction who, if either nature or kindness had held place, must needs have been their chief defence. For Richard the Duke of Gloucester, by nature their uncle, by office their protector, to their father beholden, to themselves by oath and allegiance bound, broke all the bands that bind man and man together and, without any respect of God or the world, unnaturally contrived to bereave them, not only of their dignity, but also of their lives. But forasmuch as this duke's demeanour furnishes in effect all the whole matter whereof this book shall treat, it is therefore convenient somewhat to show you ere we further go, what manner of man this was that could find in his heart so much mischief to conceive.

Richard, Duke of York, a noble man and a mighty, had begun not by war but by law to challenge the crown, putting his claim into the Parliament. There his cause was, either for right or favour, so far forth advanced that King Henry's blood (albeit he had for son a goodly prince*) was utterly rejected and the crown was by authority of Parliament entailed unto the Duke of York and his issue male in remainder, immediately after the death of King Henry. But the Duke, not enduring so long to tarry but intending —under pretext of dissension and debate arising in the realm—to anticipate his time and to take upon him the rule in King Harry's life, was with many nobles of the realm at Wakefield slain, leaving three sons, Edward, George, and Richard.

All three, as they were great princes of birth, so were they great and princely of temper, greedy and ambitious of authority, and impatient of partners. Edward, revenging his father's death, deprived King Henry and attained the crown. George, Duke of Clarence, was a goodly noble prince and at all points fortunate, if either his own ambition had not set him against his brother, or the envy of his enemies set his brother against him. For were it due to the Queen and the lords of her blood, who highly maligned the King's kindred (as women commonly, not of malice but of nature,

* Henry VI's son, Edward, Prince of Wales, was killed at the Battle of Tewkesbury on May 4, 1471, before the death of his father.

hate them whom their husbands love), or were it due to the proud appetite of the Duke himself, intending to be king, heinous treason was laid to his charge, and finally—were he faulty, were he faultless—attainted was he by Parliament and judged to the death, and thereupon hastily drowned in a butt of Malmesey. His death King Edward (albeit he commanded it), when he knew it was done, piteously bewailed and sorrowfully repented.

Richard, the third son, of whom we now treat, was in wit and courage equal with either of them, in body and probity far under them both: little of stature, ill-featured of limbs, crook-backed, his left shoulder much higher than his right, hard-favoured of visage and such as is in princes called warlike, in other men otherwise. He was malicious, wrathful, envious, and, from before his birth, ever froward. It is for truth reported that the Duchess his mother had so much ado in her travail that she could not be delivered of him uncut, and that he came into the world with the feet forward—as men be borne out of it—and (as the fame runs) also not untoothed: either men out of hatred report above the truth or else nature changed her course in his beginning who in the course of his life many things unnaturally committed. No evil captain was he in the war, as to which his disposition was more meet than for peace. Sundry victories had he and sometimes overthrows, but never for any lack in his own person, either of hardiness or politic order. Free was he called of spending and somewhat above his power liberal: with large gifts he got him unsteadfast friendship, for which he was fain to pillage and spoil in other places, and get him steadfast hatred.

He was close and secret, a deep dissembler, lowly of countenance, arrogant of heart, outwardly companionable where he inwardly hated, not hesitating to kiss whom he thought to kill, pitiless and cruel, not for evil will always but oftener for ambition and either for the surety or increase of his position. 'Friend' and 'foe' were to him indifferent: where his advantage grew, he spared no man's death whose life withstood his purpose. He slew with his

[35]

own hands—as men constantly say--King Henry the Sixth, being prisoner in the Tower, and that without commandment or knowledge of the King, who would undoubtedly, if he had intended that thing, have appointed that butcherly office to some other than his own born brother.

Some wise men also think that his drift, covertly conveyed, lacked not in helping forth his brother of Clarence to his death, which he resisted openly, howbeit somewhat (as men deemed) more faintly than he that were heartily minded to his welfare. And they that thus deem, think that he long time in King Edward's life forethought to be king in case that the King his brother (whose life he looked that evil diet should shorten) should happen to decease (as indeed he did) while his children were young. And they deem that for this intent he was glad of the death of his brother the Duke of Clarence, whose life must needs have hindered him whether the same Duke of Clarence had kept him true to his nephew, the young King, or enterprised to be king himself. But of all this point is there no certainty, and whoso divines upon conjectures may as well shoot too far as too short. Howbeit, this have I by credible information learned, that the same night in which King Edward died, one Mistlebrook long ere morning, came in great haste to the house of one Pottier, dwelling in Redcross street without Cripplegate; and when he was with hasty rapping quickly let in, he showed unto Pottier that King Edward was departed. 'By my troth, man,' quoth Pottier, 'then will my master the Duke of Gloucester be king.' What cause he had so to think, hard it is to say: if he, being the Duke's adherent, anything knew that he such thing purposed, or otherwise had any inkling thereof, he was not likely to speak it of naught.

But now to return to the course of this history. Whether the Duke of Gloucester had of old foreminded this conclusion or was now for the first time thereunto moved and put in hope by the occasion of the tender age of the young princes his nephews (as opportunity and likelihood of success put a man in courage of that he never intended), certain is it that he contrived their destruction, with the usurpation of the regal dignity upon himself. And forasmuch as he was well aware of, and helped to maintain, a long-continued grudge and heartburning between the Queen's kindred and the King's blood—either party envying other's authority—he now thought that their division should be (as it was indeed) a favourable beginning to the pursuit of his intent and a sure ground for the foundation of all his building. Under the pretext of revenging of old displeasure, he might first play upon the anger and ignorance of the one party to the destruction of the other and then win to his purpose as many as he could; and those that could not be won might be lost ere they looked therefor. For of one thing was he certain, that if his intent were perceived, he would soon have made peace between the both parties with his own blood.

In his life King Edward, albeit that this dissension between his friends somewhat irked him, yet in his good health he somewhat the less regarded it because he thought that, whatsoever business should fall between them, he himself would always be able to rule both the parties. But in his last sickness, when he perceived his natural strength so sore enfeebled that he despaired all recovery, then he called some of them before him that were at variance. Considering the youth of his children—albeit he nothing less mistrusted than that that happened—he well foresaw that many harms might grow by their debate while his children should lack discretion of themselves and good counsel of their friends, for either party would counsel for their own advantage and seek, by pleasant advice, to win themselves favour rather than, by profitable advertisement, to do the children good. In especial he called the Lord Marquess Dorset, the Queen's son by her first husband, and William, the Lord Hastings, a noble man, then Lord Chamberlain, whom the Queen specially begrudged for the great favour the King bore him and also for that she thought him secretly familiar with the King in wanton company. Her kindred also bore him sore, as well for that the King had made him Captain of Calais (which office the Lord Rivers [Earl Rivers], brother to the Queen, claimed of the King's former promise), as for divers other great gifts which he received, that they had looked for.

When these lords, with divers others of both the parties, were come in presence, the King, lifting up himself and underset with pillows, as it is reported, in this wise said unto them:

'My lords, my dear kinsmen and allies, in what plight I lie, you see and I feel. By which, the less while I look to live with you, the more deeply am I moved to care in what case I leave you; for such as I leave you, such be my children like to find you. Who, if they should (that God forbid) find you at variance, might hap to fall themselves at war ere their discretion would serve to set you at peace. You see their youth, of which I reckon the only surety to rest in your concord. For it suffices not that all of you love them, if each of you hate the other. If they were men, your faithfulness haply would suffice. But childhood must be maintained by men's authority and unstable youth underpropped with elder counsel, which neither they can have but you give it, nor you give it if you agree not. For where each labours to break what the other makes, and for hatred of each other's person impugns each other's counsel, it must needs be long ere any good conclusion go forward. And also while either party labours to be chief, flattery shall have more place than plain and faithful advice. Then there must needs ensue the evil bringing up of the Prince, whose mind, in tender youth infected, shall readily fall to mischief and riot, and draw down with this noble realm to ruin, unless grace turn him to wisdom. And if God send him wisdom, then they that by evil means before pleased him best shall after fall farthest out of favour, so that ever at length evil drifts drive to naught and good plain ways prosper.

'Great variance has there long been between you, not always for great causes. Sometimes a thing right well intended, our misconstruction turns unto worse, or a small displeasure done us, either our own affection or evil tongues aggravate. But this know

I well: you never had so great cause of hatred as you have of love. That we be all men, that we be Christian men, this shall I leave for preachers to tell you—and yet I know not whether any preacher's words ought more to move you than his that is by and by going to the place that they all preach of. But this shall I desire you to remember, that the one part of you is of my blood, the other of mine allies, and each of you with other either of kindred or affinity, which spiritual kindred of affinity, if the sacraments of Christ's Church bear that weight with us that would God they did, should no less move us to charity than the respect of fleshly consanguinity. Our Lord forbid that you love together the worse for the very cause that you ought to love the better. And yet that happens. And nowhere find we so deadly debate as among them who by nature and law most ought to agree together.

'Ambition and desire of vainglory and sovereignty is such a pestilent serpent that, once it enters among princes, it creeps forth so far till with division and variance it turns all to mischief—first longing to be next the best, afterwards equal with the best, and at last chief and above the best. From this immoderate appetite for great place, and thereby for debate and dissension, I pray God as well forget as we well remember what loss, what sorrow, what trouble has within these few years grown in this realm. If I could as well have foreseen these things as I have with my more pain than pleasure experienced them, by God's blessed Lady (that was ever his oath) I would never have won the courtesy of men's knees with the loss of so many heads. But since things past cannot be called back, much more should we beware, from the occasions when we have taken so great hurt before, that we soon afterwards fall not in that occasion again. Now be those griefs passed, and all is (God be thanked) quiet and likely right well to prosper in weal and peace under your cousins my children, if God send them life and you love. Of which two things, the less loss were they; for though God so did His pleasure, yet should the realm always find kings and peradventure as good kings. But if you among yourselves in a child's reign fall at debate, many a good man shall perish and haply he too, and you too, ere this land find peace again.

'Wherefore in these last words that ever I look to speak with you, I exhort you and require you all, for the love that you have ever borne to me, for the love that I have ever borne to you, for the love that our Lord bears to us all, from this time forward, all griefs forgotten, each of you love other. Which I verily trust you will, if you at all regard either God or your King, affinity or kindred, this realm, your own country, or your own surety.'

And therewithal the King, no longer enduring to sit up, laid him down on his right side, his face towards them. And none was there present that could refrain from weeping. But the lords, recomforting him with as good words as they could, and answering for the time as they thought to stand with his pleasure, there in his presence (as by their words appeared) each forgave other and joined their hands together, when (as it after appeared by their deeds) their hearts were far asunder.

As soon as the King was departed this life, the noble Prince his son drew towards London. At the time of his father's decease the Prince kept his household at Ludlow in Wales, a country which, being far off from the law and recourse to justice, had begun to be far out of good will and to wax wild, robbers and pillagers walking at liberty uncorrected. For this reason the Prince had, in the life of his father, been sent thither, to the end that the authority of his presence should refrain evil-disposed persons from the boldness of their former outrages. To the governance and ordering of this young Prince, at his sending thither, was there appointed Sir Anthony Woodville, Lord Rivers and brother unto the Queen, a right honourable man, as valiant of hand as politic in counsel. Adjoined were there unto him others of the same party, and, in effect, every one as he was nearest of kin unto the Queen so was he planted next about the Prince.

This drift that the Queen not unwisely devised so that her

blood might in his youth be rooted in the Prince's favour, the Duke of Gloucester turned unto their destruction, and upon that ground set the foundation of all his unhappy building. For whomsoever he perceived either at variance with them or bearing himself their favour, he broke unto them—some by mouth, some by writing and secret messengers—that it was neither reasonable nor in any wise to be suffered that the young King, their master and kinsman, should be in the hands and custody of his mother's kindred, sequestered in manner from the company and attendance of all others who owed him as faithful service as they. Many of these were a far more honourable part of kin than those on his mother's side, for her blood (quoth he), saving the King's pleasure, was full unmeet to be matched with his. For them, as it is said, to be removed from the King and the less noble to be left about him was (quoth he) neither honourable to his Majesty nor unto us. Moreover, it was no surety to his Grace to have the mightiest of his friends from him, and no little jeopardy unto us to suffer our well-proved evil-willers to grow in overgreat authority with the Prince, in youth especially, for youth is light of belief and soon persuaded.

'You remember, I think, King Edward himself, albeit he was a man of age and of discretion, yet was he in many things ruled by that band more than stood either with his honour or our profit, or to the advantage of any man else, except only the immoderate advancement of themselves, who, whether they sorer thirsted after their own weal or our woe, it were hard, I think, to guess. And if some folks' friendship had not held better place with the King than any respect of kindred, they might, peradventure, easily have betrapped and brought to confusion some of us ere this. Why not as easily as they have done some others already, as near of his royal blood as we? But our Lord has wrought His will, and thanks be to His grace that peril is past. Howbeit, as great a one is growing if we suffer this young King in our enemies' hand, for, without his knowing, they might abuse the name of his commandment to

[41]

any of our undoing, which thing God and good provision forbid. Of which good provision none of us has any the less need because of the late-made reconciliation, for in it the King's pleasure had more place than the parties' wills. Nor none of us, I believe, is so unwise oversoon to trust a new friend made of an old foe or to think that a passing kindness, suddenly contracted in one hour, continued yet scant a fortnight, should be deeper settled in their hearts than a long accustomed malice many years rooted.'

With these words and writings and such other, the Duke of Gloucester soon set afire them that were of themselves easy to kindle, and in especial twain, Henry, Duke of Buckingham, and William, Lord Hastings, the Chamberlain, both men of honour and of great power, the one by long succession from his ancestry, the other by his office and the King's favour. These two, not bearing each to other so much love as both bore hatred unto the Queen's party, in this point accorded together with the Duke of Gloucester that they would utterly remove from the King's company all his mother's friends, under the name of their enemies. This concluded, the Duke of Gloucester, understanding that the lords who at that time were about the King intended to bring him up to his coronation accompanied with such a power of their friends that it would be hard for him to bring his purpose to pass without the gathering and great assembly of people and in manner of open war—whereof the end, he knew, was dubious and in which, the King being on their side, his part should have the face and name of a rebellion—he secretly, by divers means, caused the Queen to be persuaded and brought in the mind that it neither were needful and also would be jeopardous, for the King to come up strong. Whereas now every lord loved other and none other thing studied upon but the coronation and honour of the King, if the lords of her kindred should assemble in the King's name much people, they should give the lords betwixt whom and them had been sometime debate, to fear and suspect lest they should gather this people not for the King's safeguard, whom no man impugned, but for their destruction, having more regard to their old variance than their new reconciliation. For this reason they would assemble on the other part much people again for their defence, and their power, she knew well, stretched far. And thus should all the realm fall on a roar. And of all the hurt that thereof should ensue—which was likely not to be little, and the most harm like to fall where she least would—all the world would put her and her kindred in the wrong and say that they had unwisely, and untruly also, broken the amity and peace that the King her husband had so prudently made between his kin and hers on his deathbed and which the other party faithfully observed.

The Queen, being in this wise persuaded, sent word unto her son and unto her brother being about the King; and over that, the Duke of Gloucester himself and other lords, the chief of his band, wrote unto the King so reverently and to the Queen's friends there so lovingly that they, nothing at all mistrusting, brought the King up in great haste, not in good speed, with a sober company.

When the King was on his way to London from Northampton, these Dukes of Gloucester and Buckingham came thither, where the Lord Rivers, the King's uncle, had remained behind, intending on the morrow to follow the King and be with him early at Stony Stratford fourteen miles thence, ere he departed.

So was there made a great while that night much friendly cheer between these Dukes and the Lord Rivers. But incontinent after they had openly with great courtesy parted and the Lord Rivers lodged, the Dukes secretly with a few of their most privy friends set them down in council, wherein they spent a great part of the night. And at their rising in the dawning of the day, they sent about privily to their servants in the inns and lodgings about, giving them commandment to make themselves shortly ready, for their lords were about to take horse. Upon which messages, many of their folk were attendant when many of the Lord Rivers' servants were unready. Now had these Dukes taken also into their custody the keys of the inn, that none should pass forth without their licence. And over this, in the highway towards Stony Stratford, where the King lay, they had bestowed certain of their folk that should send back again and compel to return any man that were got out of Northampton towards Stony Stratford, till they should give other licence; forasmuch as the Dukes themselves intended, for the show of their diligence, to be the first that should that day attend upon the King's Highness out of that town. Thus they deceived folk.

But when the Lord Rivers understood the gates closed and the ways on every side beset, with neither his servants nor himself suffered to go out, he perceived well so great a thing was not begun without his knowledge for naught and, comparing this manner present with this last night's cheer, he marvellously misliked so great a change in so few hours. Howbeit, since he could not get away, and would not keep himself close lest he should seem to hide for some secret fear of his own fault—whereof he saw no such cause in himself—he determined upon the surety of his own conscience to go boldly to them and inquire what this matter might mean. As soon as they saw him, they began to quarrel with him and say that he intended to set distance between the King and them and to bring them to confusion, but it should not lie in his power. And when he began (as he was a very well-spoken man) in goodly wise to excuse himself, they tarried not the end of his answer but shortly took him and put him in ward, and that done, forthwith went to horseback and took the way to Stony Stratford, where they found the King with his company ready to leap on horseback and depart forward, leaving that lodging for them because it was too strait for both companies.

And as soon as they came into his presence, they lighted adown with all their company about them, to whom the Duke of Buckingham said, 'Go before, gentlemen and yeomen; keep your ranks.' And thus in a goodly array they came to the King and on their knees in very humble wise saluted his Grace, who received them in very joyous and amiable manner, nothing at all knowing nor mistrusting as yet. But even by and by in his presence they picked a quarrel with the Lord Richard Grey, the King's other brother by his mother, saying that he, with the Lord Marquess his brother and the Lord Rivers his uncle, had compassed to rule the King and the realm, to set variance among the lords, and to subdue and destroy the noble blood of the realm. Towards the accomplishing whereof, they said that the Lord Marquess had entered into the Tower of London, and thence taken out the King's treasure, and sent men to the sea. All which things these Dukes knew well were done for good and necessary purposes by the whole Council at London—saving that something they must say.

Unto which words the King answered, 'What my brother Marquess has done, I cannot say; but in good faith, I dare well answer for mine uncle Rivers and my brother here, that they be innocent of any such matters.'

'Yea, my liege,' quoth the Duke of Buckingham, 'they have kept their dealing in these matters far from the knowledge of your good Grace.'

And forthwith they arrested the Lord Richard and Sir Thomas Vaughan, knight, in the King's presence and brought the King and all back unto Northampton, where they took again further counsel. And there they sent away from the King whom it pleased them and set new servants about him, such as liked better them than him. At which dealing he wept and was nothing content; but it booted not. And at dinner the Duke of Gloucester sent a dish from his own table to the Lord Rivers, praying him to be of good cheer, all should be well enough. And he thanked the Duke and prayed the messenger to bear it to his nephew the Lord Richard, with the same message for his comfort, who, he thought, had more need of comfort, as one to whom such adversity was strange. He himself had been all his days inured thereto and therefore could bear it the better. But for all this comfortable courtesy of the Duke of Gloucester, he sent the Lord Rivers and the Lord Richard, with

Sir Thomas Vaughan, into the north country into divers places to prison and afterwards all to Pomfret [Pontefract], where they were in conclusion beheaded.

In this wise the Duke of Gloucester took upon himself the order and governance of the young King, whom with much honour and humble reverence he conveyed upward towards the city. But anon the tidings of this matter came hastily to the Queen, a little before the midnight following, and that in the sorest wise—that the King her son was taken, her brother, her son and her other friends arrested and sent no man knew whither, to be done with God knew what. With which tidings the Queen, in great flutter and heaviness, bewailing her child's ruin, her friends' mischance, and her own misfortune, damning the time that ever she dissuaded the gathering of power about the King, got herself in all the haste possible with her younger son and her daughters out of the Palace of Westminster, in which she then lay, into the sanctuary [of Westminster Abbey], lodging herself and her company there in the Abbot's place.

Now came there one in like wise, not long after midnight, from the Lord Chamberlain unto the Archbishop of York, then Chancellor of England, to his place not far from Westminster. And for that he showed the servants that he had tidings of so great importance that his master gave him in charge not to spare the Archbishop's rest, they refused not to wake him nor he to admit this messenger in to his bedside, of whom he heard that these Dukes were gone back with the King's Grace from Stony Stratford unto Northampton.

'Notwithstanding, Sir,' quoth he, 'my Lord sends your Lordship word that there is no fear, for he assures you that all shall be well.'

'I assure him,' quoth the Archbishop, 'be it as well as it will, it will never be so well as we have seen it.' And thereupon, by and by, after the messenger departed, he caused in all haste all his servants to be called up, and so, with his own household about him, and every man weaponed, he took the Great Seal with him and came, yet before day, unto the Queen. About her he found much heaviness, rumble, haste, and business—carriage and conveyance of her stuff into sanctuary, chests, coffers, packs, bundles, trusses, all on men's backs, no man unoccupied, some lading, some going, some discharging, some coming for more, some breaking down the walls to bring in the nearest way, and some yet drew to them that helped to carry a wrong way.

The Queen herself sat alone, low down on the rushes, all desolate and dismayed, whom the Archbishop comforted in the best manner he could, showing her that he trusted the matter was nothing so sore as she took it for, and that he was put in good hope and out of fear by the message sent him from the Lord Chamberlain.

'Ah, woe be to him!' quoth she, 'for he is one of them that labour to destroy me and my blood.'

'Madam,' quoth he, 'be of good cheer. For I assure you if they crown any other king than your son, whom they now have with them, we shall on the morrow crown his brother, whom you have here with you. And here is the Great Seal, which, in like wise as that noble prince, your husband, delivered it unto me, so here I deliver it unto you, to the use and behoof of your son.' And therewith he presented her the Great Seal and departed home again, yet in the dawning of the day. At which time he could, from his chamber window, see all the Thames full of boats of the Duke of Gloucester's servants, watching that no man should go to sanctuary, nor none could pass unsearched. Then was there great commotion and murmur, as well in other places about as specially in the city, the people diversely divining upon this dealing. And some lords, knights, and gentlemen, either for favour of the Queen or for fear of themselves, assembled in sundry companies and went armoured in flocks—and many also for that they reckoned this demeanour attempted not so specially against other lords as against the King himself in the disturbance of his coronation.

But then, by and by, the lords assembled together at London.

Towards which meeting the Archbishop of York, fearing that it would be ascribed (as it was indeed) to his overmuch lightness that he so suddenly had yielded up the Great Seal to the Queen—to whom the custody thereof nothing pertained, without especial commandment of the King—secretly sent for the Seal again and brought it with him after the customable manner. And at this meeting the Lord Hastings, whose truth towards the King no man doubted nor needed to doubt, persuaded the lords to believe that the Duke of Gloucester was sure and steadfastly faithful to his Prince and that the Lord Rivers and Lord Richard with the other knights were, for matters attempted by them against the Dukes of Gloucester and Buckingham, put under arrest for the Dukes' surety, not for the King's jeopardy; and that they were also in safeguard, and there no longer should remain than till the matter were, not by the Dukes only, but also by all the other lords of the King's Council, impartially examined and by other discretions ordered, and either judged or appeased. But one thing he advised them beware, that they judged not the matter too far forth ere they knew the truth, nor, turning their private grudges into the common hurt, so irritate and provoke men unto anger and disturb the King's coronation—towards which the Dukes were coming up—that they might peradventure bring the matter so far out of joint that it should never be brought in frame again. Which strife, if it should hap, as it were likely, to come to a battle, yet should the authority, though both parties were in all other things equal, be on that side where the King himself was.

With these persuasions of the Lord Hastings—whereof part he himself believed, of part he knew the contrary—these commotions were somewhat appeased. They were the more so because the Dukes of Gloucester and Buckingham were so near and came so shortly on with the King, in no other manner, with no other voice or semblance, than to his coronation, and also since they caused the rumour to be blown about that those lords and knights who were taken had contrived the destruction of the Dukes of Gloucester and Buckingham and of other noble blood of the realm, to the end that themselves would alone manage and govern the King at their pleasure. And for the plausible proof thereof, such of the Dukes' servants as rode with the carts laden with the stuff of them that were taken (among which stuff, no marvel though some were armour, which at the breaking up of that household must needs either be brought away or cast away) they showed unto the people all the way as they went: 'Lo, here be the barrels of armour that these traitors had privily conveyed in their baggage to destroy the noble lords withal.' This device, albeit that it made the matter to wise men more unlikely—well perceiving that the intenders of such a purpose would rather have had their armour on their backs than to have bound it up in barrels—yet much part of the common people were therewith very well satisfied and said it were alms to hang them.

When the King approached near to the city, Edmund Shaa, goldsmith, then Mayor, with William White and John Matthew, Sheriffs, and all the other Aldermen in scarlet, with five hundred horse of the citizens in violet, received him reverently at Hornsey, and riding from thence, accompanied him into the city, which he entered the fourth day of May, the first and last year of his reign. But the Duke of Gloucester bore him in open sight so reverently to the Prince, with all semblance of lowliness, that from the great obloquy in which he was so late before, he was suddenly fallen in so great trust that, at the Council next assembled, he was made the only man chosen and thought most meet to be Protector of the King and his realm, so that (were it destiny or were it folly) the lamb was delivered to the wolf to keep.

At this Council also, the Archbishop of York, Chancellor of England, who had delivered the Great Seal to the Queen, was thereof greatly reproved, and the Seal taken from him and delivered to Doctor [John] Russell, Bishop of Lincoln, a wise man and a good and of much experience and one of the best learned men undoubtedly that England had in his time. Divers lords and knights were appointed unto divers offices. The Lord Chamberlain, and some others, kept still their offices that they had before.

Now, although the Protector so sore thirsted for the finishing of that he had begun that he thought every day a year till it were achieved, yet durst he no further attempt as long as he had but half his prey in hand, well knowing that if he deposed the one brother, all the realm would fall to the other, if he either remained in sanctuary or should haply be shortly conveyed to liberty farther off.

Wherefore incontinent at the next meeting of the lords at the Council, he proposed unto them that it was a heinous deed of the Queen, and proceeding of great malice towards the King's Councillors, that she should keep in sanctuary the King's brother from him, whose special pleasure and comfort were to have his brother with him. She had so done to no other intent but to bring all the lords in obloquy and murmur of the people, as though those were not to be trusted with the King's brother who by the assent of the nobles of the land were appointed, as the King's nearest friends, to the tuition of his own royal person. 'The prosperity of whom stands,' quoth he, 'not all in keeping from enemies or ill viands, but partly also in recreation and moderate pleasure, which he cannot, in this tender youth, take in the company of ancient persons, but in the familiar conversation of those that be neither far under nor far above his age and nevertheless of station convenient to accompany his noble Majesty. Wherefore, with whom rather than with his own brother? And if any man think this consideration light (which I think no man thinks that loves the King), let him consider that sometimes without small things greater cannot stand. And verily it redounds greatly to the dishonour both of the King's Highness and of all us that be about his Grace, to have it run in every man's mouth, not in this realm only but also in other lands (as evil words walk far), that the King's brother should be fain to keep sanctuary. For every man will think that no man will so do for naught. And such evil opinion once fastened in men's hearts, hard it is to wrest out, and may grow to more grief than any man here can divine.

'Wherefore, methinks it were not worst to send unto the Queen for the redress of this matter some honourable trusty man such as has a tender regard both for the King's weal and for the honour of his Council, and is also in favour and trust with her. For all which considerations none seems to me more meet than our reverend father here present, my Lord Cardinal, who may in this matter do most good of any man, if it please him to take the pain. Which, I doubt not, of his goodness he will not refuse, for the King's sake and ours, and for the welfare of the young Duke himself, the King's most honourable brother and, after my Sovereign Lord himself, my most dear nephew. Thereby shall be ceased the slanderous rumour and obloquy now going, and the hurts avoided that thereof might ensue, and much rest and quiet grow to all the realm.

'And if she be perchance so obstinate and so precisely set upon her own will that neither his wise and faithful advertisement can move her nor any man's reason content her, then shall we, by my advice, by the King's authority fetch him out of that prison and bring him to his noble presence, in whose continual company he shall be so well cherished and so honourably treated that all the world shall, to our honour and her reproach, perceive that it was only malice, frowardness, or folly that caused her to keep him there.

'This is my mind in this matter for this time, except any of your lordships anything perceive to the contrary. For never shall I, by God's grace, so wed myself to mine own will but that I shall be ready to change it upon your better advices.'

When the Protector had said, all the Council affirmed that the motion was good and reasonable, and to the King and the Duke his brother honourable, and a thing that should cease great murmur in the realm, if the mother might be by good means induced to deliver him. Which thing [Cardinal Bourchier], the Archbishop of Canterbury, whom they all agreed also to be thereto most convenient, took upon him to move her and therein to do his uttermost endeavour. Howbeit, if she could be in no wise entreated with good will to deliver him, then thought he, and such others as were of the spirituality present, that it were not in any wise to be attempted to take him out against her will.

It would be a thing that should turn to the great grudge of all men, and high displeasure of God, if the privilege of that holy place should now be broken, which had so many years been kept. Both kings and popes so good had granted it, so many had confirmed it, and that holy ground had, more than five hundred years ago by Saint Peter, his own person in spirit, accompanied with great multitude of angels, by night been so specially hallowed and dedicated to God (for the proof whereof they have yet in the Abbey, Saint Peter's cope to show) that from that time hitherward was there never so undevout a king that durst that sacred place violate, or so holy a bishop that durst it presume to consecrate.*
'And therefore,' quoth the Archbishop of Canterbury, 'God forbid that any man should for any reason undertake to break the immunity and liberty of that sacred sanctuary, which has been the safeguard of so many a good man's life. And I trust,' quoth he, 'with God's grace, we shall not need it. But for any manner of need I would not we should do it. I trust that she shall be with reason contented, and all thing in good manner obtained. And if it happen that I bring it not so to pass, yet shall I towards it so far forth do my best that you shall all well perceive that no lack of my endeavour but the mother's dread and womanish fear shall be the hindrance.'

'Womanish fear! Nay, womanish frowardness!' quoth the Duke of Buckingham. 'For I dare take it upon my soul, she well knows

* According to the legendary report of a fisherman who witnessed the scene, on the night in the early seventh century before the Abbey was to be consecrated by the first Bishop of London, St Peter in celestial splendour, aided by a host of angels, himself dedicated the church, leaving his cloak there.

she needs no such thing to fear, either for her son or for herself. For as for her, here is no man that will be at war with women. Would God some of the men of her kin were women too, and then should all be soon in rest! Howbeit, there is none of her kin the less loved for that they be her kin, but for their own evil deserving. And nevertheless, if we loved neither her nor her kin, yet were there no cause to think that we should hate the King's noble brother, to whose Grace we ourself be of kin. Whose honour if she as much desired as our dishonour, and as much regard took to his welfare as to her own will, she would be as loath to suffer him from the King as any of us be. For if she have any wit (as would God she had as good will as she has cunning wit) she reckons herself no wiser than she thinks some that be here, of whose faithful mind she nothing doubts but verily believes and knows that they would be as sorry of his harm as herself, and yet would have him from her if she bide there. And we all, I think, be content that both be with her, if she come thence and bide in such place where they may with their honour be.

'Now then, if she refuse, in the deliverance of him, to follow the counsel of them whose wisdom she knows, whose truth she well trusts, it is easy to perceive that frowardness prevents her, and not fear. But suppose that she fear (as who may prevent her fearing her own shadow?), the more she fears to deliver him, the more ought we fear to leave him in her hands. For if she conceive such foolish doubts that she fear his hurt, then will she fear that he shall be fetched thence. For she will soon think that if men were set (which God forbid) upon so great a mischief, the sanctuary would little hinder them—which good men might, methinks, without sin somewhat less regard than they do.

'Now then, if she fear lest he might be fetched from her, is it not likely enough that she shall send him somewhere out of the realm? Verily, I look for none other. And I doubt not but she now as earnestly intends it as we the preventing thereof. And if she might happen to bring that to pass (as it were no great accomplishment, we letting her alone), all the world would say that we were a wise sort of counsellors about a king, that let his brother be cast away under our noses. And therefore, I assure you faithfully, for my mind I will rather, despite her mind, fetch him away than leave him there till her frowardness or foolish fear convey him away.

'And yet will I break no sanctuary therefor. For verily, since the privileges of that place and others like have been of long continued, I am not he that would be about to break them. And, in good faith, if they were now to begin, I would not be he that should be about to make them. Yet will I not say nay, that it is a deed of pity that such men as the sea or their evil debtors have brought in poverty should have some place of liberty to keep their bodies out of the danger of their cruel creditors. And also if the crown happen (as it has done) to come in question, while either party takes other as traitors, I am well willing there be some places of refuge for both. But as for thieves, of whom these places be full and who never fall from the craft after they once fall thereto, it is pity the sanctuary should serve them. And much more, mankillers, whom God bade to take from the altar and kill them if their murder were wilful. And where it is otherwise, there need we not the sanctuaries that God appointed in the old law. For if either necessity, his own defence, or misfortune draw him to that deed, a pardon serves, which either the law grants of course, or the King of pity may.

'Then look me now, how few sanctuary men there be whom any commendable necessity compelled to go thither. And then see, on the other side, what a sort there be commonly therein of them whom wilful unthriftiness has brought to naught.

'What a rabble of thieves, murderers, and malicious, heinous traitors! And that in two places specially—the one at the elbow of the city [Westminster Abbey], the other in the very bowels [the church of St Martin le Grand]. I dare well avow it—weigh the good that they do with the hurt that comes of them, and ye shall find it much better to lack both than have both. And this I say: although they were not abused as they now be and so long have been, I fear me ever they will be while men be afraid to set their hands to the amendment—as though God and Saint Peter were the patrons of ungracious living!

'Now unthrifts riot and run into debt, upon the boldness of these places. Yea, and rich men run thither with poor men's goods; there they build, there they spend, and bid their creditors go whistle them. Men's wives run thither with their husbands' plate, and say they dare not abide with their husbands for beating. Thieves bring thither their stolen goods, and there live thereon. There devise they new robberies; nightly they steal out; they rob and pillage and kill and come in again as though those places gave them not only a safeguard for the harm they have done but a licence also to do more. Howbeit, much of this mischief, if wise men would set their hands to, it might be amended, with great thank of God and no breach of the privilege. The residue—since, so long ago, I know never what pope and what prince more piteous than politic have granted it, and other men since of a certain religious fear have not broken it—let us take pains therewith, and let it in God's name stand in force, as far forth as reason will. Which is not fully so far as may serve to prevent us from the fetching forth of this noble man to his honour and welfare, out of that place in which he neither is nor can be a sanctuary man.

'A sanctuary serves always to defend the body of that man that stands in danger abroad, not of great hurt only but also of lawful hurt. For against unlawful harms, never pope nor king intended to privilege any one place. For that privilege has every place. Knows any man any place wherein it is lawful, one man to do another wrong? That no man unlawfully take hurt, the King, the law, and very nature forbid the liberty [to do an injury] in every place, and make in that regard for every man every place a sanctuary. But where a man is by lawful means in peril, there needs he the tuition of some special privilege, which is the only ground and

[55]

cause of all sanctuaries.* From which necessity this noble prince is far. His love to his King, nature and kindred prove; his innocence, to all the world his tender youth proves. And so for sanctuary, neither none he needs, nor also none can have.

'Men come not to sanctuary as they come to baptism, to require it by their godfathers. He must ask it himself who must have it. And reasonably, since no man has cause to have it but whose consciousness of his own fault makes him need to require it. What will then has yonder babe? And if he had discretion to require it if need were, I dare say he would now be right angry with them that keep him there. And I would think, without any scruple of conscience, without any breach of privilege, to be somewhat more downright with them that be there sanctuary men indeed. For if one go to sanctuary with another man's goods, why should not the King, leaving his body at liberty, recover the part of his goods even within the sanctuary? For neither king nor pope can give any place such a privilege that it shall discharge a man of his debts, if he be able to pay.'

And with that, divers of the clergy that were present, whether they said it for his pleasure or as they thought, agreed plainly that by the law of God and of the Church the goods of a sanctuary man should be delivered in payment of his debts, and stolen goods to the owner, and only liberty reserved him to get his living with the labour of his hands.

'Verily,' quoth the Duke, 'I think you say very truth. And what if a man's wife will take sanctuary because she wishes to run from her husband? I would think, if she can allege no other cause, he may lawfully, without any displeasure to St Peter, take her out of St Peter's church [Westminster Abbey] by the arm. And if nobody

* From the middle of the fifteenth century onward, the abuses of sanctuary enumerated by Buckingham had become an increasingly bitter source of friction between laity and clergy. For a brief account of fifteenth-century English customs and attitudes regarding sanctuary, see Paul Kendall, *The Yorkist Age*, 1962, pp. 247–9 and p. 279.

may be taken out of sanctuary that says he will bide there, then if a child will take sanctuary because he fears to go to school, his master must let him alone. And as foolish as that example is, yet is there less reason in our case than in that. For therein though it be a childish fear, yet is there at the least some fear. And herein is there none at all. And verily I have often heard of sanctuary men. But I never heard before of sanctuary children. And therefore, as for the conclusion of my mind, whoso may have deserved to need it, if they think it for their surety, let them keep it. But he can be no sanctuary man that neither has wisdom to desire it nor malice to deserve it, whose life or liberty can by no lawful process stand in jeopardy. And he that takes one out of sanctuary to do him good, I say plainly that he breaks no sanctuary.'

When the Duke had done, the temporal men all, and good part of the spiritual also, thinking no hurt at all meant toward the young babe, agreed in effect that if he were not delivered he should be fetched. Howbeit, they thought it all best, in the avoiding of all manner of rumour, that the Lord Cardinal should first essay to get him with her good will. And thereupon all the Council came unto the Star Chamber at Westminster. And the Lord Cardinal, leaving the Protector with the Council in the Star Chamber, departed into the sanctuary to the Queen with divers other lords with him. This may have been for the respect of his honour, or that she should by presence of so many perceive that this errand was not one man's mind. Or it may be that the Protector intended not in this matter to trust any one man alone; or else that if finally she were determined to keep him, some of that company had haply secret instruction incontinent in spite of her mind to take him and to leave her no respite to convey him away, which she was likely to have in mind after this matter should be broken to her, if her time would in any wise serve her.

When the Queen and these lords were come together in presence, the Lord Cardinal showed unto her that it was thought by the Protector and by the whole Council that her keeping of the

King's brother in that place was the thing which caused, not only great rumbles of disapproval among the people, but also insupportable grief and displeasure to the King's royal Majesty. To whose Grace it were a singular comfort to have his natural brother in company, as it was dishonourable to both princes and to all of them and to her also to suffer him in sanctuary—as though the one brother stood in danger and peril of the other. And he showed her that the Council therefore had sent him unto her to require of her the delivery of him, that he might be brought unto the King's presence at his liberty, out of that place which they reckoned as a prison. And there should he be treated according to his station. And she in this doing would do great good to the realm, pleasure to the Council and profit to herself, would give succour to her friends that were in distress, and over that (which, he knew well, she specially valued), give not only great comfort and honour to the King but also to the young Duke himself. Their great welfare it were to be together, as well for many greater causes as also for their disport and recreation—which thing the lords esteemed not slight, though it seem light, well pondering that their youth without recreation and play cannot endure, nor was there any stranger for the convenience of their ages and stations so meet in that point for either of them as either of them for other.

'My lord,' quoth the Queen, 'I say not nay that it were very convenient that this gentleman whom you require were in the company of the King his brother. And, in good faith, methinks it were as great an advantage to them both for yet a while to be in the custody of their mother, the tender age considered not only of the elder, but specially of the younger. For he, besides his infancy that also needs good looking to, has a while been so sore distressed with sickness and is so newly rather a little amended than well recovered, that I dare put no person earthly in trust with his keeping but myself only, considering that there is—as physicians say and as we also find—double the peril in the relapse that was in the first sickness, with which disease, nature, being forlaboured, forwearied, and weakened, becomes the less able to bear a new attack. And albeit there might be found others that would haply do their best unto him, yet is there none that either knows better how to order him than I that so long have kept him, or is more tenderly like to cherish him than his own mother that bore him.'

'No man denies, good madam,' quoth the Cardinal, 'but that your Grace were of all folk most necessary about your children; and so would all the Council not only be content but also glad that you were, if it might stand with your pleasure to be in such place as might stand with their honour. But if you appoint yourself to tarry here, then think they yet more convenient that the Duke of York were with the King honourably at his liberty to the comfort of them both, than here as a sanctuary man to the dishonour and obloquy of them both. For there is not always so great necessity to have the child be with the mother but that occasion may some-time be such that it should be more expedient to keep him else-where. In this well appears that, at such time as your dearest son, then Prince and now King, did for his honour and good order of the country keep household in Wales far out of your company, your Grace was well content therewith yourself.'

'Not very well content,' quoth the Queen. 'And yet the case is not like, for the one was then in health and the other is now sick. In which case I marvel greatly that my lord Protector is so desirous to have him in his keeping, where, if the child in his sickness mis-carried naturally, yet might he run into slander and suspicion of fraud. And where they call it a thing so sore against my child's honour and theirs also, that he bides in this place, it is to all their honours there to suffer him bide where, no man doubts, he shall be best kept. And that is here, while I am here, who as yet intend not to come forth and jeopardize myself like others of my friends—who would God were rather here in surety with me than I were there in jeopardy with them!'

'Why, madam,' quoth another lord, 'know you any thing why they should be in jeopardy?'

'Nay verily, sir,' quoth she, 'nor why they should be in prison neither, as they now be. But it is, I believe, no great marvel, though I fear lest those that have not refrained from putting them in duress without reason will refrain as little from procuring their destruction without cause.'

The Cardinal made a countenance to the other lord, that he should harp no more upon that string. And then he said to the Queen that he nothing doubted but that those lords of her honourable kin who as yet remained under arrest should, upon the matter examined, do well enough. And as towards her noble person, neither was nor could be any manner of jeopardy.

'Whereby should I trust that?' quoth the Queen. 'In that I am guiltless? As though they were guilty. In that I am by their enemies better beloved than they? When they hate them for my sake. In that I am so near of kin to the King? And how far be they off, if that would help, as God send grace it hurt not? And therefore as for me, I purpose not as yet to depart hence. And as for this gentleman my son, I intend that he shall be where I am till I see further. For I assure you, for that I see some men so greedy, without any substantial cause, to have him, this makes me much the more further from delivering him.'

'Truly, madam,' quoth he, 'and the further that you be from delivering him, the further be other men from suffering you to keep him, lest your causeless fear might cause you farther to convey him. And many be there that think that he can have no privilege in this place who neither can have will to ask it nor malice to deserve it. And therefore they reckon no privilege broken, though they fetch him out. Which, if ye finally refuse to deliver him, I verily think they will. So much dread has my Lord his uncle, for the tender love he bears him, lest your Grace should hap to send him away.'

'Ah, sir,' quoth the Queen, 'has the Protector so tender zeal to him that he fears nothing but lest he should escape him? Thinks he that I would send him hence who is in no condition to send out.

And in what place could I reckon him sure if he be not sure in this the sanctuary, whereof was there never tyrant yet so devilish that he durst presume to break it? And I trust God as strong now to withstand His adversaries as ever He was. But my son can deserve no sanctuary, and therefore he cannot have it. Forsooth, he has found a goodly gloss—by which that place that may defend a thief may not save an innocent! But he is in no jeopardy nor has no need thereof. Would God he had not!

'Believes the Protector (I pray God he may prove a protector!), believes he that I perceive not whereunto his painted process draws?

'It is not honourable that the Duke bide here; it were comfortable for them both that he were with his brother because the King lacks a playfellow, be you sure. I pray God send them both better play-fellows than him that makes so high a matter upon such a trifling pretext. As though there could none be found to play with the King unless his brother—that has, for sickness, no desire to play—come out of sanctuary, out of his safeguard, to play with him. As though princes as young as they be, could not play but with their peers, or children could not play but with their kindred, with whom for the more part they agree much worse than with strangers. But the child cannot require the privilege—who told him so? He shall hear him ask it, and he will. Howbeit, this is a gay matter!

'Suppose he could not ask it, suppose he would not ask it, sup-pose he would ask to go out—if I say he shall not, if I ask the privi-lege but for myself, I say he that against my will takes out him breaks the sanctuary. Serves this liberty for my person only, or for my goods too? Ye may not hence take my horse from me; and may you take my child from me? He is also my ward, for, as my learned counsel shows me, since he has nothing by descent held by knight's service [and holding no such tenure cannot be re-garded as an independent person], the law makes his mother his guardian. Then may no man, I suppose, take my ward from me out of sanctuary, without the breach of the sanctuary. And if my privilege could not serve him, nor he ask it for himself, yet since the law commits to me the custody of him, I may require it for him—except the law give a child a guardian only for his goods and his lands, discharging him of the care and safekeeping of his body, for which alone both lands and goods serve.

§ 'And if examples be sufficient to obtain privilege for my child, I need not far to seek. For in this place in which we now be (and which is now in question whether my child may take benefit of it) my other son now King was born, and kept in his cradle, and preserved to a more prosperous fortune, which I pray God long to continue. As all you know, this is not the first time that I have taken sanctuary, for when my Lord my husband was banished and thrust out of his kingdom, I fled hither being great with child, and here I bore the Prince. And when my Lord my husband returned safe again and had the victory, then went I hence to welcome him home, and from hence I brought my babe the Prince unto his father, when he first took him in his arms. I pray God that my son's palace may be as great safeguard to him now reigning, as this place was some time to him when an enemy reigned. §

'Wherefore, here I intend to keep his brother, since man's law serves the guardian to keep the infant. The law of nature wills that the mother keep her child. God's law privileges the sanctuary, and the sanctuary my son, since I fear to put him in the Protector's hands, for he has his brother already and would be, if both failed, inheritor to the crown. The cause of my fear has no man to-do to examine. Yet fear I no further than the law fears, which, as learned men tell me, forbids every man the custody of them by whose death he may inherit less land than a kingdom. I can say no more. But whosoever he be that breaks this holy sanctuary, I pray God shortly send him need of sanctuary, when he may not come to it. For I would not my mortal enemy were taken out of sanctuary.'

The Lord Cardinal, perceiving that the Queen waxed ever the

§ The text between the § marks was not part of the English *History* but translated from the Latin version.

[62]

longer the farther off, and also that she began to kindle and chafe and speak sore biting words against the Protector, and such as he neither believed and was also loath to hear, he said unto her for a final conclusion that he would no longer dispute the matter. But if she were content to deliver the Duke to him and to the other lords there present, he durst lay his own body and soul both in pledge, not only for his surety but also for his princely state. But if she would give them a resolute answer to the contrary, he would forthwith depart therewithal and, manage whoso would this business afterwards, he never intended more to move her in a matter, in which she thought that he and all others also, save herself, lacked either wit or truth. Wit, if they were so dull that they could nothing perceive what the Protector intended; truth, if they would procure her son to be delivered into his hands in whom they could perceive towards the child any evil intended.

The Queen, with these words, stood a good while in a great study. And forasmuch as she thought the Cardinal more ready to depart than some of the remnant—and for that the Protector himself was ready at hand—she also verily thought she could not keep her son there, but that he should incontinent be taken thence. To convey him elsewhere neither had she time to serve her, nor place determined, nor persons appointed. The message came on her so suddenly that all things were unready. Nothing less had she looked for than to have him fetched out of sanctuary, which now she thought to be so guarded about that he could not be conveyed out untaken. Partly, therefore, since she thought it might fortune her fear to be false, and since she knew so well it was either needless or bootless to resist, she deemed it best, if he should needs go from her, to deliver him. And over that, of the Cardinal's faith she nothing doubted, nor of some other lords neither whom she there saw. Which lords, as she feared lest they might be deceived, so was she well assured they would not be corrupted. Then, thought she, it should yet make them the more warily to look to him and the more circumspectly to see to his surety if she with her own hands delivered him to them of trust. And at the last she took the young Duke by the hand and said unto the lords:

'My Lord,' quoth she, 'and all my lords, I neither am so unwise to mistrust your wits nor so suspicious to mistrust your truths. Of which thing I purpose to make you such a proof as, if either or both lacked in you, might turn both me to great sorrow, the realm to much harm, and you to great reproach. For, lo, here is,' quoth she, 'this gentleman, whom I doubt not but I could here keep safe if I would, whatsoever any man say. And I doubt not also but there be some abroad so deadly enemies unto my blood that if they knew where any of it lay in their own body, they would let it out. We have also had experience that the desire of a kingdom knows no kindred. The brother has been the brother's bane. And may the nephews be sure of their uncle? Each of these children is the other's defence while they be asunder, and each of their lives lies in the other's body. Keep one safe and both be sure, and nothing for them both be more perilous than to be both in one place. For what wise merchant adventures all his goods in one ship?

'All this notwithstanding, here I deliver him, and his brother in him, to keep into your hands, of whom I shall ask them both before God and the world. Faithful you be, that know I well, and I know well you be wise. Power and strength to keep him, if you please, neither lack you of yourself nor can lack help in this cause. And if you cannot elsewhere, then may you leave him here. But only one thing I beseech you, for the trust that his father put in you ever and for the trust that I put in you now, that as far as ye think that I fear too much, be you well wary that you fear not as far too little.'

And therewithal she said unto the child, 'Farewell, my own sweet son. God send you good keeping. Let me kiss you once yet ere you go, for God knows when we shall kiss together again.' And therewith she kissed him and blessed him, turned her back and wept and went her way, leaving the child weeping as fast.

When the Lord Cardinal and these other lords with him had received this young Duke, they brought him into the Star Chamber, where the Protector took him in his arms and kissed him with these words: 'Now welcome, my Lord, even with all my heart.' And he said, in that, of likelihood as he thought. Thereupon forthwith they brought him to the King his brother into the Bishop's Palace at Paul's, and from thence through the city honourably into the Tower, out of which, after that day, they never came abroad.

§ When the Protector had both the children in his hands, he opened himself more boldly, both to certain other men and also chiefly to the Duke of Buckingham, although I know that many thought that this duke was privy to all the Protector's counsel even from the beginning. And some of the Protector's friends said that the Duke was the first mover of the Protector to this matter, sending a privy messenger unto him straight after King Edward's death. But others again, who knew better the subtle wit of the Protector, deny that he ever opened his enterprise to the Duke until he had brought to pass the things before rehearsed. But when he had imprisoned the Queen's kinsfolk and got both her sons into his own hands, then he opened the rest of his purpose, with less fear, to them whom he thought meet for the matter, and specially to the Duke, who, being won to his purpose, he thought his strength more than half increased.

The matter was broken unto the Duke by subtle folks and such as were masters of their craft in the handling of such wicked devices. These declared unto him that the young King was offended with him for his kinsfolk's sakes and that if he were ever able, he would revenge them, while they, if they escaped (for they would remember their imprisonment), would prick him forward thereunto or else, if they were put to death, without doubt the young King would be full of grief for their deaths, for their imprisonment was grievous unto him. With repenting the Duke should nothing avail. There was no way left to redeem his offence by benefits, but that he should sooner destroy himself than save the King, whom

§ The text between the § here and the § on p. 67 was not part of the English *History*, but was translated from the Latin version.

with his brother and his kinsfolk he saw in such places imprisoned as the Protector might with a nod destroy them all. It were no doubt but he would do it indeed if there were any new enterprise attempted. And it was likely that as the Protector had provided privy guard for himself, so had he spies for the Duke and traps to catch him, if he should be against him—and that peradventure from them whom he least suspected. For the state of things and the dispositions of men were then such that a man could not well tell whom he might trust or whom he might fear.

These things and such like, being beaten into the Duke's mind, brought him to the point that, although he had repented the way that he had entered, yet would he go forth in the same; and since he had once begun, he would stoutly go through. And therefore to this wicked enterprise, which he believed could not be avoided, he bent himself and went through, and determined that, since the common mischief could not be amended, he would turn it as much as he might to his own advantage.

Then it was agreed that the Protector should have the Duke's aid to make him King, that the Protector's only lawful son should marry the Duke's daughter, and that the Protector should grant him the quiet possession of the earldom of Hereford, which he claimed as his inheritance and could never obtain in King Edward's time. Besides these requests of the Duke, the Protector of his own mind promised him a great quantity of the King's treasure and of his household stuff. And when they were thus in agreement between themselves, they went about to prepare for the coronation of the young King, as they would have it seem. And that they might turn both the eyes and minds of men from perceiving their drifts elsewhere, the lords, being sent for from all parts of the realm, came thick to that solemnity.

But the Protector and the Duke, after they had set the Lord Cardinal [Thomas Bourchier, Archbishop of Canterbury], the Archbishop of York, the Bishop of Ely, the Lord Stanley, and the Lord Hastings, then Lord Chamberlain, with many other noble men§ to confer and devise about the coronation in one place, as fast were they in another place contriving the contrary, and to make the Protector king. To which council albeit there were invited very few, and they very secret, yet began there, here and there about, some manner of muttering among the people, as though all should not long be well, though they neither knew what they feared nor wherefore—were it that, before such great things, men's hearts of a secret instinct of nature misgive them, as the sea without wind swells of itself sometimes before a tempest; or were it that some one man, haply something perceiving, filled many men with suspicion, though he showed few men what he knew. Howbeit, somewhat the dealing itself made men to muse on the matter, though the council were close. For little by little all folk withdrew from the Tower and drew to Crosby's Place in Bishopsgate Street where the Protector kept his household. The Protector had the resort, the King in manner desolate. While some for their business made suit to them that had the doing, some were by their friends secretly warned that it might haply turn them to no good to be too much attendant about the King without the Protector's appointment, who removed also divers of the Prince's old servants from him and set new about him.

Thus many things coming together, partly by chance, partly of purpose, caused at length, not common people only that wave with the wind, but wise men also and some lords too, to mark the matter and muse thereon; so much that the Lord Stanley, that was after Earl of Derby, wisely mistrusted it and said unto the Lord Hastings that he much misliked these two separate councils. 'For while we,' quoth he, 'talk of one matter in the one place, little know we whereof they talk in the other place.'

'My Lord,' quoth the Lord Hastings, 'on my life, never doubt you. For while one man is there, who is never thence, never can there be thing once intended that should appear amiss towards me but it should be in my ears ere it were well out of their mouths.' By this meant he Catesby, who was of his near, secret counsel, whom he very familiarly used and in his most weighty matters put no man in so special trust. He reckoned himself to no man so dear since he well knew there was no man to him so much beholden as was this Catesby, who was a man well learned in the laws of this land and, by the special favour of the Lord Chamberlain, was in good authority and bore much rule in all the county of Leicester, where the Lord Chamberlain's power chiefly lay. But surely great pity was it that he had not had either more truth or less wit. For his dissimulation only, kept all that mischief up. If the Lord Hastings had not put so special trust in him, the Lord Stanley and he had departed with divers other lords and broken all the dance, but that the many ill signs he saw, he now construed all to the best. So surely thought the Lord Hastings that there could be no harm towards him in that council intended where Catesby was.

And of truth, the Protector and the Duke of Buckingham made very good semblance unto the Lord Hastings and kept him much in company. And undoubtedly the Protector loved him well and loath was to have lost him, saving for fear lest his life should have quelled their purpose. For which cause he moved Catesby to test, with some words cast out afar off, whether he could think it possible to win the Lord Hastings unto their party. But Catesby, whether he essayed him or essayed him not, reported unto them that he found him so steadfast and heard him speak so terrible words that he durst no further proceed. And of truth, the Lord Chamberlain of very trust showed unto Catesby the mistrust that others began to have in the matter. And therefore Catesby, fearing lest their warnings might with the Lord Hastings diminish his credit—whereunto only all the matter leaned—procured the Protector hastily to be rid of him. And much the rather, for that he trusted by his death to obtain much of the rule that the Lord Hastings bore in his country, the only desire whereof was the enticement that induced him to be partner and one special contriver of all this horrible treason.

Whereupon, soon after—to wit, on the Friday, the thirteenth

of June—many lords assembled in the Tower and there sat in council, devising the honourable solemnity of the King's coronation, of which the time appointed then so near approached that the pageants and subtleties [elaborate sculptures in pastry served at feasts] were in making day and night at Westminster, and much victual killed therefor, that was afterwards cast away.

These lords so sitting together conferring about this matter, the Protector came in among them, first about nine of the clock, saluting them courteously and excusing himself that he had been from them so long, saying merrily that he had been asleep that day. And after a little talking with them, he said unto the Bishop of Ely, 'My Lord, you have very good strawberries at your garden in Holborn; I request you, let us have a mess of them.'

'Gladly, my Lord,' quoth he. 'Would God I had some better thing as ready to your pleasure as that.' And therewith in all haste he sent his servant for a mess of strawberries.

The Protector set the lords fast in conferring and, thereupon praying them to spare him for a little while, departed thence. And soon after one hour, between ten and eleven, he returned into the chamber among them, all changed, with a wonderfully sour angry countenance, knitting the brows, frowning, and fretting and gnawing on his lips, and so sat him down in his place—all the lords much dismayed and sore marvelling at this manner of sudden change, and at what thing should ail him.

Then, when he had sat still a while, thus he began: 'What are they worthy to have that compass and plot the destruction of me, being so near of blood unto the King, and Protector of his royal person and his realm?'

At this question, all the lords sat sore astonished, musing much who by this question should be meant, of which every man knew himself clear. Then the Lord Chamberlain, as he that for the love between them thought he might be boldest with him, answered and said that they were worthy to be punished as heinous traitors, whosoever they were. And all the others affirmed the same.

'That is,' quoth the Protector, 'yonder sorceress, my brother's wife, and others with her'—meaning the Queen.

At these words many of the other lords were greatly abashed that favoured her. But the Lord Hastings was in his mind better content that it was moved against her than against any other whom he loved better, albeit his heart somewhat grudged that he was not before made of counsel in this matter, as he had been in the taking of her kindred and of their putting to death. These were, by his assent before, to be beheaded at Pomfret this self same day—on which he was not aware that it was by others devised that himself should be beheaded at London.

Then said the Protector, 'You shall all see in what wise that sorceress and that other witch of her counsel, Shore's wife, with their affinity have by their sorcery and witchcraft wasted my body.' And therewith he plucked up his doublet sleeve to his elbow upon his left arm, where he showed a shrivelled withered arm and small, as it was never otherwise. And thereupon every man's mind sore misgave them, well perceiving that this matter was but a quarrel. For well they knew that the Queen was too wise to go about any such folly. And also if she would, yet would she of all folk least make Shore's wife of counsel, whom of all women she most hated as that concubine whom the King her husband had most loved. And also no man was there present but well knew that his arm was ever such since his birth.

Nevertheless the Lord Chamberlain (who, from the death of King Edward, kept Shore's wife, on whom he somewhat doted in the King's life, saving, as it is said, he that while forbore her, of reverence towards his King or else of a certain kind of fidelity to his friend) answered and said, 'Certainly, my Lord, if they have so heinously done, they be worthy heinous punishment.'

'What!' quoth the Protector. 'Thou servest me, I think, with *ifs* and with *ands*! I tell thee, they have so done! And that, I will make good on thy body, traitor!'

And therewith, as in a great anger, he clapped his fist upon the board a great rap. At which token given, one cried 'Treason!' without the chamber. Therewith a door clapped, and in came there rushing men in armour, as many as the chamber might hold.

And at once the Protector said to the Lord Hastings, 'I arrest thee, traitor.'

'What, me, my Lord?' quoth he.

'Yea, thee, traitor!' quoth the Protector.

And another let fly at the Lord Stanley, who shrank at the stroke and fell under the table—or else his head had been cleft to the teeth, for as hastily as he shrank, yet ran the blood about his ears.

Then were they all quickly bestowed in divers chambers, except the Lord Chamberlain, whom the Protector bade speed and shrive him apace. 'For by St Paul,' quoth he, 'I will not to dinner till I see thy head off.' It booted him not to ask why, but heavily he took a priest at random and made a short shrift. A longer would not be suffered, since the Protector made so much haste to dinner, which he might not go to till this were done, for saving of his oath.

So was he brought forth unto the green beside the chapel within the Tower, and his head laid down upon a long log of timber, and there struck off, and afterwards his body with the head interred at Windsor beside the body of King Edward—our Lord pardon both their souls.

A marvellous case is it to hear either the warnings of that he should have avoided, or the tokens of that he could not avoid. For the very night before his death, the Lord Stanley had sent a trusty secret messenger unto him at midnight in all the haste, requiring him to rise and ride away with him. He was disposed utterly no longer to bide, for he had so fearful a dream—in which he thought that a boar with his tusks so slashed them both by the heads that the blood ran about both their shoulders. And forasmuch as the Protector gave the boar for his cognisance [badge worn by his followers], this dream made so fearful an impression in his heart that he was thoroughly determined no longer to tarry but had his horse ready, if the Lord Hastings would go with him to ride so far the same night that they should be out of danger ere day.

'Oh, good Lord!' quoth the Lord Hastings to this messenger. 'Leans my Lord thy master so much to such trifles and has such faith in dreams, which either his own fear fancies or do rise in the night's rest by reason of his day thoughts? Tell him it is plain witchcraft to believe in such dreams. If they were tokens of things to come, why thinks he not that we might be as likely to make them true by our going, if we were caught and brought back (as friends fail fugitives); for then had the boar a cause likely to slash us with his tusks, as folk that fled for some falseness. Therefore, either is there no peril—nor none there is indeed—or if any be, it is rather in going than biding. And if we should of necessity fall in peril one way or other, yet had I rather that men should see it were by other men's falseness than think it were either our own fault or faint heart. And therefore go to thy master, man, and commend me to him, and pray him be merry and have no fear; for I assure him, I am as sure of the man that he knows of as I am of my own hand.'

'God send grace, sir,' quoth the messenger, and went his way.

Certain is it also that in the riding towards the Tower the same morning in which he was beheaded, his horse twice or thrice stumbled with him almost to the falling, which thing, albeit each man knows well daily happens to them to whom no such mischance is towards, yet has it been, of an old rite and custom, observed as a token often times notably foregoing some great misfortune.

Now this that follows was no warning but an enemy's scorn. The same morning ere he were up, came a knight unto him, as it were of courtesy to accompany him to the council but of truth sent by the Protector to haste him thitherwards. He was of secret confederacy in that purpose, being a mean man at that time and now of great authority. This knight, when it happed the Lord Chamberlain by the way to stay his horse and converse a while with a priest whom he met in the Tower Street, broke his tale and said merrily to him, 'What, my Lord, I pray you come on. Whereto talk you so long with that priest? You have no need of a priest yet!' And therewith he laughed upon him as though he would say, ye shall have soon. But so little knew the other what he meant, and so little mistrusted, that he was never merrier nor never so full of good hope in his life, which very thing is often seen as a sign of change. But I shall rather let anything pass me by than the vain surety of man's mind so near his death.

Upon the very Tower wharf, so near the place where his head was off so soon after, there met he with one Hastings, a pursuivant of his own name. And at their meeting in that place he was put in remembrance of another time in which it had happened them before to meet in like manner together in the same place. At which other time the Lord Chamberlain had been accused unto King Edward by the Lord Rivers, the Queen's brother, in such wise that he was for the while (but it lasted not long) far fallen into the King's indignation and stood in great fear of himself. And forasmuch as he now met this pursuivant in the same place, that jeopardy so well passed, it gave him great pleasure to talk with him thereof.

And therefore he said, 'Ah, Hastings, are you remembered when I met you here once with an heavy heart?'

'Yea, my Lord,' quoth he, 'that remember I well; and thanked be God they got no good nor you no harm thereby.'

'You would say so,' quoth he, 'if you knew as much as I know, which few know else as yet and more shall shortly.' By that meant he the lords of the Queen's kindred that were taken before and should that day be beheaded at Pomfret, which he well knew, but was nothing aware that the axe hung over his own head. 'In faith, man,' quoth he, 'I was never so sorry nor never stood in so great dread in my life as I did when you and I met here. And lo! how the world is turned! Now stand mine enemies in the danger (as you may hap to hear more hereafter) and I never in my life so merry nor never in so great surety.'

[73]

O good God, the blindness of our mortal nature! When he most feared, he was in good surety; when he reckoned himself surest, he lost his life, and that within two hours after. Thus ended this honourable man, a good knight and a gentle, of great authority with his prince, of living somewhat dissolute, plain and open to his enemy and secret to his friend, easy to beguile as he that of good heart and courage forestudied no perils. A loving man and passing well beloved. Very faithful, and trusty enough, trusting too much.

Now flew the rumour of this lord's death swiftly through the city, and so forth farther about, like a wind in every man's ear. But the Protector immediately after dinner, intending to set some colour upon the matter, sent in all the haste for many substantial men out of the city into the Tower. And at their coming, himself with the Duke of Buckingham stood armoured in old ill-faring brigandines [leather coats covered with overlapping pieces of metal], such as no man should think that they would vouchsafe to have put upon their backs except that some sudden necessity had constrained them. And then the Protector showed them that the Lord Chamberlain and others of his conspiracy had contrived to have suddenly destroyed him and the Duke, there the same day in the council. And what they intended further was as yet not well known. Of which treason he never had knowledge before ten of the clock the same forenoon. Which sudden fear drove them to put on for their defence such armour as came next to hand. And so had God helped them that the mischief turned upon them that would have done it. And this he required them to report. Every man answered him fair, as though no man mistrusted the matter, which of truth no man believed.

Yet for the further appeasing of the people's mind, he sent immediately after dinner in all the haste one herald of arms with a proclamation to be made through the city in the King's name, containing that the Lord Hastings with divers others of his traitorous purpose had before conspired the same day to have slain the Lord Protector and the Duke of Buckingham sitting in the council, and after to have taken upon them to rule the King and the realm at their pleasure, and thereby uncontrolled to pillage and spoil whom they pleased. And much matter was there in the proclamation devised to the slander of the Lord Chamberlain: as that he was an evil counsellor to the King's father—enticing him to many things highly redounding to the diminishing of his honour and to the universal hurt of his realm—by his evil company, sinister procuring, and ungracious example, as well in many other things as in the vicious living and inordinate abuse of his body, both with many others and also specially with Shore's wife—who was one also of his most secret counsel of this heinous treason—with whom he lay nightly, and especially the night last passed before his death. It was, therefore, the less marvel if ungracious living brought him to an unhappy ending—which he was now put unto by the most dread commandment of the King's Highness and of his honourable and faithful Council, both for his demerits, being so openly taken in his falsely conceived treason, and also lest the delaying of his execution might have encouraged other mischievous persons, partners of his conspiracy, to gather and assemble themselves together in making some great commotion for his deliverance. Their hope now being by his well deserved death politicly repressed, all the realm should, by God's grace, rest in good quiet and peace.

Now was this proclamation made within two hours after he was beheaded, and it was so elaborately endited and so fair written in parchment in so well-set a hand, and therewith of itself so long a process, that every child might well perceive that it was prepared before. For all the time between his death and the proclaiming could scarce have sufficed unto the bare writing alone, although it had been but in paper and scribbled forth in haste at random. So that upon the proclaiming thereof, one that was schoolmaster of Paul's, of chance standing by and comparing the shortness of the time with the length of the matter, said unto them that stood about him, 'Here is a gay goodly cast [artifice] foully cast away for haste.' And a merchant answered him that it was written by prophecy.

Now then, by and by, as it were for anger, not for covetousness, the Protector sent into the house of Shore's wife (for her husband dwelt not with her) and spoiled her of all that ever she had, about the value of two or three thousand marks,* and sent her body to prison. And when he had a while laid unto her, for the manner's sake, that she went about to bewitch him and that she was of counsel with the Lord Chamberlain to destroy him, and when, in conclusion, no plausibility could he fasten upon these matters, then he laid heinously to her charge the thing that herself could not deny, that all the world knew was true—and that nevertheless every man laughed at to hear it then so suddenly so highly taken—that she was free of her body.

And for this cause (as a goodly continent prince, clean and fault-less of himself, sent out of heaven into this vicious world for the amendment of men's manners) he caused the Bishop of London to put her to open penance, to go before the cross in procession upon a Sunday with a taper in her hand. In which she went in coun-tenance and pace demure, so womanly, and albeit she were out of all array save her kirtle only, yet went she so fair and lovely—especially while the wondering of the people cast a comely red in her cheeks (of which she before had most lack)—that her great shame won her much praise among those that were more amorous of her body than concerned for her soul. And many good folk also, that hated her living and glad were to see sin corrected, yet pitied they more her penance than rejoiced therein, when they con-sidered that the Protector procured it more of a corrupt intent than any virtuous feeling.

This woman was born in London, worthily friended, honour-ably brought up, and very well married, saving somewhat too soon, her husband an honest citizen, young and goodly and of good substance. But forasmuch as they were coupled ere she were well ripe, she not very fervently loved for whom she never longed. Which was haply the thing that the more easily made her incline

* The mark was worth two-thirds of a pound.

[76]

unto the King's appetite when he required her. Howbeit, the respect of his royalty, the hope of gay apparel, ease, pleasure, and other lavish lures, were able soon to pierce a soft tender heart. But when the King had misused her, at once her husband (as he was an honest man and one that knew his good, not presuming to touch a King's concubine) left her to him altogether. When the King died, the Lord Chamberlain took her, who, in the King's days, albeit he was sore enamoured upon her, yet he forbore her, either for reverence or for a certain friendly faithfulness.

Proper she was and fair: nothing in her body that you would have changed, unless you would have wished her somewhat higher. Thus say they that knew her in her youth, albeit some that now see her (for yet she lives) deem her never to have been well visaged. Their judgement seems to me somewhat like as though men should guess the beauty of one long before departed by her scalp taken out of the charnel house; for now is she old, lean, withered, and dried up, nothing left but shrivelled skin and hard bone. And yet being even such, whoso well regards her visage might guess and imagine which parts, how filled, would make it a fair face.

Yet delighted not men so much in her beauty as in her pleasant behaviour. For a proper wit had she and could both read well and write, merry in company, ready and quick of answer, neither mute nor full of babble, sometimes taunting without displeasure and not without disport. The King would say that he had three concubines, who in three diverse properties diversely excelled. One, the merriest; another, the wiliest; the third, the holiest harlot in his realm, as one whom no man could get out of the church lightly to any place but it were to his bed. The other two were somewhat greater personages, and nevertheless of their humility content to be nameless and to forgo the praise of those properties. But the merriest was this Shore's wife, in whom the King therefor took special pleasure. For many he had, but her he loved—whose favour, to say truth (for sin it were to belie the devil), she never abused to any man's hurt, but to many a man's comfort and relief. Where the

[77]

King took displeasure, she would mitigate and appease his mind; where men were out of favour, she would bring them in his grace. For many that had highly offended, she obtained pardon; of great forfeitures she got men remission. And finally in many weighty suits she stood many men in great stead, either for none or very small rewards, and those rather gay than rich, either for that she was content with the deed's self well done, or for that she delighted to be sued unto and to show what she was able to do with the King, or for that wanton women and well-to-do be not always covetous.

I doubt not some shall think this woman too slight a thing to be written of and set among the remembrances of great matters, which they shall specially think that haply shall esteem her only by what they now see her. But methinks the chance so much the more worthy to be remembered in how much she is now in the more beggarly condition—unfriended and worn out of acquaintance [cast aside by the world] after good substance, after as great favour with the Prince, after as great suit and seeking to by all those that those days had business to speed, as many other men had in their times who be now famous only by the infamy of their ill deeds. Her doings were not much less, albeit they be much less remembered because they were not so evil. For men use, if they have an evil turn, to write it in marble; and whoso does us a good turn, we write it in dust—which is not worst proved by her, for at this day she begs of many at this day living, that at this day had begged if she had not been.

Now was it so devised by the Protector and his council that the very day in which the Lord Chamberlain was beheaded in the Tower of London and about the selfsame hour, were there—not without his assent—beheaded at Pomfret the foreremembered lords and knights that were taken from the King at Northampton and Stony Stratford. Which thing was done in the presence and by the order of Sir Richard Ratcliffe, knight, whose service the Protector specially used in the counsel and in the execution of such lawless enterprises, as a man that had been long secret with him, having experience of the world and a shrewd wit, short and rude in speech, rough and boisterous of behaviour, bold in mischief, as far from pity as from all fear of God. This knight, bringing them out of the prison to the scaffold and showing to the people about that they were traitors, not suffering them to speak and declare their innocence lest their words might have inclined men to pity them and to hate the Protector and his party, caused them hastily, without judgement, process, or manner of order, to be beheaded—and without any other guilt but only that they were good men, too true to the King and too nigh to the Queen.

Now, when the Lord Chamberlain and these other lords and knights were thus beheaded and got out of the way, then thought the Protector that, while men mused what the matter meant, while the lords of the realm were about him and out of their own strongholds, while no man knew what to think nor whom to trust, ere ever they should have space to discuss and digest the matter and make parties, it were best hastily to pursue his purpose and put himself in possession of the crown, ere men could have time to devise any ways to resist.

Now was all the study by what means this matter, being of itself so heinous, might be first broken to the people in such wise that it might be well taken. Into this counsel they took divers, such as they thought meet to be trusted, likely to be induced to the party and able to stand them in stead either by power or policy. Among whom, they made of counsel Edmund Shaa, knight, then Mayor of London, who upon trust of his own advancement, whereof he was of a proud heart highly desirous, should frame the city to their appetite. Of spiritual men they took such as had wit and were in authority among the people for opinion of their learning, and who had no scrupulous conscience.

Among these had they Ralph Shaa, clerk, brother to the Mayor, and Friar Penketh, Provincial of the Augustine Friars, both Doctors of Divinity, both great preachers, both of more learning than virtue, of more fame than learning. For they were before greatly esteemed among the people, but after that never. Of these two, the one had a sermon in praise of the Protector before the coronation, the other after; both so full of tedious flattery that no man's ears could abide them. Penketh in his sermon so lost his voice that he was glad to leave off and come down in the midst. Doctor Shaa by his sermon lost his reputation and soon after his life, for very shame of the world, into which he durst never after come abroad. But the friar had no care for shame, and so it harmed him the less. Howbeit, some doubt and many think that Penketh was not of counsel in the matter before the coronation, but after the common manner fell to flattery after, especially since his sermon was not immediately upon it but at St Mary's Hospital at the Easter after. But certain is it that Doctor Shaa was of counsel in the beginning, so much that they determined that he should first break the matter in a sermon at Paul's Cross, in which he should by the authority of his preaching incline the people to the Protector's holy purpose.

But now was all the labour and study in the devising of some convenient pretext, for which the people should be content to depose the Prince and accept the Protector for King. In which, divers things they devised. But the chief thing and the most weighty of all that invention rested in this, that they should allege bastardy either in King Edward himself or in his children or both, so that he should seem disabled from inheriting the crown through the Duke of York [his father], and the Prince through him.

To lay bastardy in King Edward redounded openly to the rebuke of the Protector's own mother, who was mother to them both, for in that point could be no other colour but to pretend that his own mother was an adulteress. This notwithstanding, to further his purpose he omitted not to do. Nevertheless, he would the point should be more or less favourably handled, not even, fully plain, and directly, but that the matter should be touched aslant, craftily, as though men forbore in the point to speak all the truth for fear of his displeasure. But the other point concerning the bastardy that they devised to surmise in King Edward's children, that, wished he, should be openly declared and enforced to the uttermost. The colour and pretext whereof cannot be well perceived unless we first repeat to you some things long before done about King Edward's marriage.

After King Edward the Fourth had deposed King Henry the Sixth and was in peaceable possession of the realm, determining himself to marry—as it was requisite both for himself and for the realm—he sent over in embassy the Earl of Warwick with other noble men in his company unto Spain, to treat for and conclude a marriage between King Edward and the King's daughter of Spain.* In which thing the Earl of Warwick found the parties so towards and willing that he speedily, according to his instructions, without any difficulty brought the matter to very good conclusion. Now happed it that in the mean season there came to make a suit by petition to the King, Dame Elizabeth Grey, who was after his Queen, at that time a widow born of noble blood, specially by her mother who was Duchess of Bedford ere she married the Lord Woodville [Richard Woodville, Lord Rivers], Elizabeth's father. Howbeit, this Dame Elizabeth, herself being in service with Queen Margaret, wife unto Henry the Sixth, was married unto one John Grey, esquire, whom King Henry made knight upon the field fought on Shrove Tuesday at St Albans against King Edward.† And little while enjoyed he that knighthood, for he was on the same field slain.

After which done, and the Earl of Warwick being in his embassy about the foreremembered marriage, this poor lady made humble suit unto the King that she might be restored unto such small lands as her late husband had given her in jointure. Whom when the King beheld and heard her speak, as she was both fair, of goodly

* Warwick negotiated, through embassies, with Louis XI of France for Bona of Savoy.
† Second battle of St Albans, February 1461, in which Queen Margaret defeated Warwick.

appearance, moderate of stature, well made and very wise, he not only pitied her but also waxed enamoured on her. And taking her afterwards secretly aside, began to enter into talking more familiarly. Whose appetite when she perceived, she virtuously denied him, but so wisely and with so good manner and words so well set that she rather kindled his desire than quenched it. And finally, after many a meeting, much wooing, and many great promises, she well espied the King's affection towards her so greatly increased that she durst somewhat the more boldly say her mind to him whose heart she perceived more firmly set than to fall off for a word. And in conclusion she showed him plain that as she knew herself too simple to be his wife, so thought she herself too good to be his concubine.

The King, much marvelling of her constancy, as he that had not been wont elsewhere to be so stiffly said nay, so much esteemed her continence and chastity that he set her virtue in the stead of possession and riches. And thus taking counsel of his desire, determined in all possible haste to marry her. And after he was thus decided, and had between them twain assured her, then asked he counsel of his other friends, and that in such manner as they might easily perceive it booted not greatly to say nay.

Notwithstanding, the Duchess of York, his mother, was so sore moved therewith that she opposed the marriage as much as she possibly might, alleging that it was his honour, profit, and surety also to marry into a noble family out of his realm, whereupon depended great strength to his estate by the affinity and great possibility of increase of his possessions. And that he could not well otherwise do, seeing that the Earl of Warwick had so far moved already, and he were not likely to take it well if all his voyage were in such wise frustrated and his negotiations mocked. And she said also that it was not princely to marry his own subject, no great occasion leading thereunto, no possessions or other advantages depending thereupon, but only, as it were, a rich man that would marry his maid only for a little wanton dotage upon her person. In which marriage, many more commend the maiden's fortune than the master's wisdom. And yet therein, she said, was more honesty, than honour in this marriage, forasmuch as there is between no merchant and his own maid so great difference as between the King and this widow. In her person, albeit there was nothing to be misliked, yet was there, she said, nothing so excellent but that it might be found in divers others, 'that were more meet,' quoth she, 'for your station, and also maidens. The widowhood of Elizabeth Grey alone, though she were in all other things convenient for you, should yet suffice, as meseems, to refrain you from her marriage, since it is an unfitting thing, and a very blemish and high disparagement to the sacred majesty of a Prince—that ought as nigh to approach priesthood in purity as he does in dignity—to be defouled with bigamy in his first marriage.'

The King, when his mother had said, made her answer part in earnest, part in play merrily, as he that knew himself out of her rule. And albeit he would gladly that she should take it well, yet was he at a conclusion in his own mind, took she it well or otherwise. Howbeit, somewhat to satisfy her he said that albeit marriage, being a spiritual thing, ought rather to be made for the respect of God—where His grace inclines the parties to love together, as he trusted it was in his—than for the regard of any temporal advantage, yet, nevertheless, it seemed to him that this marriage, even worldly considered, was not unprofitable. For he reckoned the amity of no other nation so necessary for him as the friendship of his own, which he thought likely to bear him so much the more hearty favour in that he disdained not to marry with one of his own land. And yet if outward alliance were thought so requisite, he would find the means to enter thereinto much better by others of his kin, where all the parties could be contented, than to marry himself one whom he should haply never love and, for the possibility of more possessions, lose the fruit and pleasure of this that he had already. For small pleasure takes a man in all that ever he has besides, if he be wived against his appetite.

'And I doubt not,' quoth he, 'but there be, as you say, others that be in every point comparable with her. And therefore I prevent not them that like them from wedding them. No more is it reasonable that it mislike any man that I marry where it likes me. And I am sure that my cousin of Warwick neither loves me so little as to resent what I love, nor is so unreasonable as to look that I should in choice of a wife rather be ruled by his eye than by mine own, as though I were a ward that were bound to marry by the appointment of a guardian. I would not be a King with that condition, to forgo mine own liberty in choice of my own marriage. As for possibility of more inheritance by new affinity in foreign lands, it is often the occasion of more trouble than profit. And we have already title [the English claim to France] by those means to so much as suffices to get and keep well in one man's days.

'That she is a widow and has already children—by God's blessed Lady, I am a bachelor and have some too! And so each of us has a proof that neither of us is like to be barren. And therefore, Madam, I pray you be content; I trust in God she shall bring forth a young prince that shall please you. And as for the bigamy, let the bishop indeed lay it in my way—when I come to take [Holy] Orders. For I understand it is forbidden a priest, but I never knew it yet that it was forbidden a prince.'

The Duchess, with these words nothing appeased and seeing the King so set thereon that she could not pull him back, so highly disdained it that, under pretext of her duty towards God, she devised to disturb this marriage and rather to help that he should marry one Dame Elizabeth Lucy, whom the King had also not long before got with child. Wherefore the King's mother objected openly against his marriage, as it were in discharge of her conscience, that the King was ensured [betrothed] to Dame Elizabeth Lucy and was her husband before God. By reason of which words, such obstacle was made in the matter that either the bishops durst not, or the King would not, proceed to the solemnizing of this wedding, till these same were clearly purged and the truth well and openly testified.

Whereupon Dame Elizabeth Lucy was sent for, and albeit that she was by the King's mother and many others put in good comfort to affirm that she was ensured unto the King, yet when she was solemnly sworn to say the truth, she confessed that they were never ensured. Howbeit, she said his Grace spake so loving words unto her that she verily hoped he would have married her, and that if it had not been for such kind words, she would never have showed such kindness to him, to let him so kindly* get her with child. This examination solemnly taken, when it was clearly perceived that there was no impediment, the King with great feast and honourable solemnity married Dame Elizabeth Grey, and her crowned Queen that was his enemy's wife and many times had prayed full heartily for his loss. In which God loved her better than to grant her her boon.

But when the Earl of Warwick learned of this marriage, he took it so highly that his embassy was mocked, that for very anger and disdain he at his return assembled a great puissance against the King and came so fast upon him, ere he could be able to resist, that he was fain to leave the realm and flee into Holland for succour. There he remained for the space of two years, leaving his new wife in Westminster in sanctuary, where she was delivered of Edward the Prince, of whom we before have spoken.

In which meantime the Earl of Warwick took out of prison and set up again King Henry the Sixth, who was before by King Edward deposed, and that mostly by the power of the Earl of Warwick. This same Earl was a wise man and a courageous warrior and of such strength, what with his lands, his allies, and favour with all the people, that he made kings and put down kings almost at his pleasure—and it were not impossible for him to have attained it himself if he had not reckoned it a greater thing to make a king than to be a king. But nothing lasts always; for in conclusion King Edward returned, and, with much less number, at Barnet on

* This *double entendre* is typical of More's exuberant word-play: *kindly* also means *naturally*.

the Easter Day field slew the Earl of Warwick with many other great lords of that party. Thus, so stably attained he the crown again that he peaceably enjoyed it until his dying day, and in such condition left it that it could not be lost but by the discord of his true friends or falsehood of his feigned friends.

I have rehearsed this business about this marriage somewhat the more at length because it might thereby the better appear upon how slippery a ground the Protector built his pretext, by which he pretended King Edward's children to be bastards. But that invention, foolish as it was, pleased them to whom it sufficed to have somewhat to say, while they were sure to be compelled to no larger proof than themselves desired to make.

Now then, as I began to show you, it was by the Protector and his council concluded that this Doctor Shaa should in a sermon at Paul's Cross signify to the people that neither King Edward himself nor the Duke of Clarence were lawfully begot, nor were the very children of the Duke of York who were got unlawfully by other persons by the adultery of the Duchess their mother. And that also Dame Elizabeth Lucy was verily the wife of King Edward, and so the Prince, and all his children, bastards that were got upon the Queen.

According to this device, Doctor Shaa the Sunday after [June 22] at Paul's Cross in a great audience (as always, assembled great numbers to his preaching), he took for his theme *Spuria vitulamina non agent radices altas*. That is to say, bastard slips shall never take deep root. Thereupon, when he had showed the great grace that God gives and secretly pours into the right generation after the laws of matrimony, then declared he that commonly those children lacked that grace—and for the punishment of their parents were for the more part unhappy—who were got in bastardy and specially in adultery. Of whom, though some, by the ignorance of the world and the truth hid from knowledge, inherited for the season other men's lands, yet God always so provides that it continues not in their blood long, but, the truth coming to light, the rightful inheritors be restored, and the bastard slip pulled up ere it can be rooted deep. And when he had laid for the proof and confirmation of this saying certain examples taken out of the Old Testament and other ancient histories, then began he to descend into the praise of the Lord Richard, late Duke of York, calling him father to the Lord Protector, and declaring the title of his heirs unto the crown, to whom it was, after the death of King Henry the Sixth, entailed by authority of Parliament. Then showed he that his very right heir of his body lawfully begot was only the Lord Protector. For he declared then that King Edward was never lawfully married unto the Queen but was, before God, husband unto Dame Elizabeth Lucy, and so his children bastards. And besides that, neither King Edward himself nor the Duke of Clarence were reckoned, among those that were secret in the household, very surely for the children of the noble Duke, as those that in their features more resembled other known men than him. From whose virtuous conditions, he said also that King Edward was far off. But the Lord Protector, he said, that very noble prince, that special pattern of knightly prowess, as well in all princely behaviour as in the lineaments and features of his visage, represented the very face of the noble Duke his father. 'This is,' quoth he, 'the father's own figure, this is his own countenance, the very print of his visage, the sure undoubted image, the plain express likeness, of that noble Duke!'

Now, was it before devised that, in the speaking of these words, the Protector should have come in among the people to the sermon, to the end that those words meeting with his presence might have been taken among the hearers as though the Holy Ghost had put them in the preacher's mouth, and should have moved the people even there to cry 'King Richard! King Richard!' so that it might have been after said that he was specially chosen by God and, in a manner, by miracle.

But this device failed, either by the Protector's negligence or by the preacher's overmuch diligence. For while the Protector found means of tarrying by the way lest he should arrive before those words, the Doctor, fearing that he should come ere his sermon could come to those words, hastened his matter thereto: he was come to them and past them and entered into other matters ere the Protector came. Whom when he beheld coming, he suddenly left the matter with which he was in hand and without any transition thereunto, out of all order and out of all design, began to repeat those words again: 'This is the very noble prince, the special pattern of knightly prowess, which as well in all princely behaviour as in the lineaments and features of his visage represents the very face of the noble Duke of York his father. This is the father's own figure, this his own countenance, the very print of his visage, the sure undoubted image, the plain express likeness, of the noble Duke, whose remembrance can never die while he lives.'

While these words were being spoken, the Protector, accompanied by the Duke of Buckingham, went through the people into the place where the doctors commonly stand in the upper story, where he stood to hearken to the sermon. But the people were so far from crying 'King Richard!' that they stood as if they had been turned into stones, for wonder of this shameful sermon. After which, once ended, the preacher got him home and never after durst look out, for shame, but kept him out of sight like an owl. And when he once asked one that had been his old friend, what the people talked of him, although his own conscience well showed him that they talked no good, yet when the other answered him that there was in every man's mouth spoken of him much shame, it so struck him to the heart that within few days after he withered and consumed away.

Then, on the Tuesday following this sermon [June 24], there came unto the Guildhall in London the Duke of Buckingham, accompanied by divers lords and knights, more than perhaps knew the message that they brought. And there in the east end of the hall where the Mayor keeps the [Court of] Hustings, the Mayor and all the Aldermen being assembled about him, all the commons of the city [the principal citizens] gathered before them, after silence commanded upon great pain in the Protector's name, the Duke stood up and (as he was neither unlearned, and of nature marvellously well spoken) he spoke unto the people with a clear and a loud voice in this wise:

'Friends, for the zeal and hearty favour that we bear you, we be come to break unto you a matter right great and weighty, and no less weighty than pleasing to God and profitable to all the realm; nor to no part of the realm more profitable than to you, the citizens of this noble city. For why? That thing that we know well you have long time lacked and sore longed for, that you would have given great goods for, that you would have gone far to fetch, that thing we be come hither to bring you, without your labour, pain, cost, adventure, or jeopardy.

'What thing is that? Certes, the surety of your own bodies, the quiet of your wives and your daughters, the safeguard of your goods; of all which things in time passed you stood ever more in doubt. For who was there of you all that would reckon himself lord of his own goods, among so many snares and traps as were set therefor, among so much pillaging and plundering, among so many taxes and tallages, of which there was never end and often time no need, or if any were, it rather grew of riot and unreasonable waste than any necessary or honourable charge? So that there was daily plundered from good men and honourable, great substance of goods, to be lavished among unthrifts so extravagantly that Fifteenths* sufficed not, nor any usual names of known taxes; but, under an easy name of "benevolence and good will," the commissioners so much of every man took, as no man would with his good will have given. As though the name of benevolence had signified that every man should pay, not what himself of his good will was pleased to grant, but what the King of his good will was

---

* 'Fifteenth and Tenth' (one-fifteenth in the country and one-tenth in towns) was a tax on personal property granted by Parliament to the King, supposedly to meet extraordinary needs.

[89]

pleased to take. Who never asked little, but every thing was raised above the measure: amercements turned into fines, fines into ransoms, small trespass to misprision, misprision into treason.

'Whereof, I think, no man expects that we should remind you with examples by name—as though Burdet were forgotten, that was for a word spoken in haste cruelly beheaded, through the misconstruing of the laws of this realm for the Prince's pleasure. But no less honour was there to Markham, then Chief Justice—who left his office rather than he would assent to that judgement—than dishonour to those that either for fear or flattery gave that judgement.

'What of Cook, your own honoured neighbour, Alderman and Mayor of this noble city? Who is of you either so negligent that he knows not, or so forgetful that he remembers not, or so hard-hearted that he pities not, that honoured man's loss? What, speak we of loss? His utter despoiling and undeserved destruction, only for that it happed those to favour him whom the Prince favoured not.*

'We need not, I suppose, rehearse these any more by name, since there be, I doubt not, many here present that either in themselves or their near friends have known as well their goods as their persons greatly endangered, either by feigned quarrels or small

*Thomas Burdet was charged with complicity in the schemes of the Duke of Clarence and executed in 1477. The 'word spoken in haste' probably refers to the story, preserved in Stow's *Annals*, that Burdet, on learning that King Edward, while hunting in Burdet's park, had slain a pet white buck of his, exclaimed that he wished the buck's head in the belly of him who did the killing.

Sir John Markham did not preside at Burdet's trial but at the trial of Sir Thomas Cook, a wealthy draper, accused of treason in 1467 for secretly lending money to Queen Margaret. Because Markham directed the jury to bring in a verdict of misprision of treason only, he was removed from his office of Chief Justice a few months later, probably at the urging of his enemies, the Woodvilles.

matters exaggerated by heinous names. And also there was no accusation so great of which there could lack a pretext. For since the King, anticipating the time of his inheritance, attained the crown by battle, it sufficed in a rich man, for a pretext of treason, to have been of kindred or alliance, near familiarity or light acquaintance, with any of those that were at any time the King's enemies—which meant, at one time and other, more than half the realm.

'Thus were neither your goods in surety, and yet they brought your bodies in jeopardy—besides the general risk of open war. Albeit that this is ever the source and occasion of much mischief, yet is it never so mischievous as where any people fall into discord among themselves, nor in no nation on earth so deadly and so pestilent as when it happens among us, and among us never so long-continued dissension, nor so many battles in the season, nor so cruel and so deadly fought, as was in the King's days that dead is, God forgive it his soul.

'In his time and by his occasion, the getting of the garland, keeping it, losing and winning again, cost more English blood than has twice the winning of France. In which inward war among ourselves was so great effusion of the ancient noble blood of this realm that scarcely the half remains, to the great enfeebling of this noble land, besides many a good town ransacked and spoiled by them that have been going to the field or coming from thence. And peace long after not much surer than war. So that no time was there in which rich men for their money, and great men for their lands, or some other for some fear or some displeasure, were out of peril.

'For whom trusted he that mistrusted his own brother? Whom spared he that killed his own brother? Or who could perfectly love him if his own brother could not? What manner of folk he most favoured, we shall for his honour spare to speak of; howbeit, this know you well all, that whoso was best, bore always least rule; and more suit was in his days unto Shore's wife, a vile and an abominable strumpet, than to all the lords in England, except unto those that made her their patron. And this simple woman was well named and chaste till the King for his wanton lust and sinful affection snatched her from her husband, a right honest, substantial young man among you.

'And in that point, which, in good faith, I am sorry to speak of, saving that it is in vain to keep secret that thing that all men know, the King's greedy appetite was insatiable, and everywhere over all the realm intolerable. For no woman was there anywhere, young or old, rich or poor, whom he set his eye upon, in whom he anything liked—either person or face, speech, pace, or countenance—but without any fear of God or respect of his honour, murmur or grudge of the world, he would importunately pursue his appetite and have her, to the great destruction of many a good woman, and great dolour to their husbands and their other friends. They, being honourable people of themselves, so much regard the purity of their house, the chastity of their wives and their children, that they would rather lose all that they have besides than to have such a villainy done them. And although with this and other insupportable dealing, the realm was in every part annoyed, yet specially you here, the citizens of this noble city, as well for that among you is most plenty of all such things as furnish matter for such injuries, as for that you were nearest at hand, since near hereabout was commonly his place of dwelling.

'And yet be you the people whom he had as singular cause well and kindly to treat as any part of his realm, not only for that the Prince by this noble city, as his special chamber and the special well renowned city of his realm, much honourable fame receives among all other nations; but also for that you, not without your great cost and sundry perils and jeopardies in all his wars, bore ever your special favour to his party, which your kind minds cherished towards the House of York.

'Although he has nothing worthily requited this favour, there is one of that House that now by God's grace better shall, which thing to show you is the whole sum and effect of this our present errand.

'It shall not, I know well, need that I rehearse to you again what you have already heard from him that can better tell it and of whom, I am sure, you will better believe it. And reasonable is it that it so be. I am not so proud to look therefor, that you should reckon my words of as great authority as the preacher's of the word of God, especially a man so learned and so wise that no man better knows what he should say, and thereto so good and virtuous that he would not say the thing which he knew he should not say, in the pulpit especially, into which no honest man comes to lie. This honourable preacher, you well remember, substantially declared unto you at Paul's Cross on Sunday last past the right and title that the most excellent Prince Richard, Duke of Gloucester, now Protector of this realm, has unto the crown and kingdom of the same.

'For as that honoured man thoroughly made open unto you, the children of King Edward the Fourth were never lawfully begot, forasmuch as the King (his very wife Dame Elizabeth Lucy still living) was never lawfully married unto the Queen their mother, whose blood, saving that he set his voluptuous pleasure before his honour, was full unmeet to be matched with his, and the mingling of whose bloods together has been the effusion of great part of the noble blood of this realm. Whereby it may well seem, that marriage was not well made, from which there is so much mischief grown. For lack of which lawful coupling, and also of other things, which the said honoured Doctor rather signified than fully explained and which things shall not be spoken by me, as the thing wherein every man forbears to say what he knows in avoiding the displeasure of my noble Lord Protector, who bears, as nature requires, a filial reverence to the Duchess his mother— for these causes, I say, that is, for lack of other issue lawfully coming of the late noble Prince Richard, Duke of York, to whose royal blood the crown of England and of France is by the high authority of Parliament entailed, the right and title of the same is by the just course of inheritance according to the common law of this land devolved and come unto that most excellent Prince, the Lord Protector, as to the very lawfully begot son of the foreremembered noble Duke of York.

'Which thing well considered, and the great knightly prowess pondered, with manifold virtues which in his noble person singularly abound, the nobles and commons also of this realm, and specially of the north parts, not willing any bastard blood to have the rule of the land nor the abuses in the same any longer to continue, have agreed and fully determined to make humble petition unto that most puissant Prince, the Lord Protector, that it may like his Grace at our humble request to take upon him the guiding and governance of this realm, to the welfare and increase of the same, according to his very right and just title. Which thing, I know it well, he will be loath to take upon him, as he whose wisdom well perceives the labour and study both of mind and of body that shall come therewith to whosoever well holds that position, as I dare say he will if he take it. Which position, I warn you well, is no child's office. And that the great wise man* well perceived when he said, "*Veh regno cuius rex puer est*—Woe is that realm that has a child to their King."

'Wherefore so much the more cause have we to thank God that this noble personage, who is so rightfully entitled thereunto, is of so mature age and thereto of so great wisdom joined with so great experience. Albeit he will be loath, as I have said, to take it upon him, yet shall he to our petition in that behalf the more graciously incline if you, the honoured citizens of this the chief city of this realm, join with us the nobles in our said request. Which for your own weal we doubt not but you will, and nevertheless I heartily pray you so to do. Thereby you shall do great profit to all this

---

* Solomon, as the reputed author of *Ecclesiastes*; Buckingham paraphrases 10:16 in the Vulgate: 'Vae tibi, terra, cuius rex puer est—Woe to thee, land, whose King is a child.'

realm both in choosing them so good a king and yourselves special advantage, for His Majesty shall ever after bear you so much the more tender favour, in how much he shall perceive you the more prone and benevolently minded towards his election. Wherein, dear friends, what mind you have, we request you plainly to show us.'

When the Duke had spoken, and stood in expectation that the people—whom he hoped that the Mayor had prepared before—should after this proposition made, have cried 'King Richard! King Richard!', all was hushed and mute, and not one word answered thereunto.

Wherewith the Duke was marvellously abashed and, taking the Mayor nearer to him, with others that were about him privy to that matter, said unto them softly, 'What means this, that this people be so still?'

'Sir,' quoth the Mayor, 'perhaps they understand you not well.'

'That shall we mend,' quoth he, 'if that will help.'

And by and by, somewhat louder, he rehearsed them the same matter again in other order and other words, so well and ornately, and nevertheless so clearly and plain, with voice, gesture, and countenance so comely and so becoming, that every man much marvelled that heard him, and thought that they never had in their lives heard so evil a tale so well told. But were it for wonder or fear, or that each looked that other should speak first, not one word was there answered, by all the people that stood before; but all was as still as the midnight, not so much as whispering among them by which they might seem to confer about what was best to do.

When the Mayor saw this, he with other partners of that counsel drew about the Duke and said that the people had not been accustomed there to be spoken unto but by the Recorder, who is the mouth of the city, and haply to him they will answer. With that, the Recorder—called [Sir Thomas] Fitzwilliam, a serious man and an honourable, who was so newly come into that office that he never had spoken to the people before, and loath was with that matter to begin—thereunto commanded by the Mayor, made rehearsal to the commons of what the Duke had twice rehearsed them himself. But the Recorder so tempered his tale that he showed everything as the Duke's words and no part his own.

But all this no change made in the people, who still in the same way stood as if they had been men amazed. Whereupon the Duke whispered unto the Mayor and said, 'This is a marvellous obstinate silence'; and therewith he turned unto the people again with these words:

'Dear friends, we come to move you to that thing—which peradventure we not so greatly needed to do but that the lords of this realm and the commons of other parts might have sufficed, saving that we such love bear you and so much set by you that we would not gladly do without you—that thing in which to be partners is your weal and honour, which, as it seems, either you see not or weigh not. Wherefore we require you give us answer one or other, whether you be minded, as all the nobles of this realm be, to have this noble Prince, now Protector, to be your King, or not.'

At these words the people began to whisper among themselves secretly, so that the voice was neither loud nor distinct but, as it were, the sound of a swarm of bees, till at the last in the nether end of the hall, a concealed group of the Duke's servants and of [John] Nesfield's and others belonging to the Protector, with some 'prentices and lads that thrust into the hall among the press, began suddenly at men's backs to cry out as loud as their throats would give 'King Richard! King Richard!' and threw up their caps in token of joy. And they that stood before, cast back their heads, marvelling thereof, but nothing they said.

And when the Duke and the Mayor saw this manner, they wisely turned it to their purpose and said it was a goodly cry and a joyful to hear, every man with one voice, no man saying nay.

'Wherefore, friends,' quoth the Duke, 'since we perceive it is all your whole minds to have this noble man for your king—

whereof we shall make his Grace so effectual report that we doubt not but it shall redound unto your great weal and advantage—we request you that you tomorrow go with us and we with you unto his noble Grace, to make our humble request unto him in the manner before rehearsed.'

And therewith the lords came down, and the company dissolved and departed, the more part all sober, some with glad semblance that were not very merry; and some of those that came thither with the Duke, not able to dissemble their sorrow, were fain at his back to turn their face to the wall while the dolour of their heart burst out at their eyes.

Then on the morrow after, the Mayor with all the Aldermen and chief commoners of the city in their best manner apparelled, assembling themselves, together resorted unto Baynard's Castle where the Protector lay. To which place repaired also, according to their appointment, the Duke of Buckingham with divers noblemen with him, besides many knights and other gentlemen. And thereupon the Duke sent word unto the Lord Protector of the being there of a great and honourable company to move a great matter unto his Grace. Whereupon the Protector made difficulty to come out unto them unless he first knew some part of their errand, as though he doubted and partly distrusted the coming of such number unto him so suddenly, without any warning or knowledge whether they came for good or harm.

Then the Duke when he had showed this unto the Mayor and others that they might thereby see how little the Protector looked for this matter, they sent unto him by the messenger such loving message again, and therewith so humbly besought him to vouchsafe that they might resort to his presence to propose their intent, of which they would unto no other person any part disclose, that at the last he came forth from his chamber. And yet he came not down unto them, but stood above in a gallery over them where they might see him and speak to him, as though he would not yet come too near them till he knew what they meant.

And thereupon the Duke of Buckingham first made humble petition unto him, on the behalf of them all, that his Grace would pardon them and license them to propose unto his Grace the intent of their coming without his displeasure, without which pardon obtained they durst not be bold to move him of that matter. In which, albeit they meant as much honour to his Grace as weal to all the realm besides, yet were they not sure how his Grace would take it, whom they would in no wise offend.

Then the Protector, as if he was very tractable by nature, and also longed sore to know what they meant, gave him leave to propose what he liked, verily trusting for the good mind that he bore them all, none of them anything would intend towards him wherewith he ought to be grieved.

When the Duke had this leave and pardon to speak, then waxed he bold to show him their intent and purpose, with all the causes moving them thereunto as ye before have heard. Finally he besought his Grace that he would be willing, out of his accustomed goodness and zeal unto the realm, now with his eye of pity to behold the long continued distress and decay of the same and to set his gracious hands to the redress and amendment thereof, by taking upon him the crown and governance of this realm, according to his right and title lawfully descended unto him, and to the laud of God, profit of the land, and unto his Grace so much the more honour and less pain in that never prince reigned upon any people that were so glad to live under his rule as the people of this realm under his.

When the Protector had heard the proposition, he looked very strangely thereat, and answered that although he partly knew the things alleged by them to be true, yet such entire love he bore unto King Edward and his children and so much more regarded his honour in other realms about than the crown of any one—of which he was never desirous—that he could not find in his heart in this point to incline to their desires. For in all other nations where the truth were not well known, it should peradventure be thought that it were his own ambitious mind and devising, to depose the Prince and take himself the crown. With which infamy he would not have his honour stained for any crown, in which he had ever perceived much more labour and pain than pleasure to him that so would so use it, while he that would not, were not worthy to have it. Notwithstanding, he not only pardoned them the offer that they made him but also thanked them for the love and hearty favour they bore him, praying them for his sake to give and bear the same to the Prince, under whom he was and would be content to live; and with his labour and counsel, as far as should like the King to use him, he would do his uttermost devoir to set the realm in good state. This, in the little while of his protectorship (the praise given to God) was already well begun, in that the malice of such as were before occasion of the contrary and of new intended to be, were now, partly by good policy, partly more by God's special providence than man's provision, repressed.

Upon this answer given, the Duke, by the Protector's licence, a little while whispered as well with other noblemen about him as with the Mayor and Recorder of London. And after that, upon like pardon desired and obtained, he showed aloud unto the Protector that, for a final conclusion, the realm was agreed King Edward's line should not any longer reign upon them, both for that they had so far gone that it was now no surety to retreat, as for that they thought it for the weal universal to take that way although they had not yet begun it. Wherefore, if it would like his Grace to take the crown upon him, they would humbly beseech him thereunto. If he would give them a resolute answer to the contrary, which they would be loath to hear, then must they needs seek, and should not fail to find, some other nobleman that would.

These words much moved the Protector—who else, as every man may know, would never of likelihood have inclined thereunto! But when he saw there was no other way but that either he must take it or else he and his both go from it, he spoke thus unto the lords and commons. 'Since we perceive well that all the realm is so set, though we be very sorry that they will not suffer in any wise King Edward's line to govern them whom no man on earth can govern against their wills, and since we well also perceive that no man is there to whom the crown can by so just title appertain as to ourself, as very right heir lawfully begot of the body of our most dear father Richard, late Duke of York—to which title is now joined your election, the nobles and commons of this realm, which we of all titles possible take for most effectual—we be content and agree favourably to incline to your petition and request. According to the same, here we take upon us the royal estate, pre-eminence, and kingdom of the two noble realms, England and France, the one from this day forward by us and our heirs to rule, govern, and defend, the other by God's grace and your good help to get again and subdue and establish forever in due obedience unto this realm of England, the advancement whereof we never ask of God longer to live than we intend to procure.'

With this there was a great shout crying 'King Richard! King Richard!' And then the lords went up to the King (for so was he from that time called), and the people departed, talking diversely of the matter, every man as his fancy prompted him. But much they talked and marvelled at the manner of this dealing, that the matter was on both parts made so strange, as though neither had ever conferred with other thereof before, when that themselves well knew there was no man so dull that heard them but he perceived well enough that all the matter was already arranged between them.

Howbeit, some excused that in reply, and said all must be done in good order, though. And men must sometimes for the manner's sake not seem to know what they know. For at the consecration of a bishop every man knows well by the paying for his papal bulls that he purposes to be one—though he pay for nothing else. And yet must he be twice asked whether he will be bishop or no, and he must twice say nay and at the third time take it as if compelled thereunto by his own will. And in a stage play all the people know right well that he that plays the Sultan is perchance a shoemaker. Yet if one should have so little sense, to show out of season what acquaintance he has with him and call him by his own name while he stands in his majesty, one of his tormentors might hap to break his head, and rightly for marring of the play. So they said that these matters be Kings' games, as it were stage plays, and for the more part played upon scaffolds. In them poor men be but the lookers on, and they that wise be, will meddle no further. For they that sometimes step up and play with them, when they cannot play their parts, they disorder the play and do themselves no good.*

§ The next day the Protector with a great train went to Westminster Hall and there, when he had placed himself in the Court of the King's Bench, declared to the audience that he would take upon him the crown in that place there, where the King himself sits and ministers the law, because he considered that it was the chiefest duty of a king to minister the laws.

---

* More was probably thinking of the miracle plays performed by the craft gilds, in which an infidel tyrant—Herod or a Pharaoh—appeared surrounded by his 'tormentors'. The acrid pun on 'scaffolds' suggests both the high waggons on which miracle plays were performed and the rude stage of boards set up in inn-yards by players of moralities and interludes. In the six decades between the first skirmish in the Wars of the Roses, at St Albans in 1455, and the year 1513 when More began to compose his *History*, something like forty magnates, Lancastrian and Yorkist, were beheaded on scaffolds. According to the biography of More written by his son-in-law, William Roper, young Thomas himself used to 'step up and play' with players: in the household of Cardinal Morton, 'though he was young of years, yet would he at Christmas-tide suddenly sometimes step in among the players, and never studying for the matter, make a part of his own there presently among them, which made the lookers-on more sport than all the players beside'. The advice embodied in the metaphor has for the reader a bitter irony unintended by the author: as a result of meddling in Kings' games, i.e. accepting the rôle of Chancellor to Henry VIII, More mounted a scaffold to die by the headsman's axe in 1535.

§ The text between the § here and the § on p. 102 was not part of the English *History*, but was translated from the Latin version.

[101]

Then, with as pleasant an oration as he knew how to make, he went about to win unto him the nobles, the merchants, the artificers, and, in conclusion, all kinds of men. But specially the lawyers of this realm. And finally, to the intent that no man should hate him for fear and that his deceitful clemency might get him the good will of the people, when he had declared the disadvantages of discord and the advantages of concord and unity, he made an open proclamation that he did put out of his mind all enmities and that he there did openly pardon all offences committed against him. And to the intent that he might show a proof thereof, he commanded that one Fogge [Sir John Fogge, an adherent of the Woodvilles], whom he had long deadly hated, should be brought then before him. Who being brought out of the sanctuary nearby [Westminster Abbey]—for thither had he fled for fear of him—in the sight of the people he took him by the hand. Which thing the common people rejoiced at and praised, but wise men took it for a vanity. In his return homeward, whomsoever he met he saluted. For a mind that knows itself guilty is, in a manner, reduced to a servile flattering.

When he had begun his reign, the twenty-sixth day of June, after this mock election, then was he crowned the sixth day of July. And that solemnity was furnished for the most part with the selfsame provision that was appointed for the coronation of his nephew. §

Now fell there mischiefs thick. And as the thing evilly got is never well kept, through all the time of his reign never ceased there cruel death and slaughter, till his own destruction ended it. But as he finished his time with the best death and the most righteous—to wit, his own—so began he with the most piteous and wicked, I mean the lamentable murder of his innocent nephews, the young King and his tender brother.

Whose death and final misfortune has nevertheless so far come in question that some remain yet in doubt whether they were in his days destroyed or no. Not only for that Perkin Warbeck, by many folk's malice and more folk's folly so long space deceiving the world, was as well by princes as the poorer people reputed and taken for the younger of those two; but also for that all things were in late days so covertly managed, one thing pretended and another meant, that there was nothing so plain and openly proved but that yet for the common custom of close and covert dealing men had it ever inwardly suspect, as many well-counterfeited jewels make the true mistrusted. Howbeit, concerning that opinion, with the occasions moving either party, we shall have place more at large to treat if we hereafter happen to write the time of the late noble Prince of famous memory, King Henry the Seventh, or perchance that history of Perkin in a compendious account by itself.

But in the meantime for this present matter, I shall rehearse you the dolorous end of those babes, not after every way that I have heard, but after that way that I have so heard by such men and by such means as methinks it were hard but it should be true.

King Richard after his coronation, taking his way to Gloucester to visit, in his new honour, the town of which of old he bore the name, devised as he rode to fulfil that thing which he before had intended. And forasmuch as his mind misgave him that, his nephews living, men would not reckon that he could have right to the realm, he thought therefore without delay to be rid of them, as though the killing of his kinsmen could amend his cause and make him a kindly king.*

Whereupon he sent one John Green, whom he specially trusted, unto Sir Robert Brakenbury, Constable of the Tower, with a letter and credentials also that the same Sir Robert should in any wise put the two children to death. This John Green did his errand unto Brakenbury, kneeling before Our Lady in the Tower, who plainly answered that he would never put them to death, though he should die therefor; with which answer John Green returning, re-counted the same to King Richard at Warwick, yet on his progress.

Wherewith he took such displeasure and thought, that the same

* A bitter pun: 'kindly' also meaning 'natural'.

night he said unto a secret page of his: 'Ah, whom shall a man trust? Those that I have brought up myself, those that I had thought would most surely serve me, even those fail me, and at my commandment will do nothing for me.'

'Sir,' quoth his page, 'there lies one on your pallet without that, I dare well say, to do your Grace pleasure, the thing would be right hard that he would refuse'—meaning by this Sir James Tyrell, who was a man of right goodly personage and, for nature's gifts, worthy to have served a much better Prince, if he well served God and by grace obtained as much truth and good will as he had strength and wit.

The man had a high heart and sore longed upward, not rising yet so fast as he had hoped, being hindered and kept under by the means of Sir Richard Ratcliffe and Sir William Catesby, who, longing for no more partners of the Prince's favour, and especially not for him, whose pride, they knew, would bear no peer, kept him by secret drifts out of all secret trust. Which thing this page well had marked and known. Wherefore, this occasion offered of very special friendship, he took the opportunity to put him forward and by such wise do him good—such that all the enemies he had, except the devil, could never have done him so much hurt.

For upon this page's words King Richard arose (for this communication had he sitting on the stool—a fitting carpet for such a counsel) and came out into the pallet-chamber, on which he found in bed Sir James and Sir Thomas Tyrell, of person like and brethren of blood but nothing of kin in qualities. Then said the King merrily to them, 'What, sirs, be ye in bed so soon?' and calling up Sir James, broke to him secretly his mind in this mischievous matter. In which he found him nothing unwilling. Wherefore on the morrow he sent him to Brakenbury with a letter, by which he was commanded to deliver Sir James all the keys of the Tower for one night, to the end he might there accomplish the King's pleasure in such thing as he had given him commandment. After which letter delivered and the keys received, Sir James appointed the night next ensuing to destroy them, devising before and preparing the means.

The Prince, as soon as the Protector left that name and took himself as King, had it showed unto him that he should not reign but his uncle should have the crown. At which word the Prince, sore abashed, began to sigh and said: 'Alas, I would my uncle would let me have my life yet, though I lose my kingdom.' Then he that told him the tale, used him with good words and put him in the best comfort he could. But forthwith were the Prince and his brother both shut up and all others removed from them; only one, called Black Will or William Slaughter, was set to serve them and see them sure. After which time the Prince never tied his laces nor in any way cared for himself, but with that young babe his brother lingered in thought and heaviness till this traitorous death delivered them of that wretchedness.

For Sir James Tyrell devised that they should be murdered in their beds. To the execution whereof he appointed Miles Forest, one of the four that kept them, a fellow fleshed in murder before time. To him he joined one John Dighton, his own horsekeeper, a big broad strong knave. Then all the others being removed from them, this Miles Forest and John Dighton about midnight (the innocent children lying in their beds) came into the chamber, and suddenly lapped them up among the bedclothes—so bewrapped them and entangled them, keeping down by force the featherbed and pillows hard unto their mouths, that within a while, smothered and stifled, their breath failing, they gave up to God their innocent souls into the joys of heaven, leaving to the tormentors their bodies dead in the bed.

After the wretches perceived them—first by the struggling with the pains of death and after, long lying still—to be thoroughly dead, they laid their bodies naked out upon the bed and fetched Sir James to see them. Who, upon the sight of them, caused those murderers to bury them at the stair-foot, meetly deep in the ground under a great heap of stones.

Then rode Sir James in great haste to King Richard and showed him all the manner of the murder, who gave him great thanks and, as some say, there made him knight. But he allowed not, as I have heard, the burying in so vile a corner, saying that he would have them buried in a better place because they were a King's sons. Lo, the honourable heart of a King!

Whereupon they say that a priest of Sir Robert Brakenbury took up the bodies again and secretly interred them in such place as, by the occasion of his death—for he alone knew it—could never since come to light. Very truth is it and well known that at such time as Sir James Tyrell was in the Tower, for treason committed against the most famous Prince, King Henry the Seventh, both Dighton and he were examined, and confessed the murder in manner above written, but whither the bodies were removed they could nothing tell.

And thus, as I have learned of them that much knew and little cause had to lie, were these two noble princes, these innocent tender children—born of most royal blood, brought up in great prosperity, likely long to live to reign and rule in the realm—by traitorous tyranny taken, deprived of their state, shortly shut up in prison, and privily slain and murdered, their bodies cast God knows where, by the cruel ambition of their unnatural uncle and his pitiless tormentors.

Which things on every part well pondered, God never gave this world a more notable example, neither in what unsurety stands this worldly state, or what mischief works the proud enterprise of a high heart, or finally what wretched end ensues from such pitiless cruelty. For, first to begin with the agents—Miles Forest at St Martin's piecemeal rotted away. Dighton indeed yet walks alive, in good possibility to be hanged ere he die. But Sir James Tyrell died at Tower Hill, beheaded for treason. King Richard himself—as ye shall hereafter hear—slain in the field, hacked and hewed by his enemies' hands, haled on horseback dead, his hair contemptuously torn and pulled like a cur dog. And this mischief he took within less than three years of the mischief that he did. And yet all the meantime he spent in much pain and trouble outward, much fear, anguish, and sorrow within. For I have heard by credible report of such as were secret with his chamber-men, that after this abominable deed done he never had quiet in his mind, he never thought himself sure. Where he went abroad, his eyes whirled about, his body secretly armoured, his hand ever on his dagger, his countenance and manner like one always ready to strike back. He took ill rest a-nights; lay long waking and musing, sore wearied with care and watch; rather dozed than slept, troubled with fearful dreams—suddenly sometimes start up, leap out of his bed and run about the chamber—so was his restless heart continually tossed and tumbled with the galling impression and stormy remembrance of his abominable deed.

Now had he outward no long time in rest. For hereupon soon after began the conspiracy, or rather good confederation, between the Duke of Buckingham and many other gentlemen against him. The occasion whereupon the King and the Duke fell out is, by divers folk, divers ways asserted.

This Duke, as I have for certain been informed, as soon as the Duke of Gloucester upon the death of King Edward came to York and there had solemn funeral service for King Edward, sent thither in the most secret wise he could, one Percival, his trusty servant. This servant came to John Ward, a chamber-man of like secret trust with the Duke of Gloucester, desiring that, in the most close and covert manner, he might be admitted to the presence and speech of his master. And the Duke of Gloucester, advertised of his desire, caused him in the dead of the night after all other folk departed, to be brought unto him in his secret chamber. There Percival, after his master's recommendation, showed him that the Duke had secretly sent him to show him that in this new world he would take such part as he [Richard] wished, and would wait upon him with a thousand good fellows if need were.

The messenger, sent back with thanks and some secret instruction of the Protector's mind, yet met him again with further message from the Duke his master within few days after at Nottingham, whither the Protector was come from York with many gentlemen of the North Country, to the number of six hundred horse, on his way to London. After secret meeting and communication, he soon departed. Whereupon at Northampton the Duke himself met with the Protector, with three hundred horse, and from thence still continued with him, partner of all his plans, till after his coronation they parted, as it seemed very great friends, at Gloucester.

From whence, as soon as the Duke came home, he so lightly turned from him and so highly conspired against him that a man would marvel whereof the change grew. And surely the occasion of their variance is by divers men diversely reported. Some have I heard say that the Duke, a little before the coronation, among other things requested of the Protector the Duke of Hereford's lands, to which he pretended himself just inheritor. And forasmuch as the title which he claimed by inheritance was somewhat interlaced with the title to the crown by the line of King Henry [VI], before deprived, the Protector conceived such indignation that he rejected the Duke's request with many spiteful and minatory words. Which so wounded his heart with hatred and mistrust that he never after could endure to look right at King Richard but ever feared for his own life, so much so that when the Protector rode through London towards his coronation, he feigned himself sick because he would not ride with him. And the other, taking it in evil part, sent him word to rise and come ride, or he would make him be carried. Whereupon he rode on with evil will and, that notwithstanding, on the morrow rose from the [coronation] feast feigning himself sick, and King Richard said it was done in hatred and spite of him. And they say that ever after continually each of them lived in such hatred and distrust of other that the Duke verily looked to have been murdered at Gloucester. From which, nevertheless, he in fair manner departed.

But surely some right secret [with 'inside information'] at those days deny this; and many right wise men think it unlikely (the deep dissimulating nature of both those men considered, and what need in that green world the Protector had of the Duke, and in what peril the Duke stood if he fell once under suspicion of the tyrant) that either the Protector would give the Duke occasion of displeasure or the Duke the Protector occasion of mistrust. And utterly men think that if King Richard had any such opinion conceived, he would never have suffered the Duke to escape his hands.

Very truth it is, the Duke was a proud-minded man and evilly could bear the glory of another, so that I have heard, of some that said they saw it, that the Duke at such time as the crown was first set upon the Protector's head, his eye could not abide the sight thereof, but he twisted his head another way. But men say that he was, of truth, not well at ease, and that to King Richard both well known and not ill taken; nor any demand of the Duke's discourteously rejected, but he both with great gifts and high promises in most loving and trusty manner departed at Gloucester. But soon after his coming home to Brecon [his chief castle in Wales], having there in his custody by the commandment of King Richard, Doctor [John] Morton, Bishop of Ely, who as ye before heard was taken in the council at the Tower [June 13], he waxed with him familiar. Whose wisdom deceived the Duke's pride, to his own deliverance and the Duke's destruction.

The Bishop was a man of great natural wit, very well learned, and honourable in behaviour, lacking no wise ways to win favour. He had been steadfast upon the party of King Henry [VI] while that party was in prosperity, and nevertheless left it not nor forsook it in woe, but fled the realm with the Queen [Margaret of Anjou] and the Prince [Edward, Lancastrian Prince of Wales], and, while King Edward had the King in prison, never came home but to the field [Battle of Tewkesbury, 1471]. After this was lost, and that party utterly subdued, the other [Edward IV] for his steadfast faith and wisdom not only was content to receive him but also wooed him to come and had him from thenceforth both in secret trust and very special favour. Which he nothing deceived.

For he, being, as ye have heard, after King Edward's death first taken by the tyrant for his truth to the King, found the means to set this Duke in his top [get the better of him] and joined gentlemen together in aid of King Henry [VII]. He first devised the marriage between him and King Edward's daughter [Elizabeth], by which he declared his faith and good service to both his masters [Edward IV and Henry VI] at once, with infinite benefit to the realm by the conjunction of those two bloods in one whose separate titles had long unquieted the land. He then fled the realm, went to Rome, never intending more to meddle with the world, till the noble Prince, King Henry the Seventh, got him home again, made him Archbishop of Canterbury and Chancellor of England, whereunto the Pope joined the honour of Cardinal. Thus living many days in as much honour as one man might well wish, ended them so godly that his death, with God's mercy, well changed his life.

This man, therefore, as I was about to tell you, by the long and often alternate proof, as well of prosperity as adverse fortune, had got by great experience—the very mother and mistress of wisdom —a deep insight into politic worldly drifts. Whereby, perceiving the Duke of Buckingham glad to converse with him, he fed him with fair words and many pleasant praises. And perceiving in the process of their communications, the Duke's pride now and then belch out a little burst of envy towards the glory of the King, and thereby sensing him easy to fall out [ripe to be moved against Richard] if the matter were well handled, he craftily sought the ways to prick him forwards, using always the opportunity of his coming and so keeping himself close within his bonds [carefully acting the rôle of prisoner and respectful listener] that he rather appeared to follow him than to lead him.

For when the Duke first began to praise and boast of the King and show how much profit the realm should take by his reign, my lord Morton answered, 'Surely, my Lord, folly were it for me to lie—for if I would swear the contrary, your lordship would not, I think, believe—but that if the world would have gone as I would have wished, King Henry's son had had the crown and not King Edward. But after God had ordered him to lose it and King Edward to reign, I was never so mad that I would with a dead man strive against the quick. So was I to King Edward faithful chaplain and glad would have been that his child had succeeded him. Howbeit, if the secret judgement of God have otherwise provided, I purpose not to spurn against a prick nor labour to set up what God pulls down. And as for the late Protector and now King—' And even there he left off, saying that he had already meddled too much with the world and would from that day meddle with his book and his beads and no further.

Then longed the Duke sore to hear what he would have said—because he ended with the King and there so suddenly stopped—and exhorted him familiarly between them twain to be bold to say whatsoever he thought, whereof he faithfully promised there should never come hurt and peradventure more good than he would think. For he himself intended to use his faithful secret advice and counsel, which, he said, was the only cause for which he procured of the King to have him in his custody, where he might reckon himself at home, and else had he been put in the hands of them with whom he should not have found the like favour.

The Bishop right humbly thanked him and said, 'In good faith, my Lord, I love not much to talk much of princes, as some thing not all out of peril though the word be without fault, forasmuch as it shall not be taken as the party meant it but as it pleases the Prince to construe it. And ever I think on Aesop's tale—that when the lion had proclaimed that on pain of death there should no horned beast abide in that wood, one that had in his forehead a bunch of flesh fled away a great pace. The fox that saw him run so fast asked him whither he made all that haste. And he answered, "In faith, I neither know nor care, so I were once hence because of this proclamation made of horned beasts." "What, fool," quoth the fox, "thou mayest abide well enough; the lion meant not thee, for it is no horn that is in thine head." "No, marry," quoth he, "that know I well enough. But what and he call it a horn, where am I then?" '

The Duke laughed merrily at the tale and said, 'My Lord, I warrant you, neither the lion nor the boar shall pick any matter out of anything here spoken, for it shall never come near their ear.'

'In good faith, Sir,' said the Bishop, 'if it did, the thing that I was about to say, taken as well as, before God, I meant it, could deserve but thanks. And yet taken as I think it would, might happen to turn me to little good and you to less.'

Then longed the Duke yet much more to know what it was. Whereupon the Bishop said, 'In good faith, my Lord, as for the late Protector, since he is now King in possession, I purpose not to dispute his title. But for the weal of this realm, whereof his Grace has now the governance and whereof I am myself one poor member, I was about to wish that to those good abilities whereof he has already right many little needing my praise, it might yet have pleased God, for the better store, to have given him some of such other excellent virtues meet for the rule of a realm as our Lord has planted in the person of your Grace.'

The Continuation

BY RICHARD GRAFTON

With which words the Duke, perceiving that the Bishop bore unto him his good heart and favour, mistrusted not to enter into more plain communication with him, so far that at the last the Bishop declared himself to be one of them that would gladly help in order that Richard, who then usurped the crown, might be deposed, if he knew how it might conveniently be brought to pass that such a person as had true title of inheritance unto the same, might be restored thereunto. Upon this, the said Duke, knowing the Bishop to be a man of prudence and fidelity, opened to him all his whole heart and intent, saying, 'My Lord, I have devised the way how the blood both of King Edward and of King Henry the Sixth, that is left, being coupled by marriage and affinity, may be restored unto the crown which, by just and true title, is due unto them both.' King Richard he called not the brother of King Edward the Fourth, but his enemy and mortal foe.

The way that the Duke had devised was this. They should with all speed and celerity find means to send for Henry, Earl of Richmond (who, the rumour went, immediately upon knowledge of King Edward's death had been delivered out of prison by Francis, Duke of Brittany), and to help the same Henry with all their power and strength, provided that the said Henry would first, by his faithful oath, promise that immediately upon obtaining the crown he would marry and take to wife Elizabeth, the eldest daughter of Edward the Fourth. The Bishop of Ely right well allowed both the device and purpose of the Duke, and also the manner and way how the matter should be brought to effect, and found means that Reynold Bray, servant with Margaret, mother of the said Henry, then married to Thomas Stanley, came to the Duke into Wales. The Duke's mind thoroughly perceived and known, with great speed he returned to the said Margaret, advertising the same of all things which between the Duke and him—concerning as well the common weal of the realm as also the advancement of her and her blood—had been discussed.

Now it came so to pass that the Duke of Buckingham and the Lady Margaret, mother to the said Henry, had been in communication of the same matter before, and that the said Lady Margaret had devised the same means and ways for the deposition of King

Richard and bringing in of Henry her son, the which the Duke now broke unto the Bishop of Ely. Whereupon there remained no more to do, forasmuch as she perceived the Duke now willing to prosecute and further the said device, but that she should find the means that this matter might be broken unto Queen Elizabeth, the wife of King Edward the Fourth, then being in the sanctuary.

And hereupon she caused one Lewis, that was her physician, in his own name and as though it came of himself to break this matter unto the Queen, saying that, if she would consent and agree thereunto, a means might be found how to restore again the blood of King Edward and King Henry the Sixth unto the crown, and to be avenged of King Richard for the murder of King Edward's children. He then declared that there was beyond the sea Henry, Earl of Richmond, who was of the blood of Henry the Sixth, whom if she would be content that he marry Elizabeth her eldest daughter, there should of his side be made right many friends, and she for her part might help in like manner, whereby no doubt it should come to pass that he should possess the crown by most rightful inheritance.

Which matter when she heard it, it pleased her exceedingly well, insomuch that she counselled the said physician to break the same unto his mistress, the Lady Margaret, and know her mind therein. She promised upon her word that she would make all the friends of King Edward to take part with the said Henry, if he would be sworn that when he came into the possession of the crown, he would immediately take in marriage Elizabeth, her eldest daughter, or else if she lived not until that time, that then he would take Cecily, her younger daughter.

Whereupon the said Lewis returned unto the Lady Margaret, his mistress, declaring unto her the whole mind and intent of the Queen. Thus it was shortly agreed between these two women that with all speed this matter should be set forward, insomuch that the Lady Margaret broke this matter unto Reynold Bray, willing him to move and set forward the same with all such as he should perceive either able to do good or willing thereunto. Then had the Queen devised that one Christopher [Urswick] (whom the foresaid Lewis the physician had promoted into her service) should be sent into Brittany to Henry to give him knowledge of their minds here, and that Henry should prepare and appoint himself ready and come into Wales, where he should find aid and help enough ready to receive him.

But then shortly after, it came unto her knowledge that the Duke of Buckingham had of himself before intended the same matter, whereupon she thought it should be meet to send some messenger of more reputation and credit than was this Christopher, and so kept him at home and then sent Hugh Conway with a great sum of money, willing him to declare unto Henry all things, and that he should haste him to come and to land in Wales, as is aforesaid. And after him one Richard Guildford out of Kent sent one Thomas Romney with the same message, the which two messengers came in manner both at one time into Brittany to the Earl Henry and declared unto him all their commissions.

When Henry had perceived and thoroughly heard this message, it rejoiced his heart and he gave thanks unto God, fully purposing with all convenient speed to take his journey towards England, desiring the aid and help of the Duke of Brittany, with promise of thankful recompense when God should send him to come to his right. The Duke of Brittany—notwithstanding that he had not long before been requested by Thomas Hutton, purposely sent to him from King Richard in message with money, immediately to imprison the said Henry, Earl of Richmond, and there continually to keep and hold the same from coming into England—yet with all gladness and favour inclined to the desire of Henry and aided him as he might with men, money, ships, and other necessaries. But Henry, while he might accordingly appoint and furnish himself, remained in Brittany, sending before the aforesaid Hugh Conway and Thomas Romney, which two were to him very true and faithful, to bear tidings into England unto his friends of his coming, to the end that they might providently order all things, as well for the commodious receiving of him at his coming as also foreseeing such dangers as might befall and avoiding such traps and snares as by Richard the Third and his accomplices might be set for him and for all his other company that he should bring with him.

In the meantime the friends of Henry with all care, study, and diligence wrought all things unto their purpose belonging.

And though all this were as secretly wrought and conveyed as among so great a number was possible to be, yet privy knowledge thereof came to the ears of King Richard, who, although he were at the first hearing much abashed, yet thought best to dissemble the matter as though he had no knowledge thereof, while he might secretly gather unto him power and strength and by secret espial among the people get more perfect knowledge of the whole matter and of the chief authors and contrivers of the same. And because he knew the Duke of Buckingham to be chief and principal of them—as unto whom his own conscience knew that he had given most just causes of enmity—he thought it necessary first of all to dispatch the same Duke out of the way.

Wherefore, unto the Duke he addressed letters stuffed and replenished with all humanity, friendship, familiarity, and sweetness of words, willing and desiring the same to come unto him with all convenient speed. And further gave in commandment to the messenger that carried the letters that he should in his behalf make many high and gay promises unto the Duke, and by all gentle means persuade the same to come unto him. But the Duke, mistrusting the fair words and promises so suddenly offered by him of whose wily crafts and means he knew sundry examples before practised, desired the King's pardon, excusing himself that he was diseased and sick, and declaring that King Richard might be assured that if it possible were for him to come, he would not absent himself from his Grace. This excuse the King would not admit but immediately directed unto the Duke other letters of a more rough sort, not without menacing and threatening unless he would, according to his duty, repair unto him at his calling; whereunto the Duke plainly made answer that he would not come unto him whom he knew to be his enemy.

And immediately the Duke prepared himself to make war against him and persuaded all his accomplices and partakers of his intent with all possible expedition, some in one place and some in another, to stir against King Richard. And by this means, at one time and hour, Thomas, Marquess of Dorset, raised an army within the country of York—being himself late come forth from sanctuary and by the means and help of Thomas Lovell preserved and saved from peril of death. Also, in Devonshire, Edward Courtenay with his brother Peter, Bishop of Exeter, raised in like manner an army; and in Kent, Richard Guildford, accompanied with certain other gentlemen, raised up the people as is aforesaid; and all this was done, as it were, in one moment.

But the King, who had in the meantime gathered together great power and strength, thinking it not to be best by pursuing every one of his enemies to scatter his company in small flocks, determined to let pass all the others and with his whole puissance to set upon the chief head, that is to say, the Duke of Buckingham. So, taking his journey from London, he went towards Salisbury to the intent that—in case he received sure knowledge that the same lay in a field embattled—he might set upon the said Duke.

And now was the King within two days' journey of Salisbury when the Duke attempted to meet him, being accompanied with great strength of Welshmen, whom he had thereunto enforced and coerced more by lordly commandment than by liberal wages and hire; which thing, indeed, was the cause that they fell from him and forsook him.

Wherefore being suddenly forsaken by his men, he was of necessity constrained to flee; in which doing, as a man cast in sudden and therefore great fear of this the sudden change of fortune, and by reason of the same fear not knowing where to go nor where to hide his head nor what in such case best to do, he secretly conveyed himself into the house of Humphrey Banaster, in whom he had conceived a sure hope and confidence to find faithful and trusty unto him because the same had been and then was his servant. He intended there to remain in secret until he might either raise a new army or else by some means convey himself into Brittany to Henry, Earl of Richmond.

But as soon as the others who had attempted the same enterprise against the King, had knowledge that the Duke was forsaken by his company and had fled and could not be found, they—being stricken with sudden fear—made every man for himself such shift as he might, and being in utter despair of their health and life, either got them to sanctuaries or solitary places or else essayed to escape over sea. Many of them, indeed, arrived safely in Brittany, among whom were these whose names ensue: Peter Courtenay, Bishop of Exeter, with his brother Edward, Earl of Devonshire; Thomas, Marquess of Dorset, with his son Thomas, being a very young child; John Bourchier; John Welsh; Edward Woodville, a stout man of arms and brother to Elizabeth the Queen; Robert Willoughby; Giles Daubeney; Thomas Arundel; John Cheyney, with his two brothers; William Berkeley; William Brandon, with Thomas his brother; Richard Edgecombe—and all these for the most part knights; also John Hallwell; Edward Poynings, an excellent good captain; and Christopher Urswick. But John Morton, Bishop of Ely, at the selfsame time, together with sundry of the nobles and gentlemen, sailed into Flanders.

But Richard the King, who was now come to Salisbury and had got perfect knowledge that all these parties sought to fly the realm, with all diligence and haste that might be, sent to all the port towns thereabout to make sure stay that none of them might pass untaken, and made proclamation that whosoever would bring him knowledge where the Duke of Buckingham were to be had, should have for his reward, if he were a bondman, his freedom, and if he were free, his pardon and besides that a thousand pounds of money.

Furthermore, because he understood from Thomas Hutton, newly returned out of Brittany—who before is mentioned—that Francis, Duke of Brittany, would not only not hold Henry, Earl of Richmond, in prison for his sake but also was ready to help the same Henry with men, money, and ships in all that he might against him, he set divers and sundry ships in places suitable along all the seacoasts towards Brittany, that if Henry should come that way, he might either be taken before his arrival or else might be kept from landing on any coast of England. And furthermore, in every coast and corner of the realm he laid wonderful wait and watch to take any other of his enemies and specially the said Duke of Buckingham. Whereupon the said Humphrey Banaster (were it for reward or for fear of losing his life and goods) disclosed him unto the King's inquisitors, who immediately took him and forthwith brought him to Salisbury, where King Richard was.

The Duke, being diligently examined, uttered, without any manner of refusal or sticking, all such things as he knew, trusting that for his plain confession he should have liberty to speak with the King, which he made most instant and humble petition that he might do. But as soon as he had confessed his offence towards King Richard, he was out of hand beheaded. And this death the Duke received at the hands of King Richard, whom he had before helped in his affairs and purposes beyond all God's forbidding [to an outrageous extreme].

While these things were in hand in England, Henry, Earl of Richmond, made ready his host and strength to the number of five thousand Bretons and fifteen ships. The day appointed for his departure being now come, which was the twelfth day of the month of October in the year of our Lord God a thousand four hundred and eighty-three and the first year of the reign of King Richard, and having a fair wind, his ships hoisted up the sails and set forwards; but towards the night came such a tempest that they were dispersed one from another, some into Brittany and some into Normandy. But the ship in which Henry was, with one other ship, tossed all the night with the waves of the sea and tempest. When the morning came, it waxed somewhat calm and fair weather, and they were come towards the south part of England, by a haven or port called Poole; where the said Henry saw all the shores or banks set full of armoured men, who were soldiers appointed there to wait by King Richard, as we have said before, for the coming and landing of the Earl.*

While Henry there abode, he gave commandment that no man should land before the coming of the other ships. And in the meantime that he waited for them, he sent a little boat with a few in it to land, to know who they were that stood on the shore, his friends or enemies. To whom those soldiers, being before taught what they should say, answered that they were friends of Henry and were appointed by the Duke of Buckingham there to abide his coming and to conduct him to those castles and strongholds where his tents, pavilions, and artillery for the war lay, and where remained for him a great power that intended now with all speed to set upon King Richard while he was now fled for fear and clean without provision; and therefore they besought him to come a-land.

Henry suspecting this to be but fraud, after he saw none of his ships appear, hoisted up the sails, having a marvellous good wind even appointed him by God to deliver him from that great jeopardy, and sailed back again into Normandy. And after his landing there, he and his company after their labours rested them for the space of three days, determining to go from thence afoot into Brittany; and in the meantime he sent messengers unto Charles [VIII] the French King, the son of Louis [XI] that a little before had died, beseeching him for liberty and licence to pass through Normandy into Brittany. The young King Charles, being sorry for his fortune, was not only ready and well pleased to grant his

* Contemporary accounts give various dates throughout October for Henry's sailing from Brittany. It is uncertain whether he landed at Poole before or after the execution of Buckingham.

passage but also sent him money to help him forth in his journey. But Henry, before he knew the King's mind (not doubting his great humanity and gentleness), had sent away his ships towards Brittany and had set himself forwards in his journey, but made no great haste till the messengers returned. The great gentleness he received from the King, rejoiced his heart, and with a lusty will and good hope he set forwards into Brittany, there to take further counsel of his affairs.

And when he was in Brittany, he received from his friends out of England knowledge that the Duke of Buckingham was beheaded and that the Marquess of Dorset, with a great number of the noblemen of England, had been there a little before to seek him* and that they were now in Vannes, a city in Brittany. The which things being known to the Earl, he on the one part did greatly lament the death and evil chance of his chief and principal friend, but yet on the other part he greatly rejoiced in that he had so many and noble men to take his part in the battle. And therefore conceiving a good hope and opinion that his purpose should well frame and come to pass, he determined with himself with all expedition to set forward; and thereupon went to a place in Brittany called Rennes, and from thence sent to the Marquess with all the other noblemen that they should come unto him. Then when they heard that Henry was safe returned into Brittany, they rejoiced not a little for they had thought he had landed in England and so fallen into the hands of King Richard; and they made not a little haste till they were come unto him. When they met, after great ioy and gladness, as well of their part as of his, they began to talk of their matters.

And now was Christmas come, on the which day they all together assembled in the church and there swore faith and truth one to another. And Henry swore first, promising that as soon as he should possess the crown of England, he would marry Elizabeth

* Fleeing from Richard III, Dorset and his adherents had reached Brittany before Henry Tudor returned from his abortive expedition.

the daughter of Edward the Fourth; and afterwards they swore fealty and homage unto him, even as though he had already been King, and so from that time forth did take him, promising him that they would spend both their lives and goods with him and that Richard should no longer reign over them.

When this was done, Henry declared all these things to the Duke of Brittany, praying and desiring him now for help, and that he would aid him with a greater number of men and also lend him a friendly and honourable sum of money, that he might now recover his right and inheritance of the crown of England, unto the which he was called and desired by all the lords and nobility of the realm and which (God willing) he was most assured to possess. After his possession he would most faithfully restore the same again. The Duke promised him aid, upon the trust whereof he began to make ready his ships that they might with all expedition be ready to sail, that no time should be lost.

In the which time King Richard was again returned to London and had taken divers of them that were of this conspiracy—that is to say, George Browne, Roger Clifford, Thomas St Leger, knights; also Thomas Romney, Robert Clifford, and divers others—whom he caused to be put to death.

After this he called a Parliament, wherein was decreed that all those that were fled out of the land should be reputed and taken as enemies to the realm and all their lands and goods to be forfeit and confiscated. And not content with that booty, which was no small thing, he caused also a great tax and sum of money to be levied on the people—for the large gifts and liberality that he first used to buy the favours and friendships of many had now brought him in need.

Nothing was more likely than that Thomas Stanley should have been reputed and taken for one of those enemies because of the working of Margaret his wife, who was mother unto Henry, Earl of Richmond, and noted for the chief head and worker of this conspiracy. But forasmuch as it was thought that it was to small purpose that women could do, Thomas, being in no way at fault, was delivered, and commanded that he should not suffer Margaret his wife to have any servants about her, neither should she go abroad but be shut up, and that from thenceforth she should send no message, either to her son or to any of her other friends, whereby any hurt might be wrought against the King; the which commandment was accomplished. And by the authority of the same Parliament a peace was concluded with the Scots, who a little before had skirmished with the borderers.

Which things brought to pass, the King supposed all conspiracy to be entirely destroyed, forasmuch as the Duke of Buckingham, with others of his company, had been put to death, and also certain others banished. Yet for all this, King Richard was daily vexed and troubled, partly mistrusting his own strength and partly fearing the coming of Henry with his company, so that he lived but in a miserable case. And because he would not so continue any longer, he determined with himself to put away the cause of this his fear and toil, either by policy or else by strength. And after he had thus decided with himself, he thought nothing better than to tempt the Duke of Brittany yet once again, either with money, prayer, or some other special reward, because he had in keeping the Earl Henry and, most chiefly, because he knew that it was only the Duke that could deliver him from all his trouble by delivering or imprisoning the said Henry. Wherefore incontinent he sent unto the Duke certain ambassadors, who should promise unto him, besides other great rewards that they brought with them, to give him yearly all the revenues of all the lands of Henry and of all the other lords there being with him, if he would, after the receipt of the ambassadors, put them in prison.

The ambassadors, being departed and come where the Duke lay, could not have communication with him forasmuch as by extreme sickness his wits were feeble and weak. Wherefore one Peter Landois, his Treasurer, a man both of pregnant wit and of great authority, took this matter in hand, for which cause he was afterwards hated by all the lords of Brittany. With this Peter the English ambassadors had communication and, declaring to him the King's message, desired him instantly, forasmuch as they knew that he might bring their purpose to pass, that he would grant King Richard's request, and he should have the yearly revenues of all the lands of the said lords. Peter, considering that he was greatly hated by the lords of his own nation, thought that if he might bring to pass, through King Richard, to have all these great possessions and yearly revenues, he should then be able to match with them well enough and not to care a rush for them. Whereupon he answered the ambassadors that he would do what Richard did desire, if he broke not promise with him; and this did he not for any hatred that he bore unto Henry, for he hated him not, since not long before he saved his life where the Earl Henry was in great jeopardy.

But such was the good fortune of England that this crafty compact did not take place, for while the letters and messengers ran between Peter and King Richard, John, Bishop of Ely, being then in Flanders, was certified by a priest who came out of England—whose name was Christopher Urswick—of all the whole circumstance of this device and purpose. Whereupon with all speed the said Bishop caused the said priest the same day to carry knowledge thereof into Brittany to Henry, Earl of Richmond, willing him, with all the other noblemen, to dispatch themselves with all possible haste into France. Henry, then in Vannes, when he heard of this fraud, without tarrying sent Christopher unto Charles the French King, desiring licence that Henry with the other noblemen might safely come into France; the which thing being soon obtained, the messenger returned with speed to his lord and prince.

Then the Earl Henry, setting all his business in as good stay and order as he might, talked little and took few into his counsel; and for the greater expedition he caused the Earl of Pembroke [his father's brother] secretly to cause all the noblemen to take their horses, dissembling to ride unto the Duke of Brittany, but when they came to the border they should forsake the way that led them towards the Duke and make into France with all speed that ever they might. Then they, doing in everything as they were bidden, lost no time but so sped them that shortly they succeeded in getting into the county of Anjou. Henry then, within two days following, being then still at Vannes, took four or five of his servants with him and feigned as though he would have ridden to visit a friend of his—and forasmuch as there were many Englishmen left there in the town, no man suspected anything. But, after he had kept the right way for the space of five miles, he forsook that and turned straight into a wood that was thereby. There he took upon him his servant's apparel and put his apparel upon his servant and so took but one of them with him, on whom he waited as though he had been the servant and the other the master. And with all convenient and speedy haste they so set forth on their journey that no time was lost, and they made no more tarrying by the way than only the baiting of their horses, so that shortly he reached the borders of Anjou, where all his other company was.

Within four days after the Earl was thus escaped, Peter received from King Richard the confirmation of the grant and promises made for the betraying of Henry and the other nobles; wherefor the said Peter sent out after him horses and men with such expedition and speed to have taken him that scarcely the Earl was entered into France one hour but they were at his heels. The Englishmen, then being above the number of three hundred at Vannes, hearing that the Earl and all the nobles were fled so suddenly and without any of their knowledge, were astonished and, in manner, despaired of their lives.

But it happened contrary to their expectation: for the Duke of Brittany, taking the matter so unkindly that Henry should be so used with him that for fear he should be compelled to flee his land, was not a little vexed with Peter, on whom (although he was ignorant of the fraud and craft that had been wrought by him) yet

he laid the whole fault. He therefore called unto him Edward Poynings and Edward Woodville, delivering unto them the foresaid
money that Henry before had desired the Duke to lend him towards the charge of his journey, and commanded them to convey
and conduct all the Englishmen, his servants, unto him, paying
their expenses, and to deliver the said sum of money unto the Earl.

When the Earl saw his men come and heard this comfortable
news, he not a little rejoiced, desiring the messengers that returned to show unto the Duke that he trusted ere long time to
show himself not to be unthankful for this great kindness that he
now showed unto him. And within few days after, the Earl went
unto Charles the French King, to whom, after he had rendered
thanks for the great benefits and kindness that he had received of
him, first declared the cause of his coming. Then he besought him
for his help and aid, which should be an immortal benefit to him
and his lords, by whom generally he was called unto the kingdom,
forasmuch as they so abhorred the tyranny of King Richard.
Charles promised him help and bade him to be of good cheer and
to take no care, for he would gladly declare unto him his benevolence. And the same time, Charles removed and took with him
Henry and all the other noblemen.

While Henry remained there, John, Earl of Oxford (of whom it
has been before spoken), who had been put in prison by Edward
the Fourth in the castle of Hammes [an outpost of Calais], with
also James Blount, Captain of that castle, and John Fortescue,
knight, Porter of the town of Calais, came unto him. But James,
the Captain, because he left his wife in the castle, did furnish the
same with a good garrison of men before his departure.

Henry, when he saw the Earl, was out of measure glad that so
noble a man and of great experience in battle and so valiant and
hardy a knight—whom he thought to be most faithful and sure
forasmuch as he had in the time of Edward the Fourth continual
battle with him in defending of Henry the Sixth—[had succeeded
in joining him; and he]thought that now he was so well appointed

that he could not desire to be better, and therefore communicated unto him all his whole affairs, to be ordered and ruled only by him.

Not long after, Charles the French King, removed again, to Paris, whom Henry followed. There again he moved and besought the King, as he had most favourably and kindly supported him all this time not only in words but also in deeds, that it would likewise please him yet so much further to extend his favour and benevolence unto him that now he would aid and help him forwards in his journey. Thus, not only he but also all the lords and nobility of England might justly have cause to acknowledge and confess that by the means of his favour and goodness they were restored again to the possession of their inheritances, which, without him, they could not well bring to pass.

In the meanwhile his fortune was such that many Englishmen came over daily out of England unto him and many who then were in Paris. Among them were divers students that fell unto his party and specially there was one, whose name was Richard Fox, a priest, being a man of a singular good wit and learning, whom Henry straightway retained and committed all his secrets unto him, and whom also afterwards he promoted to many high positions, and at the last he made him Bishop of Winchester.

Richard then, hearing of all this conspiracy and of the great aid that daily went over unto Henry, thought yet, for all this, that if he might bring to pass that Henry should not couple in marriage with the blood of King Edward, then he should do well enough with him and keep him from the possession of the crown. Then devised he with himself all the ways and means that might be, how to bring this to pass. And first he thought it to be best with fair words and large promises to essay the Queen, whose favour obtained, he doubted not but shortly to find the means to have both her daughters out of her hands into his own. Then remained nothing but that he himself might find the means afterwards to marry one of the same daughters, whereby he thought he should make all sure and safe, to the utter undoing of Henry.

Whereupon he sent unto the Queen, then being in the sanctuary, divers and sundry messengers that should excuse and purge him of what he had before done against her, setting forth the matter with pleasant words and high promises, both to her and also her son Thomas, Lord Marquess of Dorset, of all things that could be desired. These messengers, being men of gravity, handled the Queen so craftily that soon she began to be allured and to hearken unto them favourably, so that in conclusion she promised to be obedient to the King in his request, forgetting the injuries he had done to her before and on the other part not remembering the promise that she made to Margaret, Henry's mother. And first she delivered both her daughters into the hands of King Richard; then after, she sent privily for the Lord Marquess her son, being then at Paris with Henry (as you have heard), willing him to forsake Henry, with whom he was, and speedily to return into England, for all things were pardoned and forgiven and she again in favour and friendship of the King, and it should be highly for his advancement and honour.

King Richard (when Queen Elizabeth was thus brought into a fool's paradise), after he had received all his brother's daughters from the sanctuary into his palace, thought there now remained nothing to be done but only the casting away and destroying of his own wife, which thing he had wholly purposed and decreed within himself. And there was nothing that he feared so much from this most cruel and detestable murder as the losing of the good opinion that he thought the people had conceived of him; for, as ye have heard before, he feigned himself to be a good man and thought the people had esteemed him even so.

Notwithstanding, shortly after, his foresaid ungracious purpose overcame all this honest fear. And first of all he abstained from bedding or living with her and also found himself grieved with the barrenness of his wife, that she was unfruitful and brought him forth no children, complaining thereof very grievously unto the nobles of his realm and chiefly above others unto Thomas Rotherham, then Archbishop of York—whom he had delivered a little before out of prison. The Bishop did gather from this that the Queen should be rid out of the way ere it were long after (such experience had he of King Richard's disposition, for he had practised many like things not long before); and the same time also he made divers of his secret friends privy of the same his conjecture.

After this the King caused a rumour to run among the common people (but he would not have the author known) that the Queen was dead, to the intent that she, hearing this marvellous rumour, should take so grievous a conceit that soon after she should fall into some great disease. He would essay that way, in case it should chance her afterwards to be sick, dead, or otherwise murdered, that then the people might impute her death unto the thought she took or else to the sickness. But when the Queen heard of so horrible a rumour of her death sprung abroad among the common people, she suspected the matter and supposed the world to be at an end with her; and incontinent she went to the King with a lamentable countenance, and with weeping tears asked him whether she had done anything whereby he might judge her worthy to suffer death. The King made answer with a smiling and dissimulating countenance, with flattering words bidding her to be of good comfort and to pluck up her heart for there was no such thing towards her that he knew. But howsoever it fortuned, either by sorrow or else by poisoning, within few days after, the Queen was dead, and afterwards was buried in the Abbey of Westminster. This is the same Anne, one of Richard, the Earl of Warwick's daughters, who once was contracted to Prince Edward, King Henry the Sixth's son.

The King, being thus delivered of his wife, fancied apace Lady Elizabeth, his niece, desiring in any wise to marry with her; but because all men, yea and the maiden herself, abhorred this unlawful desire as a thing most detestable, he determined with himself to make no great haste in the matter. He did so chiefly for that he was in a peck of troubles, fearing lest some of the noblemen would forsake him and run unto Henry's party, while the others at the least would favour the secret conspiracy made against him, so that of his end there was almost no doubt. Also the more part of the common people were in so great despair that many of them had rather to be accounted in the number of his enemies than to put themselves in jeopardy both of loss of body and goods in taking his part.

And among those noblemen whom he feared, first were Thomas Stanley and William his brother, Gilbert Talbot, and of others a great number; of whose purpose though King Richard was ignorant, nevertheless he trusted not one of them, and least of all Thomas Stanley because he had married Henry's mother, as it may well appear by this that follows. For when the said Thomas would have departed from the court unto his own mansion for his recreation (as he said)—but the truth was, because he would be in a readiness to receive Henry and aid him at his coming into the realm—the King did prevent him and would not suffer him to depart until such time that he had left in the court behind him George [Lord] Strange, his son and heir, for a pledge. And while King Richard was thus wrapped in fear and care of the tumult that was to come, lo, even then tidings came that the castle of Hammes was prepared to receive Henry by the means of the Earl of Oxford, who then was fled with James Blount, keeper of the castle, unto Henry.

Then King Richard, thinking at the beginning to stay all this matter, sent forth with all haste the greater part that were then at Calais to recover the said castle again. Those that were in the castle, when they saw their adversaries make towards them, speedily they armed themselves to defence and in all haste sent messengers to Henry, desiring him of aid.

Henry forthwith sent the Earl of Oxford with a chosen group of men to assist them, and at their first coming they laid siege [drew themselves up in battle formation] not far from the castle. Then, while those that were within made head against their besiegers, the Earl of Oxford so valiantly assailed those besiegers in the rear that they were glad to make proclamation to them that were within that if they would be content to give over the castle, they should have free liberty to depart with all that ever they had. The Earl of Oxford, hearing this, who came only to save his friends from hurt and especially James Blount's wife, was contented with this condition and departed safely with all his friends, returning back to Henry, who was at Paris.

After this, King Richard was informed that the French King was weary of Henry and his company and would do nothing for him. Hereby Henry was now not able in manner to help himself, so that it was not possible that he should prevail or go forwards in the enterprise that he thought to have taken in hand against King Richard.

King Richard, being brought thus into a false paradise, thought himself to be out of all fear and that there was no cause why he should, being so sure, once wake out of his sleep or trouble himself any further. He therefore called back his navy of ships that then was ready upon the sea, which was fully furnished to have scoured the seas. But yet for the more surety, lest he should be suddenly oppressed, he gave commandment to the great men dwelling by the seaside (and specially the Welshmen) to watch night and day, lest his adversaries should have any opportunity to enter into the land. The fashion is in time of war that those that dwell by the sea's side should make beacons in the highest places thereabout, which might be seen afar off; so that when it should chance their enemies to arrive towards the land, immediately they should fire their beacons and raise the country, to the intent that quickly from place to place they might be ascertained of all the whole matter, and also be able to arm themselves speedily against their enemies.

And so to come to our purpose again, King Richard, through the aforesaid tidings, began to be more careless and reckless, as who might say he had no power to withstand the destiny that hung over his head. Such is the provident justice of God, that a man does least know, provide, and beware when the vengeance of God is even at hand for his offences.

Now to go forth to the time that Henry, Earl of Richmond, remained in France, entreating and suing for aid and help from the Frenchmen. Many of the chief noblemen who had the realm in governance (because of the young age of Charles the King) fell somewhat into dissension, of the which variance Louis, the Prince of Orléans [later Louis XII], was the chief and head, who, because he had married Joanne, the King's sister [and was heir to the crown], looked to have been the chief governor of all the realm. By which means it came to pass that no one man had the principal governance of the realm; and therefore Henry the Earl was constrained to sue unto all the nobles, severally one after another, desiring and praying them for aid and help in his purpose, and thus the matter was prolonged.

In the meantime Thomas, the Marquess of Dorset (of whom we spoke before), was privily sent for to come home by his mother, partly mistrusting that Henry should not prevail and partly for the great and large promises that King Richard had made to her for him before. When the said Marquess had received these letters, he, believing all things that his mother wrote unto him and also thinking that Henry should never prevail and that the Frenchmen did but mock and dally with him, he suddenly in the night time conveyed himself out of Paris and with great speed made towards Flanders. When the Earl and others of the English lords heard of this, they were sore astonished and amazed and with all speed purchased of Charles the King a licence and commandment that the Marquess might be stayed wheresoever he were found within the dominion of France, chiefly for that he was secret of their counsel and knew all their purpose. The commandment was quickly obtained and posts made forth every way, amongst whom one Humphrey Cheyney, playing the part of a good bloodhound, so truly smelled out and followed the trace that by and by he found and took the Marquess, and so handled and persuaded him with gentle and good words that shortly after he was content to return.

Then Henry, being delivered of this chance, thought it best to prolong the matter no further, lest he should lose both the present opportunity and also weary his friends that looked for him in England. Therefore he made haste and set forward with a small army obtained from the French King, of whom he also borrowed some money, and some from others of his friends, for the which he left the Marquess and John Bourchier behind for a pledge, and so setting forwards came to Rouen.

And while he tarried there and prepared shipping at the haven of Seine [Harfleur], tidings came to him that King Richard's wife was dead and that he purposed to marry with the Lady Elizabeth, King Edward's eldest daughter and his niece, and that he had married Cecily her sister to a man's son of the land far underneath her degree. At the which thing Henry was sore amazed and troubled, thinking that by this means all his purpose was dashed, for that there was no other way for him to come to the kingdom but only by marriage to one of King Edward's daughters; and by this means also he feared lest his friends in England would shrink from him for lack of an honourable title. But after they had consulted upon the matter, they thought it best to tarry a little, to prove if they might get more help and make more friends. Among all others they thought it best to adjoin the Lord Herbert unto them, who was a man of great power in Wales, and this should be brought to pass by the means that the Lord Herbert had a sister marriageable, whom Henry would be content to marry if he would take their part. And to bring all this matter to pass, messengers were sent to Henry, the Earl of Northumberland, who had married the other sister, so that he should bring this matter about, but the ways were so beset that the messengers could not come to him.

And in the mean season came very good tidings from John ap

Morgan, a temporal lawyer, who signified unto them that Sir Rhys ap Thomas, a noble and valiant man, and John Savage both favoured his party earnestly; and also Sir Reynold Bray had prepared a great sum of money to wage battle on his part and to help him, and therefore he would they should make haste with all that ever they could assemble and make towards Wales.

Then Henry speedily prepared himself because he would keep his friends waiting no longer. And after he had made his prayer unto almighty God, that he might have good success in his journey, with only two thousand men and a few ships, in the Kalends of August [August 1], he sailed from the haven of Seine. The seventh day of August, he arrived in Wales about sunset and landed at Milford Haven, in the part which is called Dale, where he heard that there were divers laid in wait for him to keep him back. From thence, in the morning betimes he removed towards a town called Haverfordwest, within ten miles of Dale, where he was very joyfully received. Here he had tidings brought contrary to what he heard in Normandy before, that Sir Rhys ap Thomas and John Savage with all that ever they could make, were of King Richard's party.

Notwithstanding, they had such tidings sent them from the men of Pembroke, by a valiant gentleman whose name was Arnold Butler, that it rejoiced all their hearts: if all former offences might be remitted, they would be in a readiness to stick to their own Jasper, the Earl [of Pembroke]. Then Henry's company, by this means being increased, departed from Haverfordwest five miles towards Cardigan, and then while he refreshed his men, suddenly came a rumour unto him that the Lord Herbert, who dwelled at Carmarthen, was nigh at hand with a great army of men. At the which rumour there was a great stir amongst them, and every man took himself to his weapon and made himself ready if need were to fight. A little while they were all afraid, till such time as horsemen Henry had sent out to try the truth, came back and declared that all things were quiet and that there was no such thing. Most of all, Master Griffiths, a very noble man, did comfort them and gladden their hearts, for he, although before he had joined himself to Lord Herbert, at that very time cleaved to Henry with such company as he had, although they were but few; and the same time came John ap Morgan unto him.

Henry went still forwards and tarried almost in no place. Because he wished to make sure work and the better speed, he invaded such places before they were armed against him, the which places he beat down with very little strength; but afterwards having knowledge by his spies that the Lord Herbert and Sir Rhys were in a readiness to give him battle, he determined to set upon them and either to put them to flight or else to make them swear homage and fealty unto him and to take them with him in his host against King Richard. And because he would ascertain his friends in England how all the matter went forwards with him, he sent some of his most trusty friends to Lady Margaret, his mother, to Stanley, to Talbot, and to others of his most especial friends with certain commandments. The effect of the commandments was that he intended with the help of his friends to pass over Severn and, by Shrewsbury, to make towards London; therefore he desired them, with those that were of their counsel, in time and place convenient to meet him.

So, the messengers going forth with these commissions, Henry went forwards towards Shrewsbury, and on the way met with Sir Rhys ap Thomas with a great number of men, who came unto him and was of his party. For, two days before, Henry promised him (if he would come unto him), to be chief ruler of all Wales, as soon as he came to the crown, which afterwards he gave to him indeed. In the meantime the messengers, executing the message diligently, returned back again with large rewards from them to whom they were sent, and came to Henry the same day he entered Shrewsbury, and showed how all his friends were in a readiness to do the utmost that lay in them.

These tidings put Henry in such great hope that he went forth with a courage and came to the town of Newport, and there set up his tents upon a little hill and there lay all night. That night came to him Sir Gilbert Talbot with above two hundred men. After that, they went forth to Stafford, and while they were there William Stanley came to him with a few after him, and when he had talked a little with him, returned back again to his host which he had prepared. From thence Henry went to Lichfield and that night lay without the town, but in the morning betimes he entered the city and was received honourably. A day or two before, Thomas Stanley was there with five thousand men armed, who, when he knew of Henry's coming, forthwith went ahead to a village called Atherstone, there to tarry till Henry came. This he did to avoid suspicion, being afraid lest King Richard, knowing his intent, would have put his son to death, who, as I told you before, was left with him as a pledge for his father.

But King Richard in the meantime, who then was at Nottingham, hearing that Henry with a few more of banished men was entered into Wales, so lightly regarded the matter that he thought it was not much to be regarded for that he came in with so few in number, and that the Lord Herbert and Sir Rhys, who were rulers of all Wales, would either kill him or else take him and bring him alive. But afterwards, when he reminded himself that oftentimes a small matter in battle if it be not looked unto betimes, would make at the last a great stir, he thought it best to remedy the matter betimes and commanded Henry, the Earl of Northumberland, with others of the nobles of the realm (who, he thought, had set more by him than by their own goods) to raise up an army and come to him with speed. Also he sent divers messengers with letters to Robert Brakenbury, keeper of the Tower of London, commanding him to come unto him in all haste and to bring with him as fellows in battle Thomas Bourchier, Walter Hungerford, and divers other knights, whom he did not a little suspect.

In this time it was showed that Henry was come to Shrewsbury without any hurt, with the which tidings the King began to rage and made exclamation against them, that contrary to their faiths they had utterly deceived him; and then he began to mistrust all men and knew not whom he might trust, so that he thought it best to set forth himself against his adversaries. And forthwith he sent out spies to know which way Henry did take; they, when they had done their diligence, returned back again and showed him how Henry was come to Lichfield. After he knew this, immediately setting his men in array—because now there was a great number of soldiers come together—he commanded them forwards, and to go four and four together. They took that way which, they had heard said, their enemies were coming. The suspected persons he put in the midst; he himself with those he trusted came behind, with wings of horsemen running on every side, and thus keeping their order, about sunset came unto Leicester.

When Henry in the mean season had removed from Lichfield unto the next village, called Tamworth, in the midway he met with Walter Hungerford, Thomas Bourchier, and many others more who had promised to aid him before; and because they perceived that they were suspected by Richard and lest they should be brought violently unto him, being their enemy, they forsook Robert Brakenbury, their captain, and in the night time stole privily away and went to Henry. What was worthy to be marked, was that Henry, although he was a man of noble courage and also his company did daily increase, yet, for all that, he stood in great fear because he was uncertain of Thomas Stanley—who, as I told you before, for the fear of putting his son to death, inclined as yet unto no party—and for that the resources of King Richard were not so slender as report was made to him by his friends.

Wherefore, as all afraid without a cause, he took only twenty men with him and stayed in his journey as a man in despair and half musing with himself what was best to be done; and to aggravate the matter, tidings were brought him that King Richard was coming near to meet him with a great and huge host of men. And while Henry thus lingered for fear behind, his host came ahead to the town of Tamworth, and because it was then dark night he lost both his company and also his way; then wandering from place to place, at last he came to a little village three miles from his host, being full of fear. And lest he should fall into the danger of scout watch, he durst not ask a question of any man, and partly for the fear that was present, partly for that that was to come, he lay there that night, and took this for a sign or a prognostication of some great plague that was to come; and, on the other part, his host was no less abashed, seeing his absence for that time.

When in the morning Henry came to them in the light of the day, he excused the matter, saying that he was not absent because he had lost his way but rather of purpose because he wished to confer with his privy friends, who would not be seen in the day. After that he went privily to Atherstone, where Thomas Stanley and William his brother did dwell. Here Henry, Thomas, and William met and took other by the hand with loving salutations and were glad one of another; then after, they counselled together of their meeting with King Richard, whom they perceived then not to be far from them. That day when it drew towards night, in the evening John Savage, Bryan Sanford, Simon Digby, with many others, forsook King Richard and came to Henry with a great power of men, which power and strength set Henry aloft again.

In the mean season King Richard, who purposed to go through thick and thin in this matter, came to Bosworth a little beyond Leicester, where the place of battle should be—as a man would say, the high justice of God, which could not be avoided, hanging over his head, had called him to a place where he should suffer worthy punishment for his detestable offences—and there he set up his tents and rested that night.

Before he went to bed, he made an oration to his company with great vehemence, persuading and exhorting them manfully to fight; and afterwards, as it was said, he had a terrible dream in his sleep, seeming that he saw horrible devils appear unto him, pulling and haling him so that he could take no rest. Which vision filled him full of fear and also of heavy care when he waked; for by and by after, being sore grieved in his mind, he did prognosticate from this dream the evil luck and heavy chance that after came to him, and he came not with so cheerful a countenance unto his company as he was wont to do. Then, lest they should think that he had this heaviness for the fear of his enemies, he stood up and rehearsed unto them all his dream. But I think that this was not a dream but rather his conscience pricked with the sharp sting of his mischievous offences, which, although they do not prick always, yet most commonly they will bite most towards the latter day, representing unto us not only themselves but also the terrible punishment that is ordained for the same, as the sight of the devil tearing and haling us so that thereby (if we have grace) we may take an occasion to be penitent, or else for lack of the same die in desperation.

Now to come to my purpose again, the next day after, King Richard, having all things in a readiness, went forth with the army out of his tents and began to set his men in array: first the van set forth with a marvellous length both of horsemen and also of footmen, a very terrible company to them that should see them afar off, and in the foremost part of all he ordered the bowmen, as a strong fortress for them that came after. Over this John, the Duke of Norfolk, was head captain, and after him followed the King with a mighty force of men.

And in this while Henry, being departed from the communication with his friends, without any tarrying pitched his tents near his enemies and lay there all night, and commanded his men to be in a readiness; in the morning he sent also to Thomas Stanley, being then in the midst betwixt both hosts, that he should come near with his army. Stanley sent him word back that he should set his men in an order till he came [should prepare for battle and Stanley would come later], with the which answer—one otherwise than he had expected or than the matter did require—he was not a little abashed and stood as it were in doubt; yet, for all that, he tarried not but with all speed set his men in an order. The van was but slender because his numbers were but few; the archers were set in the foremost part, over whom John, the Earl of Oxford, was head captain. In the right wing he set Gilbert Talbot, in the left he put John Savage, and he himself followed with one company of horsemen and a few footmen. All his whole company were scant five thousand, apart from both Stanleys with their company, of the which William Stanley had three thousand. The King's army was double to all this.

And so, when both armies were all in a readiness and began to come within the sight of other, they thrust forth themselves on both parts, looking only for the sign and token of striking together. Betwixt both hosts there was a marsh, which Henry left on his right hand purposely as a defence of his men. He found the means also to have the bright sun on his back, that it might dazzle the eyes of his enemies.

But the King, when he saw Henry pass over the marsh, commanded his men with all violence to set upon them. They immediately with a sudden clamour let arrows fly at them. On the other side, they paid them home manfully again with the same. But when they came near together, they laid on valiantly with swords.

The Earl of Oxford, fearing lest in the meantime King Richard's multitude should have compassed in his men, who were but a few, commanded them by fives they should not move forwards past ten feet; the which commandment known, they knitted themselves together and ceased not in fighting. Their adversaries, being afraid, suspected some craft or guile and began to break off, and many of the same party were not much grieved therewith because they were as glad that the King should be lost as saved, and therefore they fought with less courage. Then the Earl of Oxford, with his men thick together, struck on more freshly. The others of the other party did likewise the same.

And while the first wards of the battle-lines had fought so manfully, Richard perceived by his spies Henry afar off with a small company of armed men; afterwards coming nearer, Richard knew him by signs and tokens. Then, being inflamed with anger, he furiously struck his horse with his spurs and ran out of the one side of the host and like a lion ran at him. On the other side, Henry, perceiving him coming, was very desirous to meet him.

Richard, at the first setting forth, killed divers that stood against him; he threw down Henry's banner and William Brandon the bearer also; he ran at Cheyney, a man of great might, who came to meet him, and with great violence overthrew him to the ground; and thus he made himself a way through them, in order to come to Henry. But Henry was a better match for him than his men would have thought, who then were almost in despair of the victory. And even at that time, lo, there came William Stanley to aid them with four thousand men, and even at the very same time the residue of King Richard's men were put to flight. Then Richard, fighting alone in the midst of all his enemies, was overthrown and slain.

In the meantime the Earl of Oxford in the van, after he had fought manfully a little while, put the residue to flight, of whom he slew a great number. But a great number more, who followed Richard more for fear than for love, held their hands from fighting and went away without hurt, for they cared less for his safety than for his destruction.

There were slain at this conflict not many more than one thousand, of whom these were noblemen: John, Duke of Norfolk, Walter Ferris, Robert Brakenbury, Richard Ratcliffe, and many others more. And within two days after, William Catesby, lawyer, with certain others of his fellows was put to death at Leicester. And amongst those that ran away were Francis [Lord] Lovell, Humphrey Stafford, with Thomas his brother, and others more that ran into sanctuary at Colchester in Essex.

There was of the captives a great number, because when Richard was slain, every man cast down his weapon and yielded himself to Henry, of whom the more part would have done so at the beginning if it had not been for fear of King Richard's spies, who then wandered in every place. And amongst these the nobles were the Earl of Northumberland, the Earl of Surrey—of whom, the Earl of Surrey was put in prison, the other as a friend was received into favour. Henry at that field lost not above an hundred men, amongst whom the chief was William Brandon, who bore Henry's banner. This battle was fought on the twenty-second day of the month of August in the year of our Lord a thousand, four hundred, eighty-five. The conflict endured more than two hours.

Richard might (as the rumour went) have saved himself if he would have fled away; for those that were about him, when they saw his men from the beginning fight but faintly and that some were run away unto the other party, suspected treason and wished him to fly; and when the matter was manifest that all hope of victory was past, they brought him a swift horse. He, putting aside all hope and trust that was in flying, made (as it was said) this answer, that this day he would have either an end of battle or else of his life. Such was his great audacity and manfulness that, because he did see certainly that in this day he should obtain the kingdom quietly all days of his life or else lose both forever, he entered in amongst them, as it was declared before, intending utterly either to lose all or else to win all.

And so the wretch died, having the end that all such were wont to have who, instead of law, honesty, and all godliness, follow their own appetite, villainy, and all wickedness. And plainly this is an example which cannot be better expressed: to fear them who will not suffer one hour to be otherwise spent than in cruelty, mischief, and all devilish fashions.

Henry, when he had thus obtained the victory, fell down on his knees and with many prayers and thanks referred all to the goodness of God. Then he stood up, being wonderfully replenished with joy, and went up upon a little hill and there gave great commendations to his soldiers, commanding them that were hurt to be healed and the dead to be buried. Afterwards he gave immortal thanks to his noble captains, promising them that he would never forget their benefit. The multitude in the meantime with one voice and one mind proclaimed him King. When Thomas Stanley saw that, he took King Richard's crown, which was found amongst the spoils, and forthwith put it upon Henry's head, as though he had been then created King by the election of the people, as it was wont to be in the old time; and this was the first token of his felicity.

After this, King Henry, with his company and baggage-train, went to Leicester towards night to bed. After he had refreshed his company well for the space of two days that they might the better go towards London, King Richard's body was brought naked over a horse's back, the head and the arms hanging on the one side and the legs on the other, and carried into the Grey Friars of Leicester (and surely it was but a miserable sight to look upon, yet it was good enough considering his wretched living), and there without any solemnity was buried two days after.

He reigned two years, one month, and twenty-seven days. He was but of a small stature, having but a deformed body, the one shoulder was higher than the other; he had a short face and a cruel look, which did betoken malice, guile, and deceit. And while he did muse upon anything, standing, he would bite his underlip continually, whereby a man might perceive his cruel nature; within his wretched body, he strived and chafed always within himself; also the dagger which he bore about him, he would always be chopping of it in and out. He had a sharp and pregnant wit, subtle, and to dissimulate and feign very meet. He had also a proud and cruel mind, which never went from him to the hour of his death, which he had rather suffer by the cruel sword, though all his company did forsake him, than by shameful flight favour his life, which after might chance by sickness or other condign punishment shortly to perish.

An Introduction to
HISTORIC DOUBTS

Though Horace Walpole (1717–97) was an indefatigable recorder of his own day—in his memoirs, his correspondence, and in topical sallies of prose or verse—he took but one plunge into the history of the past, at the age of fifty, and emerged with *Historic Doubts on the Life and Reign of King Richard the Third*, published February 1, 1768.

In his youth Walpole, like the rest of the world, had referred to Richard as 'the assassin King' ('Epistle from Florence', 1740), but later Sir George Buc's *History of Richard III* fell in his way and he became a convert to the revisionist cause.

He found ammunition to use against Thomas More's *History* in the roll of Richard III's Parliament, which, though Henry VII had ordered all copies destroyed, turned up a century later to prove that Lady Eleanor Butler, and not More's Elizabeth Lucy, was the lady of the pre-contract. However, Walpole's deduction from the roll that Edward V must have been alive when King Richard's Parliament met early in 1484, is not one of his happiest arguments.

What finally prompted his pen, apparently, was his coming across a fifteenth-century document. This discovery, he wrote jubilantly to Lord Hailes two weeks before the publication of *Doubts*, 'is one of the most marvellous that ever was made . . . the original Coronation Roll of Richard the Third. . . .' Unfortunately, as Walpole was to be informed, the Roll is in reality a Wardrobe account, the items of which do not all pertain to the coronation and which cannot bear the interpretation Walpole fastens upon it.

Indeed, the weaknesses of *Historic Doubts* catch the eye more quickly than its successes. In insisting that Perkin Warbeck was the veritable younger son of Edward IV, Walpole is flogging what has become a very dead horse; and when he solemnly declares that Shakespeare's *The Winter Evening's Tale* represents a veiled commentary on Henry VIII and Anne Boleyn, he slides into sheer rococo.

He often reaches conclusions accepted today, but he not infrequently arrives at them by unsatisfactory arguments; for, lacking fifteenth-century sources that have since come to light, he sometimes had to ground his attack upon the Tudor tradition in the materials of that tradition. Thus he dismisses a number of Richard's supposed crimes mostly by declaring the accusations to be unconvincing. He makes heavy weather over Jane Shore (pp. 228–31), who, it seems probable, became first the mistress of Dorset—hence the reference to Dorset in Richard's proclamation—and then the mistress of Hastings, whom she served as liaison with the Woodville conspirators. Walpole likewise entangles himself in the various obscure references to King Richard's bastards (p. 225). All we can be sure of is that Richard acknowledged two illegitimate children, contracting his daughter Katherine to the Earl of Huntingdon in 1484 and appointing 'our dear son, our bastard John of Gloucester' Captain of Calais the following year. In sum, as Walpole acknowledges, he is forced to limit himself to tearing down the Tudor tradition, for he has little to put in its place.

On the other hand, he industriously applied himself to seeking fresh source materials, making frequent use of the *Croyland Chronicle* as an antidote to Tudor historians. In lively style he exposes inconsistencies and improbabilities. He rightly points up the strange behaviour of Elizabeth Woodville in the reign of Henry VII (p. 207), which to this day remains a nagging mystery. Above all, he is the first to mount an intelligent attack on the story of the princes' murder as recounted by Thomas More.

Horace Walpole affected an aristocratic indifference towards his work (see his preface), but he could not altogether conceal his auctorial pride. The day after *Doubts* was published, he wrote to

Lord Hailes, 'I can attribute to nothing but the curiosity of the subject, the great demand for it; for though it was sold publicly but yesterday, and twelve hundred and fifty copies were printed, Dodsley has been with me this morning to tell me he must prepare another edition directly.' In his autobiographical notes he is careful to record for June 20 of the same year, 'Received a letter from Voltaire desiring my *Historic Doubts*. I sent them.'

Historic Doubts lit a crackling fire of controversy. The book was immediately attacked in the *Critical Review* and the *London Chronicle* and, soon after, by a lawyer who composed an *Answer to Mr Horace Walpole's Late Work . . . or an Attempt to Confute him from his own Arguments*. Meanwhile, Lord Carlisle had observed in a letter to a friend, 'The Emperor Nero's character wants a little white-washing, and so does Mrs Brownrigg's, who was hanged for murdering her apprentices the other day. I hope he will undertake them next, as they seem, next to his hero, to want it the most.'

The following year Gibbon contributed to a Continental periodical a long unsigned review, critical but chivalrous. The antiquarians, however, were not so polite. Dr John Milles, President of the Society of Antiquaries, to which Walpole himself belonged, issued in the first number of the Society's journal, *Archaeologia* (I, 1770), a blunt refutation of Walpole's claims for the so-called Coronation Roll; and two years later a Rev. Robert Masters (*Archaeologia*, II, 1773) waspishly assailed the 'boasted discoveries' of the master of Strawberry Hill. Walpole, sufficiently stung as to resign from the Society, wrote replies to these attacks, which were not printed until after his death (*Works*, II, 1798).

He was most troubled, however, by the disapproval of David Hume, with whom he maintained a somewhat fluctuating friendship. Horace Walpole, the man of society, could not forget that he was a son of the first Earl of Orford (the great Prime Minister, Sir Robert Walpole), but neither could Horace Walpole, man of genuine sensibility, forget that David Hume was the first English intellect of the day.

In the *Doubts* he had been at pains to answer Hume's defence of the Tudor tradition (pp. 216–20)—though, ironically enough, he praised Hume's 'discovery' (p. 216) that Edward IV had not been taken captive in 1469 by Warwick the Kingmaker, a conclusion that is completely untenable.

He was much disturbed, then, to discover appended to Gibbon's review (the authorship of which he apparently did not recognize) notes by David Hume strongly criticizing his treatment of the murder of the princes. Walpole penned a vigorous and quite effective rejoinder, which he made a point of showing to Hume, though this *Supplement to the Historic Doubts* likewise remained in manuscript until its appearance in the *Collected Works*, II, 1798.

On the whole, if Horace Walpole's *Doubts* are occasionally more haphazard than historic, he none the less created a sometimes illuminating and always entertaining challenge to complacent orthodoxy. This spirited defence of Richard III has enjoyed a diversity of critics and admirers: a French version, published in 1800, contains in its preface the statement that it was translated by Louis XVI . . . a king who has likewise had his detractors.

This edition is based on the first edition of 1768. In quoting More, Walpole apparently uses the somewhat corrupt version of the *History* which appears in Hall's *Chronicle*; where possible, his quotations have been brought into line with the text included in this volume. Quotations from More which do not appear in the authentic Rastell text here used, have been signalled in the notes. Similarly, other quotations from contemporary English sources have been modernized, and the spelling of proper names has been made consistent with modern usage.

Walpole deploys an elaborate 'scholarly apparatus' of notes and citations, both designed—as Gibbon remarked of the library and the concubines of the Younger Gordianus—for use rather than ostentation, but perhaps intended also to counterbalance the tendency of the author, as a civilized gentleman, to quote from memory rather than from research. A number of his notes, developing his arguments in sprightly style, continue to be of interest; others, particularly those related to his now-outmoded championing of Perkin Warbeck, add nothing to his case and have, consequently, been omitted from this edition. Walpole's notes are marked (W) to distinguish them from the editor's.

PREFACE

So incompetent has the generality of historians been for the province they have undertaken, that it is almost a question, whether, if the dead of past ages could revive, they would be able to reconnoitre the events of their own times, as transmitted to us by ignorance and misrepresentation. All very ancient history, except that of the illuminated Jews, is a perfect fable. It was written by priests, or collected from their reports; and calculated solely to raise lofty ideas of the origin of each nation. Gods and demi gods were the principal actors; and truth is seldom to be expected where the personages are supernatural. The Greek historians have no advantage over the Peruvian, but in the beauty of their language, or from that language being more familiar to us. Mango Capac, the son of the sun, is as authentic a founder of a royal race, as the progenitor of the Heraclidæ. What truth indeed could be expected, when even the identity of person is uncertain? The actions of one were ascribed to many, and of many to one. It is not known whether there was a single Hercules or twenty.

As nations grew polished, History became better authenticated. Greece itself learned to speak a little truth. Rome, at the hour of its fall, had the consolation of seeing the crimes of its usurpers published. The vanquished inflicted eternal wounds on their conquerors—but who knows, if Pompey had succeeded, whether Julius Cæsar would not have been decorated as a martyr to public liberty? At some periods the suffering criminal captivates all hearts; at others, the triumphant tyrant. Augustus, drenched in the blood of his fellow-citizens, and Charles Stuart, falling in his own blood, are held up to admiration. Truth is left out of the discussion; and odes and anniversary sermons give the law to history and credulity.

But if the crimes of Rome are authenticated, the case is not the same with its virtues. An able critic has shown that nothing is more problematic than the history of the three or four first ages of that city. As the confusions of the state increased, so do the confusions in its story. The empire had masters, whose names are only known from medals. It is uncertain of what princes several empresses were the wives. If the jealousy of two antiquaries intervenes, the point becomes inexplicable. Oriuna, on the medals of Carausius, used to pass for the moon: of late years it is become a doubt whether she was not his consort. It is of little importance whether she was moon or empress: but how little must we know of those times, when those land-marks to certainty, royal names, do not serve even that purpose! In the cabinet of the king of France are several coins of sovereigns, whose country cannot now be guessed at.

The want of records, of letters, of printing, of critics; wars, revolutions, factions, and other causes, occasioned these defects in ancient history. Chronology and astronomy are forced to tinker up and reconcile, as well as they can, those uncertainties. This satisfies the learned—but what should we think of the reign of George the Second, to be calculated two thousand years hence by eclipses, lest the conquest of Canada should be ascribed to James the First?

At the very moment that the Roman empire was resettled, nay, when a new metropolis was erected, in an age of science and arts, while letters still held up their heads in Greece; consequently, when the great outlines of truth, I mean events, might be expected to be established; at that very period a new deluge of error burst upon the world. Christian monks and saints laid truth waste; and a mock sun rose at Rome, when the Roman sun sunk at Constantinople. Virtues and vices were rated by the standard of bigotry; and the militia of the church became the only historians. The best princes were represented as monsters; the worst, at least the most useless, were deified, according as they depressed or exalted turbulent and enthusiastic prelates and friars. Nay, these men were so destitute of temper and common sense, that they dared to suppose that common sense would never revisit the earth: and accordingly wrote with so little judgment, and committed such palpable forgeries, that if we cannot discover what really happened in those ages, we can at least be very sure what did not. How many general persecutions does the church record, of which there is not the smallest trace? What donations and charters were forged, for which those holy persons would lose their ears, if they were in this age to present them in the most common court of judicature? Yet how long were these impostors the only persons who attempted to write history!

But let us lay aside their interested lies, and consider how far they were qualified in other respects to transmit faithful memorials to posterity. In the ages I speak of, the barbarous monkish ages, the shadow of learning that existed was confined to the clergy: they generally wrote in Latin, or in verse, and their compositions in both were truly barbarous. The difficulties of rhime, and the want of correspondent terms in Latin, were no small impediments to the severe march of truth. But there were worse obstacles to encounter. Europe was in a continual state of warfare. Little princes and great lords were constantly skirmishing and scrambling for trifling additions of territory, or wasting each others borders. Geography was very imperfect; no police existed; roads, such as they were, were dangerous; and posts were not established. Events were only known by rumour, from pilgrims, or by letters carried by couriers to the parties interested: the public did not enjoy even those fallible vehicles of intelligence, newspapers. In this situation did monks, at twenty, fifty, an hundred, nay, a thousand miles distance (and under the circumstances I have mentioned even twenty miles were considerable) undertake to write history—and they wrote it accordingly.

If we take a survey of our own history, and examine it with any attention, what an unsatisfactory picture does it present to us! How dry, how superficial, how void of information! How little is recorded besides battles, plagues, and religious foundations! That this should be the case, before the Conquest, is not surprizing. Our empire was but forming itself, or re-collecting its divided members into one mass, which, from the desertion of the Romans, had split into petty kingdoms. The invasions of nations as barbarous as ourselves, interfered with every plan of policy and order that might have been formed to settle the emerging state; and swarms of foreign monks were turned loose upon us with their new faith and mysteries, to bewilder and confound the plain good sense of our ancestors. It was too much to have Danes, Saxons, and Popes to combat at once.

Our language suffered as much as our government; and not having acquired much from our Roman masters, was miserably disfigured by the subsequent invaders. The unconquered parts of the island retained some purity and some precision. The Welsh and Erse tongues wanted not harmony: but never did exist a more barbarous jargon than the dialect, still venerated by antiquaries, and called *Saxon*. It was so uncouth, so inflexible to all composition, that the monks, retaining the idiom, were reduced to write in what they took or meant for Latin.

The Norman tyranny succeeded, and gave this Babel of savage sounds a wrench towards their own language. Such a mixture necessarily required ages to bring it to some standard: and, consequently, whatever compositions were formed during its progress, were sure of growing obsolete. However, the authors of those days were not likely to make these obvious reflections; and indeed seem to have aimed at no one perfection. From the Conquest to the reign of Henry the Eighth it is difficult to discover any one beauty in our writers, but their simplicity. They told their tale, like story-tellers; that is, they related without art or ornament; and they related whatever they heard. No councils of princes, no motives of conduct, no remoter springs of action, did they investigate or learn. We have even little light into the characters of the actors. A king or an archbishop of Canterbury are the only persons with whom we are made much acquainted. The barons are all represented as brave patriots; but we have not the satisfaction of knowing which of them were really so; nor whether they were not all turbulent and ambitious. The probability is, that both kings and nobles wished to encroach on each other: and if any sparks of liberty were struck out, in all likelihood it was contrary to the intention of either the flint or the steel.

Hence has it been thought necessary to give a new dress to English history. Recourse has been had to records, and they are far from corroborating the testimonies of our historians. Want of authentic materials has obliged our later writers to leave the mass pretty much as they found it. Perhaps all the requisite attention that might have been bestowed, has not been bestowed. It demands great industry and patience to wade into such abstruse stores as records and charters: and they being jejune and narrow in themselves, very acute criticism is necessary to strike light from their assistance. If they solemnly contradict historians in material facts, we may lose our history; but it is impossible to adhere to our historians. Partiality man cannot entirely divest himself of; it is so natural, that the bent of a writer to one side or the other of a question is almost always discoverable. But there is a wide difference between favouring and lying—and yet I doubt whether the whole stream of our historians, misled by their originals, have not falsified one reign in our annals in the grossest manner. The moderns are only guilty of taking on trust what they ought to have examined more scrupulously, as the authors whom they copied were all ranked on one side in a flagrant season of party. But no excuse can be made for the original authors, who, I doubt, have violated all rules of truth.

The confusions which attended the civil war between the houses of York and Lancaster, threw an obscurity over that part of our annals, which it is almost impossible to dispel. We have scarce any authentic monuments of the reign of Edward the Fourth; and ought to read his history with much distrust, from the boundless partiality of the succeeding writers to the opposite cause. That diffidence should increase as we proceed to the reign of his brother.

[157]

It occurred to me some years ago, that the picture of Richard the Third, as drawn by historians, was a character formed by prejudice and invention. I did not take Shakespeare's tragedy for a genuine representation, but I did take the story of that reign for a tragedy of imagination. Many of the crimes imputed to Richard seemed improbable; and, what was stronger, contrary to his interest. A few incidental circumstances corroborated my opinion; an original and important instrument was pointed out to me last winter, which gave rise to the following sheets; and as it was easy to perceive, under all the glare of encomiums which historians have heaped on the wisdom of Henry the Seventh, that he was a mean and unfeeling tyrant, I suspected that they had blackened his rival, till Henry, by the contrast, should appear in a kind of amiable light. The more I examined their story, the more I was confirmed in my opinion:—and with regard to Henry, one consequence I could not help drawing; that we have either no authentic memorials of Richard's crimes, or, at most, no account of them but from Lancastrian historians; whereas the vices and injustice of Henry are, though palliated, avowed by the concurrent testimony of his panegyrists. Suspicions and calumny were fastened on Richard as so many assassinations. The murders committed by Henry were indeed executions—and executions pass for prudence with prudent historians; for when a successful king is chief justice, historians become a voluntary jury.

If I do not flatter myself, I have unravelled a considerable part of that dark period. Whether satisfactorily or not, my readers must decide. Nor is it of any importance whether I have or not. The attempt was mere matter of curiosity and speculation. If any man, as idle as myself, should take the trouble to review and canvass my arguments, I am ready to yield so indifferent a point to better reasons. Should declamation alone be used to contradict me, I shall not think I am less in the right.

28 November, 1767.

HISTORIC DOUBTS

There is a kind of litterary superstition, which men are apt to contract from habit, and which makes them look on any attempt towards shaking their belief in any established characters, no matter whether good or bad, as a sort of prophanation. They are determined to adhere to their first impressions, and are equally offended at any innovation, whether the person, whose character is to be raised or depressed, were patriot or tyrant, saint or sinner. No indulgence is granted to those who would ascertain the truth. The more the testimonies on either side have been multiplied, the stronger is the conviction; though it generally happens that the original evidence is wonderous slender, and that the number of writers have but copied one another: or, what is worse, have only added to the original, without any new authority. Attachment so groundless is not to be regarded; and in mere matters of curiosity, it were ridiculous to pay any deference to it. If time brings new materials to light, if facts and dates confute historians, what does it signify that we have been for two or three hundred years under an error? Does antiquity consecrate darkness? Does a lie become venerable from its age?

Historic justice is due to all characters. Who would not vindicate Henry the Eighth or Charles the Second, if found to be falsely traduced? Why then not Richard the Third? Of what importance is it to any man living whether or not he was as bad as he is represented? No one noble family is sprung from him.

However, not to disturb too much the erudition of those who have read the dismal story of his cruelties, and settled their ideas of his tyranny and usurpation, I declare I am not going to write a vindication of him. All I mean to show, is, that though he may have been as execrable as we are told he was, we have little or no reason to believe so. If the propensity of habit should still incline a single man to *suppose* that all he has read of Richard is true, I beg no more, than that that person would be so impartial as to own that he has little or no foundation for supposing so.

I will state the list of the crimes charged on Richard; I will specify the authorities on which he was accused; I will give a faithful account of the historians by whom he was accused; and will then examine the circumstances of each crime and each evidence; and lastly, show that some of the crimes were contrary to Richard's interest, and almost all inconsistent with probability or with dates, and some of them involved in material contradictions.

SUPPOSED CRIMES OF RICHARD THE THIRD.

1st. His murder of Edward Prince of Wales, son of Henry the Sixth.
2d. His murder of Henry the Sixth.
3d. The murder of his brother George Duke of Clarence.
4th. The execution of Rivers, Gray, and Vaughan.
5th. The execution of Lord Hastings.
6th. The murder of Edward the Fifth and his brother.
7th. The murder of his own queen.

To which may be added, as they are thrown into the list to blacken him, his intended match with his own niece Elizabeth, the penance of Jane Shore, and his own personal deformities.

I. Of the murder of Edward Prince of Wales,
son of Henry the Sixth.

Edward the Fourth had indubitably the hereditary right to the crown; which he pursued with singular bravery and address, and with all the arts of a politician and the cruelty of a conqueror. Indeed on neither side do there seem to have been any scruples: Yorkists and Lancastrians, Edward and Margaret of Anjou, entered into any engagements, took any oaths, violated them, and indulged their revenge, as often as they were depressed or victorious. After the battle of Tewkesbury, in which Margaret and her son were made prisoners, young Edward was brought to the presence of Edward the Fourth; 'but after the king,' says Fabyan, the oldest historian of those times, 'had questioned with the said Sir Edward, and he had answered unto him contrary his pleasure, he then struck him with his gauntlet upon the face; after which stroke, so by him received, he was by the king's servants incontinently slain.' The Chronicle of Croyland of the same date says, the prince was slain *'ultricibus quorundam manibus;'** but names nobody.

Hall, who closes his work with the reign of Henry the Eighth, says, that 'the prince being bold of stomach and of a good courage, answered the king's question (of how he durst so presumptuously enter into his realm with banner displayed) saying, to recover my father's kingdom and inheritance, &c. at which words King Edward said nothing, but with his hand thrust him from him, or, as some say, struck him with his gauntlet, whom incontinent, they that stood about, which were George Duke of Clarence, Richard Duke of Gloucester, Thomas Marquess Dorset (son of Queen Elizabeth Woodville) and William Lord Hastynges, suddenly murdered and pitiously manquelled [killed].' Thus much had the story gained from the time of Fabyan to that of Hall.

Holinshed repeats these very words, consequently is a transcriber and no new authority.

John Stowe reverts to Fabyan's account, as the only one not grounded on hear-say, and affirms no more than that the king cruelly smote the young prince on the face with his gauntlet, and after his servants slew him.

Of modern historians, Rapin and Carte, the only two who seem not to have swallowed implicitly all the vulgar tales propagated by the Lancastrians to blacken the house of York, warn us to read with allowance the exaggerated relations of those times. The latter suspects, that at the dissolution of the monasteries all evidences were suppressed that tended to weaken the right of the prince on the throne; but as Henry the Eighth concentred in himself both

* 'By the avenging hands of certain persons'.

the claim of Edward the Fourth and that ridiculous one of Henry the Seventh, he seems to have had less occasion to be anxious lest the truth should come out; and indeed his father had involved that truth in so much darkness, that it was little likely to force its way. Nor was it necessary then to load the memory of Richard the Third, who had left no offspring. Henry the Eighth had no competitor to fear but the descendants of Clarence, of whom he seems to have had sufficient apprehension, as appeared by his murder of the old Countess of Salisbury, daughter of Clarence, and his endeavours to root out her posterity. This jealousy accounts for Hall charging the Duke of Clarence, as well as the Duke of Gloucester, with the murder of Prince Edward. But in accusations of so deep a dye, it is not sufficient ground for our belief, that an historian reports them with such a frivolous palliative as that phrase, *as some say*. A contemporary names the king's *servants* as perpetrators of the murder: is not that more probable, than that the king's own brothers should have dipped their hands in so foul an assassination? Richard, in particular, is allowed on all hands to have been a brave and martial prince: he had great share in the victory at Tewkesbury. Some years afterwards, he commanded his brother's troops in Scotland, and made himself master of Edinburgh. At the battle of Bosworth, where he fell, his courage was heroic: he fought Richmond, and endeavoured to decide their quarrel by a personal combat, slaying Sir William Brandon, his rival's standard-bearer, with his own hand, and felling to the ground Sir John Cheyney, who endeavoured to oppose his fury. Such men may be carried by ambition to command the execution of those who stand in their way; but are not likely to lend their hand, in cold blood, to a base, and, to themselves, useless assassination. How did it import Richard in what manner the young prince was put to death? If he had so early planned the ambitious designs ascribed to him, he might have trusted to his brother Edward, so much more immediately concerned, that the young prince would not be spared. If those views did not, as is probable, take root in his heart till long afterwards, what interest had Richard to murder an unhappy young prince? This crime therefore was so unnecessary, and is so far from being established by any authority, that he deserves to be entirely acquitted of it.

II. *The murder of Henry the Sixth.*

This charge, no better supported than the preceding, is still more improbable. 'Of the death of this prince, Henry the Sixth,' says Fabyan, 'divers tales were told. But the most common fame went, that he was stuck with a dagger by the handes of the Duke of Gloucester.'

The author of the Continuation of the Chronicle of Croyland says only, that the body of King Henry was found lifeless (*exanime*) in the Tower. '*Parcat Deus*', adds he, '*et spatium pœnitentiæ Ei donet, Quicunque sacrilegas manus in Christum Domini ausus est immittere. Unde et agens tyranni, patiensque gloriosi martyris titulum mereatur.*'* The prayer for the murderer, that he may live to repent, proves that the passage was written immediately after the murder was committed. That the assassin deserved the appellation of tyrant, evinces that the historian's suspicions went high; but as he calls him *Quicunque*, and as we are uncertain whether he wrote before the death of Edward the Fourth or between his death and that of Richard the Third, we cannot ascertain which of the brothers he meant. In strict construction he should mean Edward, because as he is speaking of Henry's death, Richard, then only Duke of Gloucester, could not properly be called a tyrant. But as monks were not good grammatical critics, I shall lay no stress on this objection. I do think he alluded to Richard; having treated him severely in the subsequent part of his history, and having a true monkish partiality to Edward, whose cruelty and vices he slightly

* 'May God spare,' adds he, 'and give time for repentance to whoever dared to lay sacrilegious hands on the Lord's Anointed. Hence is it that he who committed the deed has justly earned the title of tyrant while he who thus suffered has merited that of glorious martyr.'

[163]

noticed, in favour to that monarch's severity to heretics and ecclesiastic expiations. '*Is princeps, licet diebus suis cupiditatibus et luxui nimis intemperanter indulsisse credatur, in fide tamen catholicus summè, hereticorum, severissimus hostis, sapientium et doctorum hominum clericorumque promotor amantissimus, sacramentorum ecclesiæ devotissimus venerator, peccatorumque suorum omnium pænitentissimus fuit.*'* That monster Philip the Second possessed just the same virtues. Still, I say, let the monk suspect whom he would, if Henry was found dead, the monk was not likely to know who murdered him—and if he did, he has not told us.

Hall says, 'Poore King Henry the Sixth, a little before deprived of his realm and imperial crown, was now in the Tower of London spoiled of his life and all worldly felicity by Richard Duke of Gloucester (as the constant fame ran) which, to the intent that King Edward his brother should be clear out of all secret suspicion of sudden invasion, murdered the said king with a dagger.' Whatever Richard was, it seems he was a most excellent and kind-hearted brother, and scrupled not on any occasion to be the Jack Ketch of the times. We shall see him soon (if the evidence were to be believed) perform the same friendly office for Edward on their brother Clarence. And we must admire that he, whose dagger was so fleshed in murder for the service of another, should be so put to it to find the means of making away with his nephews, whose deaths were considerably more essential to him. But can this accusation be allowed gravely? If Richard aspired to the crown, whose whole conduct during Edward's reign was a scene, as we are told, of plausibility and decorum, would he officiously and unnecessarily have taken on himself the odium of slaying a saint-like monarch, adored by the people? Was it his interest to save Edward's

---

* 'This Prince, although he was believed in his day to have indulged his love of money and of women too intemperately, was nevertheless a most devout Catholic, a very severe enemy to heretics, a most loving promoter of wise and learned men and of the clergy, deeply venerating the sacraments of the Church and repenting all his sins.'

character at the expence of his own? Did Henry stand in *his* way, deposed, imprisoned, and now *childless*? The blind and indiscriminate zeal with which every crime committed in that bloody age was placed to Richard's account, makes it greatly probable, that interest of party had more hand than truth in drawing his picture. Other cruelties, which I shall mention, and to which we know his motives, he certainly commanded; nor am I desirous to purge him where I find him guilty: but mob-stories or Lancastrian forgeries ought to be rejected from sober history; nor can they be repeated, without exposing the writer to the imputation of weakness and vulgar credulity.

III. *The murder of his brother Clarence.*

In the examination of this article, I shall set aside our historians (whose gossipping narratives, as we have seen, deserve little regard) because we have better authority to direct our inquiries: and this is, the attainder of the Duke of Clarence, as it is set forth in the Parliamentary History (copied indeed from Habington's Life of Edward the Fourth) and by the editors of that history justly supposed to be taken from Stowe, who had seen the original bill of attainder. The crimes and conspiracy of Clarence are there particularly enumerated, and even his dealing with conjurers and necromancers, a charge however absurd, yet often made use of in that age. Eleanor Cobham, wife of Humphrey Duke of Gloucester, had been condemned on a parallel accusation. In France it was a common charge; and I think, so late as in the reign of Henry the Eighth, Edward Duke of Buckingham was said to have consulted astrologers and such like cattle, on the succession of the crown. Whether Clarence was guilty we cannot easily tell; for in those times neither the public nor the prisoner were often favoured with knowing the evidence on which sentence was passed. Nor was much information of that sort given to or asked by parliament itself, previous to bills of attainder. The Duke of Clarence appears to have been at once a weak, volatile, injudicious, and ambitious man. He had abandoned his brother Edward, had espoused the daughter of Warwick, the great enemy of their house, and had even been declared successor to Henry the Sixth and his son Prince Edward. Conduct so absurd must have left lasting impressions on Edward's mind, not to be effaced by Clarence's subsequent treachery to Henry and Warwick. The Chronicle of Croyland mentions the ill-humour and discontents of Clarence; and all our authors agree, that he kept no terms with the queen and her relations. Habington adds, that these discontents were secretly fomented by the Duke of Gloucester. Perhaps they were: Gloucester certainly kept fair with the queen, and profited largely by the forfeiture of his brother. But where jealousies are secretly fomented in a court, they seldom come to the knowledge of an historian; and though he may have guessed right from collateral circumstances, these insinuations are mere *gratis dicta* [gratuitous assertions], and can only be treated as surmises.* Hall, Holinshed, and Stowe say not a word of Richard being the person who put the sentence in execution; but, on the contrary, they all say he openly resisted the murder of Clarence: all too record another circumstance, which is perfectly ridiculous, that Clarence was drowned in a barrel or butt of malmsey. Whoever can believe that a butt of wine was the engine of his death, may believe that Richard helped him into it, and kept him down till he was suffocated. But the strong evidence on which Richard must be acquitted, and indeed even of having contributed to his death, was the testimony of Edward himself. Being some time afterward

* The chronicle above quoted asserts, that the Speaker of the House of Commons demanded the execution of Clarence. Is it credible that, on a proceeding so public and so solemn for that age, the brother of the offended monarch and of the royal criminal should have been deputed, or would have stooped to so vile an office? On such occasions do arbitrary princes want tools? Was Edward's court so virtuous or so humane, that it could furnish no assassin but the first prince of the blood? When the House of Commons undertook to colour the king's resentment, was every member of it too scrupulous to lend his hand to the deed? (W)

sollicited to pardon a notorious criminal, the king's conscience broke forth; 'Unhappy brother!' cried he, 'for whom no man would interceed—yet you all can be intercessors for a villain!' If Richard had been instigator or executioner, it is not likely that the king would have assumed the whole merciless criminality to himself, without bestowing a due share on his brother Gloucester. Is it possible to renew the charge, and not recollect this acquittal!

The three preceding accusations are evidently uncertain and improbable. What follows is more obscure; and it is on the ensuing transactions that I venture to pronounce, that we have little or no authority on which to form positive conclusions. I speak more particularly of the deaths of Edward the Fifth and his brother. It will, I think, appear very problematic whether they were murdered or not: and even if they were murdered, it is impossible to believe the account as fabricated and divulged by Henry the Seventh, on whose testimony the murder must rest at last; for they, who speak most positively, revert to the story which he was pleased to publish eleven years after their supposed deaths, and which is so absurd, so incoherent, and so repugnant to dates and other facts, that as it is no longer necessary to pay court to his majesty, it is no longer necessary not to treat his assertions as an impudent fiction. I come directly to this point, because the intervening articles of the executions of Rivers, Gray, Vaughan, and Hastings will naturally find their place in that disquisition.

And here it will be important to examine those historians on whose relation the story first depends. Previous to this I must ascertain one or two dates, for they are stubborn evidence and cannot be rejected: they exist every where, and cannot be proscribed even from a Court Calendar.

Edward the Fourth died April 9th 1483.

Edward, his eldest son, was then thirteen years of age.

Richard, Duke of York, his second son, was about nine.

We have but two contemporary historians, the author of the

Chronicle of Croyland, and John Fabyan. The first, who wrote in his convent, and only mentioned incidentally affairs of state, is very barren and concise: he appears indeed not to have been ill informed, and sometimes even in a situation of personally knowing the transactions of the times; for in one place we are told in a marginal note, that the doctor of the canon law, and one of the king's councellors, who was sent to Calais, was the author of the Continuation. Whenever therefore his assertions are positive, and not merely flying reports, he ought to be admitted as fair evidence, since we have no better. And yet a monk who busies himself in recording the insignificant events of his own order or monastery, and who was at most occasionally made use of, was not likely to know the most important and most mysterious secrets of state; I mean, as he was not employed in those iniquitous transactions—if he had been, we should learn or might expect still less truth from him.

John Fabyan was a merchant, and had been sheriff of London, and died in 1512: he consequently lived on the spot at that very interesting period. Yet no sheriff was ever less qualified to write a history of England. His narrative is dry, uncircumstantial, and unimportant: he mentions the deaths of princes and revolutions of government, with the same phlegm and brevity as he would speak of the appointment of churchwardens. I say not this from any partiality, or to decry the simple man as crossing my opinion; for Fabyan's testimony is far from bearing hard against Richard, even though he wrote under Henry the Seventh, who would have suffered no apology for his rival, and whose reign was employed not only in extirpating the house of York, but in forging the most atrocious calumnies to blacken their memories, and invalidate their just claim.

But the great source from whence all later historians have taken their materials for the reign of Richard the Third, is Sir Thomas More. Grafton, the next in order, has copied him verbatim: so does Holinshed—and we are told by the former in a marginal note, that Sir Thomas was under-sheriff of London when he composed his work. It is in truth a composition, and a very beautiful one. He was then in the vigour of his fancy, and fresh from the study of the Greek and Roman historians, whose manner he has imitated in divers imaginary orations. They serve to lengthen an unknown history of little more than two months into a pretty sizeable volume; but are no more to be received as genuine, than the facts they are adduced to countenance. An under-sheriff of London, aged but twenty-eight, and recently marked with the displeasure of the crown, was not likely to be furnished with materials from any high authority, and could not receive them from the best authority, I mean the adverse party, who were proscribed, and all their chiefs banished or put to death. Let us again recur to dates. Sir Thomas More was born in 1480; he was appointed under-sheriff in 1508, and three years before had offended Henry the Seventh in the tender point of opposing a subsidy. Buc, the apologist of Richard the Third, ascribes the authorities of Sir Thomas to the information of Archbishop Morton; and it is true that he had been brought up under that prelate; but Morton died 1500, when Sir Thomas was but twenty years old, and when he had scarce thought of writing history. What materials he had gathered from his master were probably nothing more than a general narrative of the preceeding times in discourse at dinner or in a winter's evening, if so raw a youth can be supposed to have been admitted to familiarity with a prelate of that rank, and prime minister. But granting that such pregnant parts as More's had leaped the barrier of dignity, and insinuated himself into the arch-bishop's favour; could he have drawn from a more corrupted source? Morton had not only violated his allegiance to Richard; but had been the chief engine to dethrone him, and to plant a bastard scyon in the throne. Of all men living there could not be more suspicious testimony than the prelate's, except the king's: and had the archbishop selected More for the historian of those dark scenes, who had so much interest to blacken Richard, as the

[169]

man who had risen to be prime minister to his rival? Take it therefore either way; that the archbishop did or did not pitch on a young man of twenty to write that history, his authority was as suspicious as could be.

It may be said, on the other hand, that Sir Thomas, who had smarted for his boldness (for his father, a judge of the king's bench, had been imprisoned and fined for his son's offence) had had little inducement to flatter the Lancastrian cause. It is very true; nor am I inclined to impute adulation to one of the honestest statesmen and brightest names in our annals. He who scorned to save his life by bending to the will of the son, was not likely to canvass the favour of the father, by prostituting his pen to the humour of the court. I take the truth to be, that Sir Thomas wrote his reign of Edward the Fifth as he wrote his *Utopia*; to amuse his leisure and exercise his fancy. He took up a paltry canvass and embroidered it with a flowing design as his imagination suggested the colours. I should deal more severely with his respected memory on any other hypothesis. He has been guilty of such palpable and material falshoods, as, while they destroy his credit as an historian, would reproach his veracity as a man, if we could impute them to premeditated perversion of truth, and not to youthful levity and inaccuracy. Standing as they do, the sole ground-work of that reign's history, I am authorized to pronounce the work, invention and romance.

Polydore Vergil, a foreigner, and author of a light Latin history, was here during the reigns of Henry the Seventh and Eighth. I may quote him now-and-then, and the Chronicle of Croyland; but neither furnish us with much light.

There was another foreign writer in that age of far greater authority, whose negligent simplicity and veracity are unquestionable; who had great opportunities of knowing our story, and whose testimony is corroborated by our records: I mean Philippe de Commynes. He and Buc agree with one another, and with the rolls of parliament; Sir Thomas More with none of them.

Buc, so long exploded as a lover of paradoxes, and as an advocate for a monster, gains new credit the deeper this dark scene is fathomed. Undoubtedly Buc has gone too far; nor are his style or method to be admired. With every intention of vindicating Richard, he does but authenticate his crimes, by searching in other story for parallel instances of what he calls policy. No doubt politicians will acquit Richard, if confession of his crimes be pleaded in defence of them. Policy will justify his taking off opponents. Policy will maintain him in removing those who would have barred his obtaining the crown, whether he thought he had a right to it, or was determined to obtain it. Morality, especially in the latter case, cannot take his part. I shall speak more to this immediately. Rapin conceived doubts; but instead of pursuing them, wandered after judgments; and they will lead a man where-ever he has a mind to be led. Carte, with more manly shrewdness, has sifted many parts of Richard's story, and guessed happily. My part has less penetration; but the parliamentary history, the comparison of dates, and the authentic monument lately come to light, and from which I shall give extracts, have convinced me, that, if Buc is too favourable, all our other historians are blind guides, and have not made out a twentieth part of their assertions.

The story of Edward the Fifth is thus related by Sir Thomas More, and copied from him by all our historians.

When the king his father died, the prince kept his court at Ludlow, under the tuition of his maternal uncle Anthony Earl Rivers. Richard Duke of Gloucester was in the north, returning from his successful expedition against the Scots. The queen wrote instantly to her brother to bring up the young king to London, with a train of two thousand horse: a fact allowed by historians, and which, whether a prudent caution or not, was the first overt-act of the new reign; and likely to strike, as it did strike, the Duke of Gloucester and the ancient nobility with a jealousy, that the queen intended to exclude them from the administration, and to govern in concert with her own family. It is not improper to observe that no precedent authorized her to assume such power. Joan, Princess dowager of Wales, and widow of the Black Prince, had no share in the government during the minority of her son Richard the Second. Catherine of Valois, widow of Henry the Fifth, was alike excluded from the regency, though her son was but a year old. And if Isabella governed on the deposition of Edward the Second, it was by an usurped power, by the same power that had contributed to dethrone her husband; a power sanctified by no title, and confirmed by no act of parliament. The first step to a female regency enacted, though it never took place, was many years afterwards, in the reign of Henry the Eighth.

Edward, on his death-bed, had patched up a reconciliation between his wife's kindred and the great lords of the court; particularly between the Marquess Dorset, the queen's son, and the lord chamberlain Hastings. Yet whether the disgusted lords had only seemed to yield, to satisfy the dying king, or whether the steps taken by the queen gave them new cause of umbrage, it appears that the Duke of Buckingham was the first to communicate his suspicions to Gloucester, and to dedicate himself to his service. Lord Hastings was scarce less forward to join in like measures: and all three, it is pretended, were so alert, that they contrived to have it insinuated to the queen, that it would give much offence if the young king should be brought to London with so great a force as she had ordered; on which suggestions she wrote to Lord Rivers to countermand her first directions.

It is difficult not to suspect, that our historians have imagined more plotting in this transaction than could easily be compassed in so short a period, and in an age when no communication could be carried on but by special messengers, in bad roads, and with no relays of post-horses.

Edward the Fourth died April 9th, and his son made his entrance into London May 4th. It is not probable, that the queen communicated her directions for bringing up her son with an armed force to the lords of the council, and her newly reconciled enemies. But she might be betrayed. Still it required some time for Buckingham to send his servant Percival (though Sir Thomas More vaunts his expedition) to York, where the Duke of Gloucester then lay;* for Percival's return (it must be observed too that the Duke of Buckingham was in Wales, consequently did not learn the queen's orders on the spot, but either received the account from London, or learnt it from Ludlow); for the two dukes to send instructions to their confederates in London; for the impression to be made on the queen, and for her dispatching her counter-orders; for Percival to post back and meet Gloucester at Nottingham, and for returning thence and bringing his master Buckingham to meet Richard at Northampton, at the very time of the king's arrival there. All this might happen, undoubtedly; and yet who will believe, that such mysterious and rapid negotiations came to the knowledge of Sir Thomas More twenty-five years afterwards, when, as it will appear, he knew nothing of very material and public facts that happened at the same period?

But whether the circumstances are true, or whether artfully imagined, it is certain that the king, with a small force, arrived at Northampton, and thence proceeded to Stony Stratford. Earl Rivers remained at Northampton, where he was cajoled by the two dukes till the time of rest, when the gates of the inn were suddenly locked, and the earl made prisoner. Early in the morning the two dukes hastened to Stony Stratford, where, in the king's presence, they picked a quarrel with his other half-brother, the

* It should be remarked too, that the Duke of Gloucester is positively said to be celebrating his brother's obsequies there. It not only strikes off part of the term by allowing the necessary time for the news of King Edward's death to reach York, and for the preparations to be made there to solemnize a funeral for him; but this very circumstance takes off from the probability of Richard having as yet laid any plan for dispossessing his nephew. Would he have loitered at York at such a crisis, if he had intended to step into the throne? (W)

Lord Richard Grey, accusing him, the Marquess Dorset, and their uncle Rivers, of ambitious and hostile designs, to which ends the marquess had entered the Tower, taken treasure thence, and sent a force to sea.

'*All which things*,' says Sir Thomas, '*the dukes knew were done for good and necessary purposes by the whole Council at London—saving that something they must say.*' As Sir Thomas has not been pleased to specify those purposes, and as in those times at least privy coun- cellors were exceedingly complaisant to the ruling powers, he must allow us to doubt whether the purposes of the queen's rela- tions were quite so innocent as he would make us believe; and whether the princes of the blood and the ancient nobility had not some reason to be jealous that the queen was usurping more power than the laws had given her. The catastrophe of her whole family so truly deserves commiseration, that we are apt to shut our eyes to all her weakness and ill-judged policy; and yet at every step we find how much she contributed to draw ruin on their heads and her own, by the confession even of her apologists. The Duke of Gloucester was the first prince of the blood, the constitution pointed him out as regent; no will, no disposition of the late king was even alledged to bar his pretensions; he had served the state with bravery, success, and fidelity; and the queen herself, who had been insulted by Clarence, had had no cause to complain of Gloucester. Yet all her conduct intimated designs of governing by force in the name of her son. If these facts are impartially stated, and grounded on the confession of those who enveigh most bitterly against Richard's memory, let us allow that at least *thus far* he acted as most princes would have done in his situation, in a lawless and barbarous age; and rather instigated by others, than from any before-conceived ambition and system. If the journeys of Percival are true, Buckingham was the devil that tempted Richard; and if Richard still wanted instigation, then it must follow, that he had not murdered Henry the Sixth, his son, and Clarence, to pave his own way to the crown. If this fine story of

Buckingham and Percival is not true, what becomes of Sir Thomas More's credit, on which the whole fabric leans?

Lord Richard, Sir Thomas Vaughan, and Sir Richard Hawte, were arrested, and with Lord Rivers sent prisoners to Pomfret, while the dukes conducted the king by easy stages to London.

The queen, hearing what had happened, took sanctuary at Westminster, with her other son the Duke of York, and the princesses her daughters. Rotheram, Archbishop of York and Lord Chancellor, repaired to her with the great seal, and endeavoured to comfort her dismay with a friendly message he had received from Hastings, who was with the confederate lords on the road. 'A woe worth him!' quoth the queen, 'for *it is he* that goeth about to destroy me and my blood!' Not a word is said of her suspecting the Duke of Gloucester. The archbishop seems to have been the first who entertained any suspicion; and yet, if all that our historian says of him is true, Rotheram was far from being a shrewd man: witness the indiscreet answer which he is said to have made on this occasion. 'Madam,' quoth he, 'be of good cheer. For I assure you if they crown any other king than your son, whom they now have with them, we shall on the morrow crown his brother, whom you have here with you.' Did the silly prelate think that it would be much consolation to a mother, whose eldest son might be murdered, that her younger son would be crowned in prison! or was she to be satisfied with seeing one son entitled to the crown, and the other enjoying it nominally?

He then delivered the seal to the queen, and as lightly sent for it back immediately after.

The dukes continued their march, declaring they were bringing the king to his coronation. Hastings, who seems to have preceded them, endeavoured to pacify the apprehensions which had been raised in the people, acquainting them that the arrested lords had been imprisoned for plotting against the Dukes of Gloucester and Buckingham. As both those princes were of the blood royal, this accusation was not ill founded, it having evidently been the intention, as I have shown, to bar them from any share in the administration, to which, by the custom of the realm, they were entitled. So much depends on this foundation, that I shall be excused from enforcing it. The queen's party were the aggressors; and though that alone would not justify all the following excesses, yet we must not judge of those times by the present. Neither the crown nor the great men were restrained by sober established forms and proceedings as they are at present; and from the death of Edward the Third, force alone had dictated. Henry the Fourth had stepped into the throne contrary to all justice. A title so defective had opened a door to attempts as violent; and the various innovations introduced in the latter years of Henry the Sixth had annihilated all ideas of order. Richard, Duke of York, had been declared successor to the crown during the life of Henry and of his son Prince Edward, and, as appears by the Parliamentary History, though not noticed by our careless historians, was even appointed Prince of Wales. The Duke of Clarence had received much such another declaration in his favour during the short restoration of Henry. What temptations were these precedents to an affronted prince! We shall see soon what encouragement they gave him to examine closely into his nephew's pretensions; and how imprudent it was in the queen to provoke Gloucester, when her very existence as queen was liable to strong objections. Nor ought the subsequent executions of Lord Rivers, Lord Richard Grey, and of Lord Hastings himself, to be considered in so very strong a light, as they would appear in, if acted in modern times. During the wars of York and Lancaster, no forms of trial had been observed. Not only peers taken in battle had been put to death without process; but whoever, though not in arms, was made prisoner by the victorious party, underwent the same fate; as was the case of Tiptoft, Earl of Worcester, who had fled and was taken in disguise. Trials had never been used with any degree of strictness, as at present; and though Richard was pursued and killed as an usurper, the Solomon that succeeded him was not a jot less a tyrant. Henry the Eighth was still less of a temper to give greater latitude to the laws. In fact, little ceremony or judicial proceeding was observed on trials, till the reign of Elizabeth, who, though decried of late for her despotism, in order to give some shadow of countenance to the tyranny of the Stuarts, was the first of our princes, under whom any gravity or equity was allowed in cases of treason. To judge impartially therefore, we ought to recall the temper and manners of the times we read of. It is shocking to eat our enemies; but it is not so shocking in an Iroquois, as it would be in the King of Prussia. And this is all I contend for, that the crimes of Richard, which he really committed, at least which we have reason to believe he committed, were more the crimes of the age than of the man; and except these executions of Rivers, Grey, and Hastings, I defy any body to prove one other of those charged to his account, from any good authority.

It is alledged that the partizans of Gloucester strictly guarded the sanctuary, to prevent farther resort thither; but Sir Thomas confesses too, that some *lords, knights, and gentlemen, either for favour of the Queen or for fear of themselves, assembled in sundry companies and went armoured in flocks.* Let us strip this paragraph of its historic buskins, and it is plain that *the queen's party took up arms.* This is no indifferent circumstance. She had plotted to keep possession of the king, and to govern in his name by force, but had been outwitted, and her family had been imprisoned for the attempt. Conscious that she was discovered, perhaps reasonably alarmed at Gloucester's designs, she had secured herself and her younger children in sanctuary. Necessity rather than law justified her proceedings—but what excuse can be made for her faction having recourse to arms? Who was authorized, by the tenour of former reigns, to guard the king's person, till parliament should declare a regency, but his uncle and the princes of the blood? Endeavouring to establish the queen's authority by force was rebellion against the laws. I state this minutely, because the fact has never been attended to; and later historians pass it over, as if Richard had hurried on the deposition of his nephews without any colour of decency, and without the least provocation to any of his proceedings. Hastings is even said to have warned the citizens that matters were likely *to come to a field* (to a battle) from the opposition of the adverse party, though as yet no symptom had appeared of designs against the king, whom the two dukes were bringing to his coronation. Nay, it is not probable that Gloucester had as yet meditated more than securing the regency; for had he had designs on the crown, would he have weakened his own claim by assuming the protectorate, which he could not accept but by acknowledging the title of his nephew? This in truth seems to me to have been the case. The ambition of the queen and her family alarmed the princes and the nobility: Gloucester, Buckingham, Hastings, and many more had checked those attempts. The next step was to secure the regency: but none of these acts could be done without grievous provocation to the queen. As soon as her son should come of age, she might regain her power and the means of revenge. Self-security prompted the princes and lords to guard against this reverse, and what was equally dangerous to the queen, the depression of her fortune called forth and revived all the hatred of her enemies. Her marriage had given universal offence to the nobility, and been the source of all the late disturbances and bloodshed. The great Earl of Warwick, provoked at the contempt shown to him by King Edward while negotiating a match for him in France, had abandoned him for Henry the Sixth, whom he had again set on the throne. These calamities were still fresh in every mind, and no doubt contributed to raise Gloucester to the throne, which he could not have attained without almost general concurrence: yet if we are to believe historians, he, Buckingham, the Mayor of London, and one Dr Shaa, operated this revolution by a sermon and a speech to the people, though the people would not even give a huzza to the proposal. The change of government in the *Rehearsal* is not effected more easily by the physician and gentleman usher,

Do you take this, and I'll seize t'other chair.*

In what manner Richard assumed or was invested with the protectorate does not appear. Sir Thomas More, speaking of him by that title, says, 'the Protector which always you must take for the Duke of Gloucester.' Fabyan, after mentioning the solemn arrival of the king in London, adds, 'Then provision was made for the king's coronation; in which pastime [interval] the duke being admitted for lord protector.' As the parliament was not sitting, this dignity was no doubt conferred on him by the assent of the lords and privy council; and as we hear of no opposition, none was probably made. He was the only person to whom that rank was due; his right could not and does not seem to have been questioned. The Chronicle of Croyland corroborates my opinion, saying, '*Accepitque dictus Ricardus dux Glocestriæ illum solennem magistratum, qui duci Humfrido Glocestriæ, stante minore ætate regis Henrici, ut regni protector appellaretur, olim contingebat. Eâ igitur auctoritate usus est, de consensu & beneplacito omnium dominorum.*'†

Thus far therefore it must be allowed that Richard acted no illegal part, nor discovered more ambition than became him. He had defeated the queen's innovations, and secured her accomplices. To draw off our attention from such regular steps, Sir Thomas More has exhausted all his eloquence and imagination to work up a piteous scene, in which the queen is made to excite our compassion in the highest degree, and is furnished by that able pen

* *The Rehearsal*, by George Villiers, second Duke of Buckingham (and others), 1671. In Act II, scene 4, the Usher says:
　　'And, since occasion now seems debonair,
　　I'll seize on this, and you shall take that chair.'
As in a later citation from Tacitus (see p. 182) Walpole here is apparently relying on his memory.
† 'And Richard, Duke of Gloucester, received that high office, called the protectorship of the realm, which Duke Humphrey of Gloucester formerly occupied during the minority of King Henry VI. He was accordingly invested with this authority by the will and consent of all the lords.'

with strains of pathetic oratory, which no part of her conduct affords us reason to believe she possessed. This scene is occasioned by the demand of delivering up her second son. Cardinal Bourchier, Archbishop of Canterbury, is the instrument employed by the protector to effect this purpose. The fact is confirmed by Fabyan in his rude and brief manner, and by the Chronicle of Croyland, and therefore cannot be disputed. But though the latter author affirms, that force was used to oblige the cardinal to take that step, he by no means agrees with Sir Thomas More in the repugnance of the queen to comply, nor in that idle discussion on the privileges of sanctuaries, on which Sir Thomas has wasted so many words. On the contrary, the chronicle declares, that the queen *'Verbis gratanter annuens, dimisit puerum.'** The king, who had been lodged in the palace of the Bishop of London, was now removed with his brother to the Tower.

This last circumstance has not a little contributed to raise horror in vulgar minds, who of late years have been accustomed to see no persons of rank lodged in the Tower but state criminals. But in that age the case was widely different. It not only appears by a map engraven so late as the reign of Queen Elizabeth, that the Tower was a royal palace, in which were ranges of buildings called the king's and queen's apartments, now demolished: but it is a known fact, that they did often lodge there, especially previous to their coronations. The queen of Henry the Seventh lay in there: Queen Elizabeth went thither after her triumphant entry into the city; and many other instances might be produced, but for brevity I omit them, to come to one of the principal transactions of this dark period: I mean Richard's assumption of the crown. Sir Thomas More's account of this extraordinary event is totally improbable, and positively false in the ground-work of that revolution. He tell us, that Richard meditating usurpation, divided the lords into two separate councils, assembling the king's or queen's party at Baynard's castle, but holding his own private junto at

* 'Graciously consenting, in words, she yielded up the boy.'

[180]

Crosby Place. From the latter he began with spreading murmurs, whispers, and reports against the legality of the late king's marriage. Thus far we may credit him—but what man of common sense can believe, that Richard went so far as publicly to asperse the honour of his own mother? That mother, Cecily Duchess dowager of York, a princess of a spotless character, was then living: so were two of her daughters, the Duchesses of Suffolk, and Burgundy, Richard's own sisters: one of them, the Duchess of Suffolk walked at his ensuing coronation, and her son the Earl of Lincoln was by Richard himself, after the death of his own son, declared heir apparent to the crown. Is it, can it be credible, that Richard actuated a venal* preacher to declare to the people from the pulpit at Paul's cross, that his mother had been an adulteress, and that her two eldest sons, Edward the Fourth and the Duke of Clarence, were spurious; and that the good lady had not given a legitimate child to her husband, but the protector, and I suppose the Duchess of Suffolk, though no mention is said to be made of her in the sermon? For as the Duchess of Suffolk was older than Richard, and consequently would have been involved in the charge of bastardy, could he have declared her son his heir, he who set aside his brother Edward's children for their illegitimacy? Ladies of the least disputable gallantry generally suffer their husbands to beget his heir; and if doubts arise on the legitimacy of their issue, the younger branches seem most liable to suspicion—but a tale so gross could not have passed even on the mob—no proof, no presumption of the fact was pretended. Were the duchess† and her

* What should we think of a modern historian, who should sink all mention of the convention parliament, and only tell us that one Dr Burnet got up into the pulpit, and assured the people that Henrietta Maria (a little more suspected of gallantry than Duchess Cecily) produced Charles the Second and James the Second in adultery, and gave no legitimate issue to Charles the First, but Mary Princess of Orange, mother of King William; that the people laughed at him, and *so* the Prince of Orange became king? (W)

† It appears from Rymer's *Foedera* [Thomas Rymer (1641–1713) issued his monumental collection of English treaties and state papers, *Foedera, etc.*, in

daughters silent on so scandalous an insinuation? Agrippina would scarce have heard it with patience. Moriar, modo imperet!* said that empress, in her wild wish of crowning her son: but had he, unprovoked, aspersed her honour in the open forum, would the mother have submitted to so unnatural an insult? In Richard's case the imputation was beyond measure atrocious and absurd. What! taint the fame of his mother to pave his way to the crown! Who had heard of her guilt? And if guilty, how came she to stop the career of her intrigues? But Richard had better pretentions, and had no occasion to start doubts even on his own legitimacy, which was too much connected with that of his brothers to be tossed and

---

fifteen volumes from 1704 to 1713], that the very first act of Richard's reign is dated from quâdam alterâ camerâ juxta capellam in hospitio dominæ Ceciliæ ducissæ Eborum [a certain lower chamber by the chapel in the dwelling of Lady Cecily, Duchess of York]. It does not look much as if he had publicly accused his mother of adultery, when he held his first council at her house. Among the Harleian MSS. in the Museum, No. 2236. art. 6. is the following letter from Richard to this very princess his mother, which is an additional proof of the good terms on which they lived: 'Madam, I recommend me to you as heartily as is to me possible, beseeching you in my most humble and earnest wise of your daily blessing to my singular comfort and defence in my need; and, madam, I heartily beseech you, that I may often hear from you to my comfort; and such news as be here, my servant Thomas Bryan this bearer shall show you, to whom please it you to give credence unto. And, madam, I beseech you to be good and gracious lady to my lord my chamberlain to be your officer in Wiltshire in such as Colinbourne had: I trust he shall therein do you good service; and that it please you, that by this bearer I may understand your pleasure in this behalf. And I pray God send you the accomplishment of your noble desires. Written at Pontefract, the third day of June, with the hand of your most humble son,

Ricardus Rex.' (W)

* In Tacitus, *Annals* XIV, Chap. ix, when astrologers told Agrippina that her son Nero would one day reign, and slay his mother, she replied: 'Let him slay, provided that he reign' (*'Occidat, inquit, dum imperet'*). Again Walpole is relying on his memory (see p. 179).

bandied about before the multitude. Clarence had been solemnly attainted by act of parliament, and his children were out of the question. The doubts on the validity of Edward's marriage were better grounds for Richard's proceedings than aspersion of his mother's honour. On that invalidity he claimed the crown, and obtained it; and with such universal concurrence, that the nation undoubtedly was on his side—but as he could not deprive his nephews, on that foundation, without bastardizing their sisters too, no wonder the historians, who wrote under the Lancastrian domination, have used all their art and industry to misrepresent the fact. If the marriage of Edward the Fourth with the widow Grey was bigamy, and consequently null, what became of the title of Elizabeth of York, wife of Henry the Seventh? What became of it? Why a bastard branch of Lancaster, matched with a bastard of York, were obtruded on the nation as the right heirs of the crown; and, as far as two negatives can make an affirmative, they were so.

Buc, whose integrity will more and more appear, affirms that, before Edward had espoused the lady Grey, he had been contracted to the lady Eleanor Butler, and married to her by the Bishop of Bath. Sir Thomas More, on the contrary (and here it is that I am unwillingly obliged to charge that great man with wilful falsehood) pretends that the Duchess of York, his mother, endeavouring to dissuade him from so disproportionate an alliance, urged him with a pre-contract to one Elizabeth Lucy, who however, being pressed, confessed herself his concubine; but denied any marriage. Dr Shaa too, the preacher, we are told by the same authority, pleaded from the pulpit the king's former marriage with Elizabeth Lucy; and the Duke of Buckingham is said to have harangued the people to the same effect. But now let us see how the case really stood; Elizabeth Lucy was the daughter of one Wyat of Southampton, a mean gentleman, says Buc, and the wife of one Lucy, as mean a man as Wyat. The mistress of Edward she notoriously was; but what if, in Richard's pursuit of the crown, no question at all was made of this Elizabeth Lucy? We have the best and most undoubted authorities to assure us, that Edward's pre-contract or marriage, urged to invalidate his match with the lady Grey, was with the lady Eleanor Talbot, widow of the Lord Butler of Sudeley, and sister of the Earl of Shrewsbury, one of the greatest peers in the kingdom; her mother was the lady Katherine Stafford, daughter of Humphrey, Duke of Buckingham, prince of the blood: an alliance in that age never reckoned unsuitable. Hear the evidence. Honest Philippe de Commynes says that the Bishop of Bath informed Richard, that he had married King Edward to an English lady; 'et dit cet évêque qu'il les avait épousés, et que n'y avait que lui et ceux deux.'* This is not positive, and yet the description marks out the lady Butler, and not Elizabeth Lucy. But the Chronicle of Croyland is more express. '*Color autem introitus et captæ possessionis hujusmodi is erat. Ostendebatur per modum supplicationis in quodam rotulo pergameni, quod filii regis Edwardi erant bastardi, supponendo illum precontraxisse cum quadam domina Alienora Boteler, antequam reginam Elizabeth duxisset uxorem; atque insuper, quod sanguis alterius fratris sui, Georgii ducis Clarenciæ, suisset attinctus; ita quod hodie nullus certus et incorruptus sanguis linealis ex parte Richardi ducis Eboraci poterat inveniri, nisi in persona dicti Richardi ducis Glocestriæ. Quo circa supplicabatur ei in fine ejusdem rotuli, ex parte dominorum et communitatis regni, ut jus suum in se assumerat.*'† Is this full? Is this evidence? Here we see the origin of the tale relating to

* 'And this bishop declared that he had married them, with only himself and the two of them present'.

† 'The pretext for this act of usurpation was as follows: it was declared by means of a petition, set forth in a certain roll of parchment, that the sons of King Edward were bastards since the king had contracted a marriage with one Eleanor Butler before his marriage to Queen Elizabeth, and that the blood of Richard's own brother, George, Duke of Clarence, had been attainted; so that at the present time no assured and uncorrupted blood of Richard, Duke of York, could be found except in the person of Richard, Duke of Gloucester. Therefore he was entreated by the lords and commons of the realm to assume his lawful right.'

the Duchess of York; *nullus certus et incorruptus sanguis*: from these mistaken or perverted words flowed the report of Richard's aspersing his mother's honour. But as if truth was doomed to emerge, though stifled for near three hundred years, the roll of parliament is at length come to light (with other wonderful discoveries) and sets forth, 'that though *the three estates* which petitioned Richard to assume the crown were not assembled in form of parliament;' yet it rehearses the supplication (recorded by the chronicle above) and declares, 'that King Edward was and stood married and troth plight to one dame Eleanor Butler, daughter to the Earl of Shrewsbury, with whom the said King Edward had made a pre-contract of matrimony, long before he made his pretended marriage with Elizabeth Grey.' Could Sir Thomas More be ignorant of this fact? Or, if ignorant, where is his competence as an historian? And how egregiously absurd is his romance of Richard's assuming the crown in consequence of Dr Shaa's sermon and Buckingham's harangue, to neither of which he pretends the people assented! Dr Shaa no doubt tapped the matter to the people; for Fabyan asserts that he durst never show his face afterwards; and as Henry the Seventh succeeded so soon, and as the slanders against Richard increased, that might happen; but it is evident that the nobility were disposed to call the validity of the queen's marriage in question, and that Richard was solemnly invited by the three estates to accept the regal dignity; and that is farther confirmed by the Chronicle of Croyland, which says, that Richard, having brought together a great force from the north, from Wales, and other parts, did on the twenty-sixth of June claim the crown, '*seque eodem die apud magnam aulam Westmonasterij in cathedram marmoream ibi intrusit;*'* but the supplication afore-mentioned had first been presented to him. This will no doubt be called violence and a force laid on the three estates; and yet that appears by no means to have been the case; for Sir Thomas More, partial as he was

* 'And on that same day in the great hall of Westminster he intruded himself into the marble chair there'.

against Richard, says, 'that to be sure of all enemies he sent for five thousand men out of the north against his coronation, which came up evil apparelled and worse harnessed, in rusty harness, neither defensible nor scoured to the sale, which mustered in Finsbury field, to the great disdain of all lookers on.'* These rusty companions, despised by the citizens, were not likely to intimidate a warlike nobility; and had force been used to extort their assent, Sir Thomas would have been the first to have told us so. But he suppressed an election that appears to have been voluntary, and invented a scene, in which, by his own account, Richard met with nothing but backwardness and silence, that amounted to a refusal. The probability therefore remains, that the nobility met Richard's claim at least half-way, from their hatred and jealousy of the queen's family, and many of them from the conviction of Edward's pre-contract. Many might concur from provocation at the attempts that had been made to disturb the due course of law, and some from apprehension of a minority. This last will appear highly probable from three striking circumstances that I shall mention hereafter. The great regularity with which the coronation was prepared and conducted, and the extraordinary concourse of the nobility at it, have not at all the air of an unwelcome revolution, accomplished merely by violence. On the contrary, it bore great resemblance to a much later event, which, being the last of the kind, we term *The Revolution*. The three estates of nobility, clergy, and people, which called Richard to the Crown, and whose act was confirmed by the subsequent parliament, trod the same steps as the convention did which elected the Prince of Orange: both setting aside an illegal pretender, the legitimacy of whose birth was called in question. And though the partizans of the Stuarts may exult at my comparing King William to Richard the Third, it will be no matter of triumph, since it appears that

* Not in the Rastell edition. This passage forms part of the six-page account of Richard III's coronation inserted in More's *History* as printed in the Hardyng and Hall chronicles.

Richard's cause was as good as King William's, and that in both instances it was a free election. The art used by Sir Thomas More (when he could not deny a pre-contract) in endeavouring to shift that objection on Elizabeth Lucy, a married woman, contrary to the specific words of the act of parliament, betrays the badness of the Lancastrian cause, which would make us doubt or wonder at the consent of the nobility in giving way to the act for bastardizing the children of Edward the Fourth. But reinstate the claim of the lady Butler, which probably was well known, and conceive the interest that her great relations must have made to set aside the queen's marriage, nothing appears more natural than Richard's succession. His usurpation vanishes, and in a few pages more, I shall show that his consequential cruelty vanishes too, or at most is very problematic: but first I must revert to some intervening circumstances.

In this whole story nothing is less known to us than the grounds on which Lord Hastings was put to death. He had lived in open enmity with the queen and her family, and had been but newly reconciled to her son the Marquess Dorset; yet Sir Thomas owns that Lord Hastings was one of the first to abet Richard's proceedings against her, and concurred in all the protector's measures. We are amazed therefore to find this lord the first sacrifice under the new government. Sir Thomas More supposes (and he could only suppose; for whatever Archbishop Morton might tell him of the plots of Henry of Richmond, Morton was certainly not entrusted with the secrets of Richard), Sir Thomas, I say, supposes, that Hastings either withstood the deposition of Edward the Fifth, or was accused of such a design by Catesby, who was deeply in his confidence; and he owns that the protector *undoubtedly loved him well, and loth he was to have him lost*. What then is the presumption? Is it not, that Hastings really was plotting to defeat the new settlement contrary to the intention of the three estates? And who can tell whether the suddenness of the execution was not the effect of necessity? The gates of the Tower were shut during that rapid scene; the protector and his adherents appeared in the first rusty armour that was at hand; but this circumstance is alledged against them, as an incident contrived to gain belief, as if they had been in danger of their lives. The argument is gratis dictum; and as Richard loved Hastings and had used his ministry, the probability lies on the other side: and it is more reasonable to believe that Richard acted in self-defence, than that he exercised a wanton, unnecessary, and disgusting cruelty. The collateral circumstances introduced by More do but weaken* his account, and take from its probability. I do not mean the silly recapitulation of silly omens which forewarned Hastings of his fate, and as omens generally do, to no manner of purpose; but I speak of the idle accusations put into the mouth of Richard, such as his baring his withered arm, and imputing it to sorcery, and to his blending the queen and Jane Shore in the same plot. Cruel or not, Richard was no fool; and therefore it is highly improbable that he should lay the withering of his arm on recent witchcraft, if it was true, as Sir Thomas More pretends, that it never had been otherwise— but of the blemishes and deformity of his person, I shall have occasion to speak hereafter. For the other accusation of a league between Elizabeth and Jane Shore, Sir Thomas More ridicules it himself, and treats it as highly unlikely. But being unlikely, was it not more natural for him to think, that it never was urged by

* Except the proclamation which, Sir Thomas says, appeared to have been prepared before hand. The death of Hastings, I allow, is the fact of which we are most sure, without knowing the immediate motives: we must conclude it was determined on his opposing Richard's claim, farther we do not know, nor whether that opposition was made in a legal or hostile manner. It is impossible to believe that, an hour before his death, he should have exulted in the deaths of their common enemies, and vaunted, as Sir Thomas More asserts, his connection with Richard, if he was then actually at variance with him; nor that Richard should, without provocation, have massacred so excellent an accomplice. This story, therefore, must be left in the dark, as we find it. (W)

Richard? And though Sir Thomas again draws aside our attention by the penance of Jane, which she certainly underwent, it is no kind of proof that the protector accused the queen of having plotted with mistress Shore. What relates to that unhappy fair one I shall examine at the end of this work.

The very day on which Hastings was executed, were beheaded Earl Rivers, Lord Richard Grey, Vaughan, and Hawte. These executions are indubitable; were consonant to the manners and violence of the age; and perhaps justifiable by that wicked code, state necessity. I have never pretended to deny them, because I find them fully authenticated. I have in another* place done justice to the virtues and excellent qualities of Earl Rivers: let therefore my impartiality be believed, when I reject other facts, for which I can discover no good authority. I can have no interest in Richard's guilt or innocence; but as Henry the Seventh was so much interested to represent him as guilty, I cannot help imputing to the greater usurper, and to the worse tyrant of the two, all that appears to me to have been calumny and misrepresentation.

All obstacles thus removed, and Richard being solemnly instated in the throne by the concurrent voice of the three estates, 'He openly,' says Sir Thomas More, 'took upon him to be king the ninth day of June, and the morrow after was proclaimed, riding to Westminster with great state; and calling the judges before him, straitly commanded them to execute the laws without favour or delay, with many good exhortations, of the which he followed not one.'† This is an invidious and false accusation. Richard, in his

*In the Catalogue of Royal and Noble Authors, vol. 1. (W)
† Like the quotation on p. 186, this citation is drawn—carelessly—from the Hardyng/Hall interpolation in More's *History*. Walpole does not follow the exact wording; he also quotes 9 June as the date on which Richard was petitioned to take the crown, correcting the date to 25 June in a footnote—whereas Hardyng/Hall give 19 June!

regal capacity, was an excellent king, and for the short time of his reign enacted many wise and wholesome laws. I doubt even whether one of the best proofs of his usurpation was not the goodness of his government, according to a common remark, that princes of doubtful titles make the best masters, as it is more necessary for them to conciliate the favour of the people: the natural corollary from which observation need not be drawn. Certain it is that in many parts of the kingdom, not poisoned by faction, he was much beloved; and even after his death the northern counties gave open testimony of their affection to his memory.

On the Sixth of July Richard was crowned, and soon after set out on a progress to York, on his way visiting Gloucester, the seat of his former duchy. And now it is that I must call up the attention of the reader, the capital and bloody scene of Richard's life being dated from this progress. The narrative teems with improbabilities and notorious falsehoods, and is flatly contradicted by so many unquestionable facts, that if we have no other reason to believe the murder of Edward the Fifth and his brother, than the account transmitted to us, we shall very much doubt whether they ever were murdered at all. I will state the account, examine it, and produce evidence to confute it, and then the reader will form his own judgment on the matter of fact.

Richard, before he left London, had taken no measures to accomplish the assassination; but on the road, 'his mind misgave him that, his nephews living, men would not reckon that he could have right to the realm. . . . Whereupon he sent one John Green . . . unto Sir Robert Brakenbury, Constable of the Tower, with a letter and credence also that the same Sir Robert should in any wise put the two children to death. This John Green did his errand unto Brakenbury, kneeling before Our Lady in the Tower, who plainly answered that he would never put them to death, though he should die therefor.'* Green returned with this answer

* Sir T. More. (W)

to the king who was then at Warwick, wherewith he took such displeasure and thought, that the same night he said unto a secret page of his, 'Ah, whom shall a man trust? Those that I have brought up myself, those that I had thought would most surely serve me, even those fail me, and at my commandment will do nothing for me.' 'Sir,' quoth the page, 'there lies one on your pallet without that, I dare well say, to do your Grace pleasure, the thing would be right hard that he would refuse;' meaning by this Sir James Tyrell, whom, says Sir Thomas a few pages afterwards, as men say, he there made a knight. 'The man,' continues More, 'had a high heart and sore longed upwards, not rising yet so fast as he had hoped, being hindered and kept under by Sir Richard Ratcliffe and Sir William Catesby, who . . . kept him by secret drifts out of all secret trust.' To be short, Tyrell voluntarily accepted the commission, received warrant to authorize Brakenbury to deliver to him the keys of the Tower for one night; and having selected two other villains called Miles Forest and John Dighton, the two latter smothered the innocent princes in their beds, and then called Tyrell to be witness of the execution.

It is difficult to crowd more improbabilities and lies together than are comprehended in this short narrative. Who can believe if Richard meditated the murder, that he took no care to sift Brakenbury before he left London? Who can believe that he would trust so atrocious a commission to a letter? And who can imagine, that on★ Brakenbury's non-compliance Richard would have

★ It appears from the *Foedera* that Brakenbury was appointed Constable of the Tower July 7th; that he surrendered his patent March 9th of the following year, and had one more ample granted to him. If it is supposed that Richard renewed this patent to Sir Robert Brakenbury, to prevent his disclosing what he knew of a murder, in which he had refused to be concerned, I then ask if it is probable that a man too virtuous or too cautious to embark in an assassination, and of whom the supposed tyrant stood in awe, would have laid down his life in that usurper's cause, as Sir Robert did, being killed

ordered him to cede the government of the Tower to Tyrell for one night only, the purpose of which had been so plainly pointed out by the preceding message? And had such weak steps been taken, could the murder itself have remained a problem? And yet Sir Thomas More himself is forced to confess at the outset of this very narration that their 'death and final misfortune has nevertheless so far come in question, that some remain yet in doubt whether they were *in his days* destroyed or no.'* Very memorable words, and sufficient to balance More's own testimony with the most sanguine believers. He adds that these doubts not only arose from the uncertainty men were in whether Perkin Warbeck was the true Duke of York, but 'for that all things were in late days so covertly managed . . . that there was nothing so plain and openly proved but that yet . . . men had it ever inwardly suspect.' Sir Thomas goes on to affirm that he does not relate the story 'after every way that I have heard, but after that way which I have so heard by such men and by such means as methinks it were hard but it should be true.' This affirmation rests on the credibility of certain reporters, we do not know whom, but who we shall find were no credible reporters at all: for to proceed to the confutation. James Tyrell, a man in no secret trust with the king, and kept down by Catesby and Ratcliffe, is recommended as a proper person by a nameless page. In the first place Richard was crowned

---

on Richard's side at Bosworth, when many other of his adherents betrayed him? (W)

* This is confirmed by Lord Bacon: 'Neither wanted there even at that time secret rumours and whisperings (which afterwards gathered strength, and turned to great trouble) that the two young sons of King Edward the Fourth, or one of them (which were said to be destroyed in the Tower) were not indeed murdered, but conveyed secretly away, and were yet living.' *Reign of Henry the Seventh*. Again, 'And all this time it was still whispered every where that at least one of the children of Edward the Fourth was living.' (W)

at York (after this transaction) September 8th.* Edward the Fourth had not been dead four months, and Richard in possession of any power not above two months, and those very bustling and active: Tyrell must have been impatient indeed, if the page had had time to observe his discontent at the superior confidence of Ratcliffe and Catesby. It happens unluckily too, that great part of the time Ratcliffe was absent, Sir Thomas More himself telling us that Sir Richard Ratcliffe had the custody of the prisoners at Pontefract,† and presided at their execution there. But a much more unlucky circumstance is, that James Tyrell, said to be knighted for this horrid service, was not only a knight before, but a great or very considerable officer of the crown; and in that situation had walked at Richard's preceding coronation. Should I be told that Sir Thomas More did not mean to confine the ill offices done to Tyrell by Ratcliffe and Catesby solely to the time of Richard's protectorate and regal power, but being all three attached to him when Duke of Gloucester, the other two might have lessened Tyrell's credit with the duke even in the preceding reign; then I answer, that Richard's appointing him master of the horse on his accession had removed those disgusts, and left the page no room to represent him as ready through ambition and despondency to lend his ministry to assassination. Nor indeed was the master of the horse likely to be sent to supersede the constable of the Tower for one night only. That very act was sufficient to point out what Richard desired to, and did, it seems, transact so covertly.

That Sir James Tyrell was and did walk as master of the horse

* Richard III was crowned only once, on 6 July. The notion of a 'double coronation', first at Westminster, 6 July, and then at York, on 8 September, arises from the fact that at York, on 8 September, King Richard, in a splendid ceremony, had his young son Edward invested with the dignity of Prince of Wales. *Foedera* XII (1727), p. 200.

† The name of the town, spelled *Pontfret* in Middle English, was corrupted to *Pomfret* in the Elizabethan age (as in Shakespeare), and is today spelled *Pontefract*.

at Richard's coronation cannot be contested. A most curious, invaluable, and authentic monument has lately been discovered, the coronation-roll of Richard the Third. Two several deliveries of parcels of stuff are there expressly entered, as made to 'Sir James Tyrell, knight, master of the horse of our said sovereign lord the kyng.' What now becomes of Sir Thomas More's informers, and of their narrative, which he thought hard but must be true?

I will go a step farther, and consider the evidence of this murder, as produced by Henry the Seventh some years afterwards, when, instead of lamenting it, it was necessary for his majesty to hope it had been true; at least to hope the people would think so. On the appearance of Perkin Warbeck, who gave himself out for the second of the brothers, who was believed so by most people, and at least feared by the king to be so, he bestirred himself to prove that both the princes had been murdered by his predecessor. There had been but three actors, besides Richard who had commanded the execution, and was dead. These were Sir James Tyrell, Dighton, and Forest: and these were all the persons whose depositions Henry pretended to produce; at least of two of them, for Forest it seems had rotted piece-meal away; a kind of death unknown at present to the college. But there were some others, of whom no notice was taken; as the nameless page, Green, one Black Will or Will Slaughter who guarded the princes, the friar who buried them, and Sir Robert Brakenbury, who could not be quite ignorant of what had happened: the latter was killed at Bosworth, and the friar was dead too. But why was no inquiry made after Green and the page? Still this silence was not so impudent as the pretended confession of Dighton and Sir James Tyrell. The former certainly did avow the fact, and was suffered to go unpunished where-ever he pleased—undoubtedly that he might spread the tale. And observe these remarkable words of Lord Bacon, 'John Dighton, who it seemeth *spake best for the king*, was forewith set at liberty.' In truth, every step of this pretended discovery, as it stands in Lord Bacon, warns us to give no heed to it.

Dighton and Tyrell agreed both in a tale, *as the king gave out.* Their confession therefore was not publickly made, and as Sir James Tyrell too was suffered to live;* but was shut up in the Tower, and put to death afterwards for we know not what treason; what can we believe, but that Dighton was some low mercenary wretch hired to assume the guilt of a crime he had not committed, and that Sir James Tyrell never did, never would confess what he had not done; and was therefore put out of the way on a fictitious imputation? It must be observed too, that no inquiry was made into the murder on the accession of Henry the Seventh, the natural time for it, when the passions of men were heated, and when the Duke of Norfolk, Lord Lovel, Catesby, Ratcliffe, and the real abettors or accomplices of Richard, were attainted and executed. No mention of such a murder was made in the very act of parliament that attainted Richard himself, and which would have been the most heinous aggravation of his crimes.† And no prosecution of the supposed assassins was even thought of till eleven years afterwards, on the appearance of Perkin Warbeck. Tyrell is not named in the act of attainder to which I have had recourse; and such omissions cannot but induce us to surmise that Henry had never been certain of the deaths of the princes, nor ever interested himself to prove that both were dead, till he had great reason to

---

* It appears by Hall, that Sir James Tyrell had even enjoyed the favour of Henry; for Tyrell is named as captain of Guïsnes in a list of valiant officers that were sent by Henry, in his fifth year, on an expedition into Flanders. Does this look as if Tyrell was so much as suspected of the murder? And who can believe his pretended confession afterwards? Sir James was not executed till Henry's seventeenth year, on suspicion of treason, which suspicion arose on the flight of the Earl of Suffolk. Vide Hall's *Chronicle.* (W)

† There is a heap of general accusations alledged to have been committed by Richard *against Henry*, in particular of his having *shed infant's blood.* Was this sufficient specification of the murder of a king? Is it not rather a base way of insinuating a slander, of which no proof could be given? Was not it consonant to all Henry's policy of involving every thing in obscure and general terms? (W)

believe that one of them was alive. Let me add, that if the confessions of Dighton and Tyrell were true, Sir Thomas More had no occasion to recur to the information of his unknown credible informers. If those confessions were not true, his informers were not creditable.

Having thus disproved the *account* of the murder, let us now examine whether we can be sure that the murder was committed.

Of all men it was most incumbent on Cardinal Bourchier, Archbishop of Canterbury, to ascertain the fact. To him had the queen entrusted her younger son, and the prelate had pledged himself for his security—unless every step of this history is involved in falsehood. Yet what was the behaviour of the archbishop? He appears not to have made the least inquiry into the reports of the murder of both children; nay, not even after Richard's death: on the contrary, Bourchier was the very man who placed the crown on the head of the latter; and yet not one historian censures this conduct. Threats and fears could not have dictated this shameless negligence. Every body knows what was the authority of priests in that age; an archbishop was sacred, a cardinal inviolable. As Bourchier survived Richard, was it not incumbent on him to show, that the Duke of York had been assassinated in spite of all his endeavours to save him? What can be argued from this inactivity of Bourchier, but that he did not believe the children were murdered?

Richard's conduct in a parallel case is a strong presumption that this barbarity was falsely laid to his charge. Edward, Earl of Warwick, his nephew, and son of the Duke of Clarence, was in his power too, and no indifferent rival, if King Edward's children were bastards. Clarence had been attainted; but so had almost every prince who had aspired to the crown after Richard the Second. Richard, Duke of York, the father of Edward the Fourth and Richard the Third, was son of Richard, Earl of Cambridge, beheaded for treason; yet that Duke of York held his father's

[196]

attainder no bar to his succession. Yet how did Richard the Third treat his nephew and competitor, the young Warwick? John Rous, a zealous Lancastrian and contemporary, shall inform us; and will at the same time tell us an important anecdote, maliciously suppressed or ignorantly omitted by all our historians. Richard actually proclaimed him heir to the crown after the death of his own son, and ordered him to be served next to himself and the queen, though he afterwards set him aside, and confined him to the castle of Sheriff-Hutton. The very day after the battle of Bosworth, the usurper Richmond was so far from being led aside from attention to his interest by the glare of his new-acquired crown, that he sent for the Earl of Warwick from Sheriff-Hutton and committed him to the Tower, from whence he never stirred more, falling a sacrifice to the inhuman jealousy of Henry, as his sister, the venerable Countess of Salisbury, did afterwards to that of Henry the Eighth. Richard, on the contrary, was very affectionate to his family: instances appear in his treatment of the Earls of Warwick and Lincoln. The lady Ann Poole, sister of the latter, Richard had agreed to marry to the Prince of Scotland.

The more generous behaviour of Richard to the same young prince (Warwick) ought to be applied to the case of Edward the Fifth, if no proof exists of the murder. But what suspicious words are those of Sir Thomas More, quoted above, and unobserved by all our historians: *'Some remain yet in doubt,'* says he, *'whether they* (the children) *were in his* (Richard's) *days destroyed or no.'* If they were not destroyed *in his days*, in *whose* days were they murdered? Who will tell me that Henry the Seventh did not find, the eldest at least, prisoner in the Tower; and if he did, what was there in Henry's nature or character to prevent our surmizes going farther?

And here let me lament that two of the greatest men in our annals have prostituted their admirable pens, the one to blacken a great prince, the other to varnish a pitiful tyrant. I mean the two chancellors, Sir Thomas More and Lord Bacon. The most senseless stories of the mob are converted to history by the former; the latter is still more culpable; he has held up to the admiration of posterity, and what is worse, to the imitation of succeeding princes, a man whose nearest approach to wisdom was mean cunning; and has raised into a legislator, a sanguinary, sordid, and trembling usurper. Henry was a tyrannic husband, and ungrateful master; he cheated as well as oppressed his subjects, bartered the honour of the nation for foreign gold, and cut off every branch of the royal family, to ensure possession to his no title. Had he had any title, he could claim it but from his mother, and her he set aside. But of all titles he preferred that of conquest, which if allowable in a foreign prince, can never be valid in a native, but ought to make him the execration of his countrymen.

There is nothing strained in the supposition of Richard's sparing his nephew. At least it is certain *now*, that though he dispossessed, he undoubtedly treated him at first with indulgence, attention, and respect; and though the proof I am going to give must have mortified the friends of the dethroned young prince, yet it showed great aversion to cruelty, and was an indication that Richard rather assumed the crown for a season, than as meaning to detain it always from his brother's posterity. It is well known that in the Saxon times nothing was more common in cases of minority than for the uncle to be preferred to the nephew; and though bastardizing his brother's children was, on this supposition, double dealing: yet I have no doubt but Richard went so far as to insinuate an intention of restoring the crown when young Edward should be of full age. I have three strong proofs of this hypothesis. In the first place Sir Thomas More reports that the Duke of Buckingham in his conversations with Morton, after his defection from Richard, told the bishop that the protector's first proposal had been to take the crown, till Edward his nephew should attain the age of twenty-four years.* Morton was certainly

---

* Not in More's *History* (nor in Grafton's *Continuation* here reprinted); but taken from that portion of Hall's *Chronicle* which recounts Richard's reign from the point at which the *History* breaks off.

competent evidence of these discourses, and therefore a credible one; and the idea is confirmed by the two other proofs I alluded to; the second of which was, that Richard's son did *not* walk at his father's coronation. Sir Thomas More indeed says that Richard created him Prince of Wales on assuming the crown; but this is one of Sir Thomas's misrepresentations, and is contradicted by fact, for Richard did not create his son Prince of Wales till he arrived at York; a circumstance that might lead the people to believe that in the interval of the two coronations, the latter of which was celebrated at York, September 8th, the princes were murdered.

But though Richard's son did not walk at his father's coronation, Edward the Fifth probably did, and this is my third proof. I conceive all the astonishment of my readers at this assertion, and yet it is founded on strongly presumptive evidence. In the coronation roll itself is this amazing entry; 'To Lord Edward, son of late King Edward the Fourth, for his apparel and array, that is to say, a short gown made of two yards and three quarters of crimson cloth of gold, lined with two yards and three quarters of black velvet, a long gown made of six yards and a half of crimson cloth of gold lined with six yards of green damask, a short gown made of two yards and three quarters of purple velvet lined with two yards and three quarters of green damask, a doublet and a stomacher made of two yards of black satin, etc.' besides two foot cloths, a bonnet of purple velvet, nine horse harness, and nine saddle houses (housings) of blue velvet, gilt spurs, with many other rich articles, and magnificent apparel for his henchmen or pages.

Let no body tell me that these robes, this magnificence, these trappings for a cavalcade, were for the use of a prisoner. Marvellous as the fact is, there can no longer be any doubt but the deposed young king walked, or it was intended should walk, at his uncle's coronation. This precious monument, a terrible reproach to Sir Thomas More and his copyists, who have been silent on so public an event, exists in the great wardrobe; and is in the highest preservation; it is written on vellum, and is bound with the coronation rolls of Henry the Seventh and Eighth. These are written on paper, and are in a worse condition; but that of King Richard is uncommonly fair, accurate and ample. It is the account of Peter Courteys keeper of the great wardrobe, and dates from the day of King Edward the Fourth his death, to the feast of the purification in the February of the following year. Peter Courteys specifies what stuff he found in the wardrobe, what contracts he made for the ensuing coronation, and the deliveries in consequence. The whole is couched in the most minute and regular manner, and is preferable to a thousand vague and interested histories. The concourse of nobility at that ceremony was extraordinarily great: there were present no fewer than three Duchesses of Norfolk. Has this the air of a forced and precipitate election? Or does it not indicate a voluntary concurrence of the nobility? No mention being made in the roll of the young Duke of York, no robes being ordered for him, it looks extremely as if he was not in Richard's custody; and strengthens the probability that will appear hereafter, of his having been conveyed away.

There is another article, rather curious than decisive of any point of history. One entry is thus; 'To the lady Bridget, one of the daughters of King Edward the Fourth being seeke (sick) in the said wardrobe for to have for her use two long pillows of fustian stuffed with down, and two pillows of Holland cloth.' The only conjecture that can be formed from this passage is, that the lady Bridget, being lodged in the great wardrobe, was not then in sanctuary.

Can it be doubted now but that Richard meant to have it thought that his assumption of the crown was only temporary? But when he proceeded to bastardize his nephew by act of parliament, then it became necessary to set him entirely aside: stronger proofs of the bastardy might have come out; and it is reasonable to infer this, for on the death of his own son, when Richard had no

[200]

longer any reason of family to bar his brother Edward's children, instead of again calling them to the succession, as he at first projected or gave out he would, he settled the crown on the issue of his sister, Suffolk, declaring her eldest son the Earl of Lincoln his successor. That young prince was slain in the battle of Stoke against Henry the Seventh, and his younger brother the Earl of Suffolk, who had fled to Flanders, was extorted from the Archduke Philip, who by contrary winds had been driven into England. Henry took a solemn oath not to put him to death; but copying David rather than Solomon, he, on his death-bed, recommended it to his son Henry the Eighth to execute Suffolk; and Henry the Eighth was too pious not to obey so scriptural an injunction.

Strange as the fact was of Edward the Fifth walking at his successor's coronation, I have found an event exactly parallel which happened some years before. It is well known that the famous Joan of Naples was dethroned and murdered by the man she had chosen for her heir, Charles Durazzo. Ingratitude and cruelty were the characteristics of that wretch. He had been brought up and formed by his uncle Louis, King of Hungary, who left only two daughters. Mary the eldest succeeded and was declared *king*; for that warlike nation, who regarded the sex of a word, more than of a person, would not suffer themselves to be governed by the term *queen*. Durazzo quitted Naples in pursuit of new ingratitude; dethroned *king Mary*, and obliged her to walk at his coronation; an insult she and her mother soon revenged by having him assassinated.

I do not doubt but the wickedness of Durazzo will be thought a proper parallel to Richard's. But parallels prove nothing: and a man must be a very poor reasoner who thinks he has an advantage over me, because I dare produce a circumstance that resembles my subject in the case to which it is applied, and leaves my argument just as strong as it was before in every other point.

They who the most firmly believe the murder of the two princes, and from what I have said it is plain that they believe it more strongly than the age did in which it was pretended to be committed; urge the disappearance of the princes as a proof of the murder, but that argument vanishes entirely, at least with regard to one of them, if Perkin Warbeck was the true Duke of York, as I shall show that it is greatly probable he was.

With regard to the elder, his disappearance is no kind of proof that he was murdered: he might die in the Tower. The queen pleaded to the Archbishop of York that both princes were weak and unhealthy. I have insinuated that it is not impossible but Henry the Seventh might find him alive in the Tower. I mention that as a bare possibility—but we may be very sure that if he did find Edward alive there, he would not have notified his existence, to acquit Richard and hazard his own crown. The circumstances of the murder were evidently false, and invented by Henry to discredit Perkin; and the time of the murder is absolutely a fiction, for it appears by the roll of parliament, which bastardized Edward the Fifth, that he was then* alive, which was seven months after

---

* Buc asserts this from the parliament roll. The annotator in Kennett's collection says, 'this author would have done much towards the credit he drives at in his history, to have specified the place of the roll and the words thereof, whence such arguments might be gathered; for,' adds he, 'all histories relate the murders to be committed before this time.' I have shown, that *all histories* are reduced to one history, Sir Thomas More's; for the rest copy him verbatim; and I have shown that his account is false and improbable. As the roll itself is now printed in the parliamentary history, vol. 2. I will point out the words that imply Edward the Fifth being alive when the act was passed. 'Also it appeareth that *all* the issue of the said King Edward *be* bastards and unable to inherit or claim any thing by inheritance, by the law and custom of England.' Had Edward the Fifth been dead, would not the act indubitably have run thus, *were and be bastards*. No, says the act, *all* the issue *are* bastards. Who were rendered uncapable to inherit but Edward the Fifth, his brother and sisters? Would not the act have specified the daughters of Edward the Fourth, if the sons had been dead? It was to bastardize the brothers, that the act was calculated and passed; and as the words *all the issue* comprehend males and females, it is clear that both were intended to be bastardized. I must however, impartially observe that Philippe

the time assigned by More for his murder. If Richard spared him seven months, what could suggest a reason for his murder afterwards? To take him off then was strengthening the plan of the Earl of Richmond, who aimed at the crown by marrying Elizabeth, eldest daughter of Edward the Fourth. As the house of York never rose again, as the reverse of Richard's fortune deprived him of any friend, and as no contemporaries but Fabyan and the author of the Chronicle have written a word on that period, and they, too slightly to inform us, it is impossible to know whether Richard ever took any steps to refute the calumny. But we do know that Fabyan only mentions the deaths of the *princes* as *reports*, which is proof that Richard never declared their deaths or the death of either, as he would probably have done if he had removed them for his own security. The confessions of Sir Thomas More and Lord Bacon that many doubted of the murder, amount to a violent presumption that they were not murdered: and to a proof that their deaths were never declared. No man has ever doubted that Edward the Second, Richard the Second, and Henry the Sixth perished at the times that were given out. Nor Henry the Fourth, nor Edward the Fourth thought it would much help their titles to leave it doubtful whether their competitors existed or not. Observe too, that the Chronicle of Croyland, after relating Richard's second coronation at York, says, it was advised by

---

de Commynes says, Richard having murdered his nephews, degraded their two sisters in full parliament. I will not dwell on his mistake of mentioning *two* sisters instead of five; but it must be remarked, that neither brothers nor sisters being specified in the act, but under the general term of King Edward's issue, it would naturally strike those who were uncertain what was become of the sons, that this act was levelled against the daughters. And as Commynes did not write till some years after the event, he could not well help falling into that mistake. For my own part I know not how to believe that Richard would have passed that act, if he had murdered the two princes. It was recalling a shocking crime, and to little purpose; for as no woman had at that time ever sat on the English throne in her own right, Richard had little reason to apprehend the claim of his nieces. (W)

some in the sanctuary at Westminster to convey abroad some of King Edward's daughters, '*ut si quid dictis masculis humanitus in Turri contingerat, nihilominus per salvandas personas filiarum, regnum aliquando ad veros rediret hæredes.*'* He says not a word of the princes being murdered, only urges the fears of their friends that it might happen. This was a living witness, very bitter against Richard, who still never accuses him of destroying his nephews, and who speaks of them as living, after the time in which Sir Thomas More, who was not then five years old, declares they were dead. Thus the parliament roll and the chronicle agree, and both contradict More. '*Interim et dum hæc agerentur* (the coronation at York) *remansurant duo predicti Edwardi regis filii sub certa deputata custodia infra Turrim Londoniarum.*'† These are the express words of the chronicle.

As Richard gained the crown by the illegitimacy of his nephews, his causing them to be murdered, would not only have shown that he did not trust to that plea, but would have transferred their claim to their sisters. And I must not be told that his intended marriage with his niece is an answer to my argument; for were that imputation true, which is very problematic, it had nothing to do with the murder of her brothers. And here the comparison and irrefragability of dates puts this matter out of all doubt. It was not till the very close of his reign that Richard is even supposed to have thought of marrying his niece. The deaths of his nephews are dated in July or August 1483. His own son did not die till April 1484, nor his queen till March 1485. He certainly therefore did not mean to strengthen his title by marrying his niece to the disinherison of his own son; and having on the loss of that son, declared his nephew the Earl of Lincoln his successor, it is plain that he still trusted to the illegitimacy of his brother's children:

---

* 'So that, if anything happened to the princes in the Tower, the realm might yet, through the daughters, be returned some day to the true heirs.'
† 'Meantime, while these things were going on, the two sons of King Edward remained, in the custody of certain persons, within the Tower of London.'

and in no case possibly to be put, can it be thought that he wished to give strength to the claim of the Princess Elizabeth.

Let us now examine the accusation of his intending to marry that niece: one of the consequences of which intention is a vague suspicion of poisoning his wife. Buc says that the queen was in a languishing condition, and that the physicians declared she could not hold out till April; and he affirms having seen in the Earl of Arundel's library a letter written in passionate strains of love for her uncle by Elizabeth to the Duke of Norfolk, in which she expressed doubts that the month of April would never arrive. What is there in this account that looks like poison? Does it not prove that Richard would *nŏt* hasten the death of his queen? The tales of poisoning for a time certain are now exploded; nor is it in nature to believe that the princess could be impatient to marry him, if she knew or thought he had murdered her brothers. Historians tell us that the queen took much to heart the death of her son, and never got over it. Had Richard been eager to wed his niece, and had his character been as impetuously wicked as it is represented, he would not have let the forward princess wait for the slow decay of her rival; nor did he think of it till nine months after the death of his son; which shows it was only to prevent Richmond's marrying her. His declaring his nephew his successor, implies at the same time no thought of getting rid of his queen, though he did not expect more issue from her: and little as Buc's authority is regarded, a contemporary writer confirms the probability of this story. The Chronicle of Croyland says, that at the Christmas festival, men were scandalized at seeing the queen and the lady Elizabeth dressed in robes similar and equally royal. I should suppose that Richard learning the projected marriage of Elizabeth and the Earl of Richmond, amused the young princess with the hopes of making her his queen; and that Richard feared that alliance, is plain from his sending her to the castle of Sheriff-Hutton on the landing of Richmond.

[205]

The behaviour of the queen dowager must also be noticed. She was stripped by her son-in-law Henry of all her possessions, and confined to a monastery, for delivering up her daughters to Richard. Historians too are lavish in their censures on her for consenting to bestow her daughter on the murderer of her sons and brother. But if the murder of her sons is, as we have seen, most uncertain, this solemn charge falls to the ground: and for the deaths of her brother and Lord Richard Grey, one of her elder sons, it has already appeared that she imputed them to Hastings. It is much more likely that Richard convinced her he had not murdered her sons, than that she delivered up her daughters to him believing it. The rigour exercised on her by Henry the Seventh on her countenancing Lambert Simnel, evidently set up to try the temper of the nation in favour of some prince of the house of York, is a violent presumption that the queen dowager believed her second son living: and notwithstanding all the endeavours of Henry to discredit Perkin Warbeck, it will remain highly probable that many more who ought to know the truth, believed so likewise; and that fact I shall examine next.

It was in the second year of Henry the Seventh that Lambert Simnel appeared. This youth first personated Richard, Duke of York, then Edward, Earl of Warwick; and was undoubtedly an impostor. Lord Bacon owns that it was whispered every-where, that *at least one* of the children of Edward the Fourth was living. Such whispers prove two things; one, that the murder was very uncertain: the second, that it would have been very dangerous to disprove the murder; Henry being at least as much interested as Richard had been to have the children dead. Richard had set them aside as bastards, and thence had a title to the crown; but Henry was himself the issue of a bastard line, and had no title at all. Faction had set him on the throne, and his match with the supposed heiress of York induced the nation to wink at the defect in his own blood. The children of Clarence and of the Duchess of

Suffolk were living; so was the young Duke of Buckingham, legiti-
mately sprung from the youngest son of Edward the Third;
whereas Henry came of the spurious stock of John of Gaunt.
Lambert Simnel appeared before Henry had had time to disgust
the nation, as he did afterwards, by his tyranny, cruelty, and ex-
actions. But what was most remarkable, the queen dowager tam-
pered in this plot. Is it to be believed, that mere turbulence and a
restless spirit could in a year's time influence that woman to
throw the nation again into a civil war, and attempt to dethrone
her own daughter? And in favour of whom? Of the issue of Clarence, whom she had contributed to have put to death, or in favour
of an impostor? There is not common sense in the supposition.
No; she certainly knew or believed that Richard, her second son,
had escaped and was living, and was glad to overturn the usurper
without risking her child. The plot failed, and the queen dowager
was shut up, where she remained till her death, 'in prison, poverty,
and solitude.' The king trumped up a silly accusation of her having
delivered her daughters out of sanctuary to King Richard, 'which
proceeding,' says the noble historian,★ 'being even at that time
taxed for rigorous and undue, makes it very probable there was
some greater matter against her, which the king, upon reason of
policy, and to avoid envy, would not publish.' How truth sometimes escapes from the most courtly pens! What interpretation can
be put on these words, but that the king found the queen dowager
was privy to the escape at least or existence of her second son, and
secured her, lest she should bear testimony to the truth, and foment
insurrections in his favour? Lord Bacon adds, 'It is likewise
no small argument that *there was some secret in it*; for that the priest
Simon himself (who set Lambert to work) after he was taken, was
never brought to execution; no, not so much as to public trial, but
was only shut up close in a dungeon. Add to this, that after the
Earl of Lincoln (a principal person of the house of York) was slain
in Stokefield, the king opened himself to some of his council, that

★ Lord Bacon. (W)

[207]

he was sorry for the earl's death, because by him (he said) he might have known the bottom of his danger.'

The Earl of Lincoln had been declared heir to the crown by Richard, and therefore certainly did not mean to advance Simnel, an impostor, to it. It will be insinuated, and Lord Bacon attributes that motive to him, that the Earl of Lincoln hoped to open a way to the crown for himself. It might be so; still that will not account for Henry's wish, that the earl had been saved. On the contrary, one dangerous competitor was removed by his death; and therefore when Henry wanted to have learned *the bottom of his danger*, it is plain he referred to Richard, Duke of York, of whose fate he was still in doubt. He certainly was; why else was it thought dangerous to visit or see the queen dowager after her imprisonment, as Lord Bacon owns it was? 'For that act,' continues he, 'the king sustained great obloquy; which nevertheless (besides the reason of state) was somewhat sweetened to him by a great confiscation.' Excellent prince! This is the man in whose favour Richard the Third is represented as a monster!

'For Lambert, the king would not take his life,' continues Henry's biographer, 'both out of magnanimity' (a most proper picture of so mean a mind!) 'and likewise out of wisdom, thinking that if he suffered death he would be forgotten too soon; but being kept alive, he would be a continual spectacle, and a kind of remedy against the *like enchantments of people* in time to come.' What! do lawful princes live in dread of a possibility of phantoms! Oh! no; but Henry knew what he had to fear; and he hoped by keeping up the memory of Simnel's imposture, to discredit the true Duke of York, as another puppet, when ever he should really appear.

That appearance did not happen till some years afterwards, and in Henry's eleventh year. Lord Bacon has taken infinite pains to prove a second imposture; and yet owns, 'that the king's manner of showing things by pieces and by dark lights, hath so muffled it, that it hath left it almost a mystery to this day.' What has he left a mystery? and what did he try to muffle? Not the imposture, but the truth. Had so politic a man any interest to leave the matter doubtful? Did he try to leave it so? On the contrary, his diligence to detect the imposture was prodigious. Did he publish his narrative to obscure or elucidate the transaction? Was it his manner to muffle any point that he could clear up, especially when it behoved him to have it cleared? When Lambert Simnel first personated the Earl of Warwick, did not Henry exhibit that poor prince on a Sunday throughout all the principal streets of London? Was he not conducted to Paul's cross, and openly examined by the nobility? 'which did in effect mar the pageant in Ireland.' Was not Lambert himself taken into Henry's service, and kept in his court for the same purpose? In short, what did Henry ever muffle and disguise but the truth? and why was his whole conduct so different in the cases of Lambert and Perkin, if their cases were not totally different? No doubt remains on the former; the gross falsehoods and contradictions in which Henry's account of the latter is involved, make it evident that he himself could never detect the imposture of the latter, if it was one. Dates, which every historian has neglected, again come to our aid, and cannot be controverted.

Richard, Duke of York, was born in 1474. Perkin Warbeck was not heard of before 1495, when Duke Richard would have been twenty-one. Margaret of York, Duchess dowager of Burgundy, and sister of Edward the Fourth, is said by Lord Bacon to have been the Juno who persecuted the pious Æneas, Henry, and set up this phantom against him. She it was, say the historians, and says Lord Bacon, 'who informed Perkin of all the circumstances and particulars that concerned the person of Richard, Duke of York, which he was to act, describing unto him the personages, lineaments, and features of the king and queen, his pretended parents, and of his brother and sisters, and divers others that were nearest him in his childhood; together with all passages, some secret, some common, that were fit for a child's memory, until the death of King Edward. Then she added the particulars of the time, from the king's death, until he and his brother were committed to the

Tower, as well during the time he was abroad, as while he was in sanctuary. As for the times while he was in the Tower, and the manner of his brother's death, and his own escape, she knew they were things that very few could control: and therefore she taught him only to tell a smooth and likely tale of those matters, warning him not to vary from it.' Indeed! Margaret must in truth have been a Juno, a divine power, if she could give all these instructions to purpose. This passage is so very important, the whole story depends so much upon it, that if I can show the utter impossibility of its being true, Perkin will remain the true Duke of York for any thing we can prove to the contrary; and for Henry, Sir Thomas More, Lord Bacon, and their copyists, it will be impossible to give any longer credit to their narratives.

I have said that Duke Richard was born in 1474. Unfortunately his aunt Margaret was married out of England in 1467, seven years before he was born, and never returned thither. Was not she singularly capable of describing to Perkin, her nephew, whom she had never seen? How well informed was she of the times of his childhood, and of all passages relating to his brother and sisters! Oh! but she had English refugees about her. She must have had many, and those of most intimate connexion with the court, if she and they together could compose a tolerable story for Perkin, that was to take in the most minute passages of so many years. Who informed Margaret, that she might inform Perkin of what passed in sanctuary? Ay; and who told her what passed in the Tower? Let the warmest asserter of the imposture answer that question, and I will give up all I have said in this work; yes, all. Forest was dead, and the supposed priest; Sir James Tyrell, and Dighton, were in Henry's hands. Had they trumpeted about the story of their own guilt and infamy, till Henry, *after* Perkin's appearance, found it necessary to publish it? Sir James Tyrell and Dighton had certainly never gone to the court of Burgundy to make a merit with Margaret of having murdered her nephews. How came she to know accurately and authentically a tale which no mortal else knew? Did Perkin or did he not correspond in his narrative with Tyrell and Dighton? If he did, how was it possible for him to know it? If he did not, is it morally credible that Henry would not have made those variations public? If Edward the Fifth was murdered, and the Duke of York saved, Perkin could know it but by being the latter. If he did not know it, what was so obvious as his detection? We must allow Perkin to be the true Duke of York, or give up the whole story of Tyrell and Dighton. When Henry had Perkin, Tyrell, and Dighton, in his power, he had nothing to do but to confront them, and the imposture was detected. It would not have been sufficient that Margaret had enjoined him *to tell a smooth and likely tale of those matters*. A man does not tell a likely tale, nor was a *likely* tale enough, of matters of which he is totally ignorant.

Still farther: why was Perkin never confronted with the queen dowager, with Henry's own queen, and with the princesses, her sisters? Why were they never asked? Is this your son? Is this your brother? Was Henry afraid to trust to their natural emotions? Yet 'he himself,' says Lord Bacon, 'saw him sometimes out of a window, or in passage.' This implies that the queens and princesses never did see him; and yet they surely were the persons who could best detect the counterfeit, if he had been one. Had the young man made a *voluntary*, coherent, and credible confession, no other evidence of his imposture would be wanted; but failing that, we cannot help asking why the obvious means of detection were not employed? Those means having been omitted, our suspicions remain in full force.

Henry, who thus neglected every means of confounding the impostor, took every step he would have done, if convinced that Perkin was the true Duke of York. His utmost industry was exerted in sifting to the bottom of the plot, in learning who was engaged in the conspiracy, and in detaching the chief supporters. It is said, though not affirmatively, that to procure confidence to his spies, he caused them to be solemnly cursed at Paul's cross. Certain it is, that, by their information, he came to the knowledge, not of the imposture, but of what rather tended to prove that Perkin was a genuine Plantagenet: I mean, such a list of great men actually in his court and in trust about his person, that no wonder he was seriously alarmed. Sir Robert Clifford, who had fled to Margaret, wrote to England, that he was positive that the claimant was the very identical Duke of York, son of Edward the Fourth, whom he had so often seen, and was perfectly acquainted with. This man, Clifford, was bribed back to Henry's service; and what was the consequence? He accused Sir William Stanley, Lord Chamberlain, the very man who had set the crown on Henry's head in Bosworth field, and own brother to the Earl of Derby, the then actual husband of Henry's mother, of being in the conspiracy? This was indeed essential to Henry to know; but what did it proclaim to the nation? What could stagger the allegiance of such trust and such connexions, but the firm persuasion that Perkin was the true Duke of York? A spirit of faction and disgust has even in later times hurried men into treasonable combinations; but however Sir William Stanley might be dissatisfied, as not thinking himself adequately rewarded, yet is it credible that he should risk such favour, such riches, as Lord Bacon allows he possessed, on the wild bottom of a Flemish counterfeit? The Lord Fitzwalter and other great men suffered in the same cause; and which is remarkable, the first was executed at Calais—another presumption that Henry would not venture to have his evidence made public. And the strongest presumption of all is, that not one of the sufferers is pretended to have recanted; they all died then in the persuasion that they had engaged in a righteous cause. When peers, knights of the garter, privy councellors, suffer death, from conviction of a matter of which they were proper judges (for which of them but must know their late master's son?) it would be rash indeed in us to affirm that they laid down their lives for an imposture, and died with a lie in their mouths.

What can be said against King James of Scotland, who bestowed a lady of his own blood in marriage on Perkin? At war with Henry, James would naturally support his rival, whether genuine or supposititious. He and Charles the Eighth both gave him aid and both gave him up, as the wind of their interest shifted about. Recent instances of such conduct have been seen; but what prince has gone so far as to stake his belief in a doubtful cause, by sacrificing a princess of his own blood in confirmation of it?

But it is needless to multiply presumptions. Henry's conduct and the narrative he published, are sufficient to stagger every impartial reader. Lord Bacon confesses *the king did himself no good* by the publication of that narrative, and that mankind was astonished to find no mention in it of the Duchess Margaret's machinations. But how could Lord Bacon stop there? Why did he not conjecture that there was no proof of that tale? What interest had Henry to manage a widow of Burgundy? He had applied to the Archduke Philip to banish Perkin: Philip replied, he had no power over the lands of the duchess's dowry. It is therefore most credible that the duchess had supported Perkin, on the persuasion he was her nephew; and Henry not being able to prove the reports he had spread of her having trained up an impostor, chose to drop all mention of Margaret, because nothing was so natural as her supporting the heir of her house. On the contrary, in Perkin's confession, as it was called, and which though preserved by Grafton, was suppressed by Lord Bacon, not only as repugnant to his lordship's account, but to common sense, Perkin affirms, that 'having sailed to Lisbon in a ship with the lady Brampton, who Lord Bacon says, was sent by Margaret to conduct him thither, and from thence having resorted to Ireland, it was at Cork that they of the town first threaped upon him that he was son of the Duke of Clarence; and others afterwards, that he was the Duke of York.' But the contradictions both in Lord Bacon's account, and in Henry's narrative, are irreconcileable and insurmountable: the former solves the likeness, which is allowing the likeness of Perkin to Edward the Fourth, by supposing that the king had an intrigue with his mother; of which he gives this silly relation: that Perkin Warbeck, whose surname it seems was Peter Osbeck, was son of a Flemish converted Jew (of which Hebrew extraction Perkin says not a word in his confession) who with his wife Katherine de Faro come to London on business; and she producing a son, King Edward, in consideration of the conversion, or intrigue, stood godfather to the child and gave him the name of *Peter*. Can one help laughing at being told that a king called *Edward* gave the name of *Peter* to his godson? But of this transfretation and christening Perkin, in his supposed confession, says not a word, nor pretends to have ever set foot in England, till he landed there in pursuit of the crown; and yet an English birth and some stay, though in his very childhood, was a better way of accounting for the purity of his accent, than either of the preposterous tales produced by Lord Bacon or by Henry. The former says, that Perkin, roving up and down between Antwerp and Tournai and other towns, and living much in English company, had the English tongue perfect. Henry was so afraid of not ascertaining a good foundation of Perkin's English accent, that he makes him learn the language twice over. 'Being sent with a merchant of Tournai, called Berlo, to the mart of Antwerp, the said Berlo set me,' says Perkin, 'to board in a skinner's house, that dwelled beside the house of the English nation. And after this the said Berlo set me with a merchant of Middelborough to service for *to learn the language*, with whom I dwelled from Christmas to Easter, and then I went into Portugal.' One does not learn any language very perfectly and with a good, nay, undistinguishable accent, between Christmas and Easter; but here let us pause. If this account was true, the other relating to the Duchess Margaret was false; and then how came Perkin by so accurate a knowledge of the English court, that he did not faulter, nor could be detected in his tale? If the confession was *not* true, it remains that it was trumped up by Henry, and then Perkin must be allowed the true Duke of York.

But the gross contradiction of all follows: 'It was in Ireland,' says Perkin, in this very narrative and confession, 'that against my will they made me to learn English, and taught me what I should do and say.' Amazing! what forced him to learn English, after, as he says himself in the very same page, he had learnt it at Antwerp! What an impudence was there in royal power to dare to obtrude such stuff on the world! Yet this confession, as it is called, was the poor young man forced to read at his execution—no doubt in dread of worse torture. Mr Hume, though he questions it, owns that it was believed by torture to have been drawn from him. What matters how it was obtained, or whether ever obtained; it could not be true: and as Henry could put together no more plausible account, commiseration will shed a tear over a hapless youth, sacrificed to the fury and jealousy of an usurper, and in all probability the victim of a tyrant, who has made the world believe that the Duke of York, executed by his own orders, had been previously murdered by his predecessor.

I have thus, I flatter myself, from the discovery of new authorities, from the comparison of dates, from fair consequences and arguments, and without straining or wresting probability, proved all I pretended to prove; not an hypothesis of Richard's universal innocence, but this assertion with which I set out, that we have no reasons, no authority for believing by far the greater part of the crimes charged on him. I have convicted historians of partiality, absurdities, contradictions, and falsehoods; and though I have destroyed their credit, I have ventured to establish no peremptory conclusion of my own. What did really happen in so dark a period, it would be rash to affirm. The coronation and parliament rolls have ascertained a few facts, either totally unknown, or misrepresented by historians. Time may bring other monuments to light: but one thing is sure, that should any man hereafter presume to repeat the same improbable tale on no better grounds than it has been hitherto urged, he must shut his eyes against conviction, and prefer ridiculous tradition to the scepticism due to most points of history, and to none more than to that in question.

I have little more to say, and only on what regards the person of Richard and the story of Jane Shore; but having run counter to a very valuable modern historian and friend of my own, I must both make some apology for him, and for myself for disagreeing with him. When Mr Hume published his reigns of Edward the Fifth, Richard the Third, and Henry the Seventh, the coronation roll had not come to light. The stream of historians concurred to make him take this portion of our story for granted. Buc had been given up as an advancer of paradoxes, and nobody but Carte had dared to controvert the popular belief. Mr Hume treats Carte's doubts as whimsical: I wonder, he did; he, who having so closely examined our history, had discovered how very fallible many of its authorities are. Mr Hume himself had ventured to contest both the flattering picture drawn of Edward the First, and those ignominious portraits of Edward the Second and Richard the Second. He had discovered from the *Foedera*, that Edward the Fourth, while said universally to be prisoner to Archbishop Nevil, was at full liberty and doing acts of royal power. Why was it whimsical in Carte to exercise the same spirit of criticism? Mr Hume could not but know how much the characters of princes are liable to be flattered or misrepresented. It is of little importance to the world, to Mr Hume, or to me, whether Richard's story is fairly told or not: and in this amicable discussion I have no fear of offending him by disagreeing with him. His abilities and sagacity do not rest on the shortest reign in our annals. I shall therefore attempt to give answers to the questions on which he pins the credibility due to the history of Richard.

The questions are these. 1. Had not the queen-mother and the other heads of the York party been fully assured of the death of both the young princes, would they have agreed to call over the Earl of Richmond, the head of the Lancastrian party, and marry him to the Princess Elizabeth?—I answer, that when the queen-mother could recall that consent, and send to her son the Marquess Dorset to quit Richmond, assuring him of King Richard's favour to him and her house, it is impossible to say what so weak and ambitious a woman would not do. She wanted to have some one of her children on the throne, in order to recover her own power. She first engaged her daughter to Richmond and then to Richard. She might not know what was become of her sons; and yet that is no proof they were murdered. They were out of her power, whatever was become of them; and she was impatient to rule. If she was fully assured of their deaths, could Henry, after he came to the crown and had married her daughter, be uncertain of it? I have shown that both Sir Thomas More and Lord Bacon own it remained uncertain, and that Henry's account could not be true. As to the heads of the Yorkists; how does it appear they concurred in the projected match? Indeed who were the heads of that party? Margaret, Duchess of Burgundy, Elizabeth, Duchess of Suffolk, and her children; did they ever concur in that match? Did not they to the end endeavour to defeat and overturn it? I hope Mr Hume will not call Bishop Morton, the Duke of Buckingham, and Margaret, Countess of Richmond, chiefs of the Yorkists.

2. The story told constantly by Perkin of his escape is utterly incredible, that those who were sent to murder his brother, took pity on him and granted him his liberty.—Answer. We do not know but from Henry's narrative and the Lancastrian historians that Perkin gave this account. I am not authorized to believe he did, because I find no authority for the murder of the elder brother; and if there was, why is it utterly incredible that the younger should have been spared?

3. What became of him during the course of seven years from his supposed death till his appearance in 1491?—Answer. Does uncertainty of where a man has been, prove his non-identity when he appears again? When Mr Hume will answer half the questions in this work, I will tell him where Perkin was during those seven years.

4. Why was not the queen-mother, the Duchess of Burgundy, and the other friends of the family, applied to, during that time,

for his support and education?—Answer. Who knows that they were not applied to? The probability is, that they were. The queen's dabbling in the affair of Simnel indicates that she knew her son was alive. And when the Duchess of Burgundy is accused of setting Perkin to work, it is amazing that she should be quoted as knowing nothing about him.

5. Though the Duchess of Burgundy at last acknowledged him for her nephew, she had lost all pretence to authority by her former acknowledgement and support of Lambert Simnel, an avowed impostor.—Answer. Mr Hume here makes an unwary confession by distinguishing between Lambert Simnel, an avowed impostor, and Perkin, whose imposture was problematic. But if he was a true prince, the duchess could only forfeit credit for herself, not for him: nor would her preparing the way for her nephew, by first playing off and feeling the ground by a counterfeit, be an imputation on her, but rather a proof of her wisdom and tenderness. Impostors are easily detected; as Simnel was. All Henry's art and power could never verify the cheat of Perkin; and if the latter was astonishingly adroit, the king was ridiculously clumsy.

6. Perkin himself confessed his imposture more than once, and read his confession to the people, and renewed his confession at the foot of the gibbet on which he was executed.—Answer. I have shown that this confession was such an awkward forgery that Lord Bacon did not dare to quote or adhere to it, but invented a new story, more specious, but equally inconsistent with probability.

7. After Henry the Eighth's accession, the titles of the houses of York and Lancaster were fully confounded, and there was no longer any necessity for defending Henry the Seventh and his title; yet all the historians of that time, when the events were recent, some of these historians, such as Sir Thomas More, of the highest authority, agree in treating Perkin as an impostor.— Answer. When Sir Thomas More wrote, Henry the Seventh was still alive; that argument therefore falls entirely to the ground:

but there *was* great necessity, I will not say to defend, but even to palliate the titles of both Henry the Seventh and Eighth. The former, all the world agrees now, had no title: the latter had none from his father, and a very defective one from his mother. If she had any right, it could only be after her brothers; and it is not to be supposed that so jealous a tyrant as Henry the Eighth would suffer it to be said that his father and mother enjoyed the throne to the prejudice of that mother's surviving brother, in whose blood the father had imbrued his hands. The murder therefore was to be fixed on Richard the Third, who was to be supposed to have usurped the throne, by murdering, and not, as was really the case, by bastardizing his nephews. If they were illegitimate, so was their sister; and if she was, what title had she conveyed to her son Henry the Eighth? No wonder that both Henrys were jealous of the Earl of Suffolk, whom one bequeathed to slaughter, and the other executed; for if the children of Edward the Fourth were spurious, and those of Clarence attainted, the right of the house of York was vested in the Duchess of Suffolk and her descendants. The massacre of the children of Clarence and the Duchess of Suffolk show what Henry the Eighth thought of the titles both of his father and mother. But, says Mr Hume, all the historians of that time agree in treating Perkin as an impostor. I have shown from their own mouths that they all doubted of it. The reader must judge between us. But Mr Hume selects Sir Thomas More as the highest authority; I have proved that he was the lowest—but not in the case of Perkin, for Sir Thomas More's history does not go so low; yet happening to mention him, he says, the man, commonly called Perkin Warbeck, was, as well with the princes as the people, held to be the younger son of Edward the Fourth; and that the deaths of the young King Edward and of Richard his brother had come so far in question, as some are yet in doubt, *whether they were destroyed or no in the days of king* Richard. Sir Thomas adhered to the affirmative, relying as I have shown on very bad authorities. But what is a stronger argument *ad hominem*, I can prove that Mr Hume did not think Sir Thomas More good authority; no, Mr Hume was a fairer and more impartial judge: at the very time that he quotes Sir Thomas More, he tacitly rejects his authority; for Mr Hume, agreeably to truth, specifies the lady Eleanor Butler as the person to whom King Edward was contracted, and not Elizabeth Lucy, as it stands in Sir Thomas More. An attempt to vindicate Richard will perhaps no longer be thought whimsical, when so very acute a reasoner as Mr Hume could find no better foundation than these seven queries on which to rest his condemnation.

With regard to the person of Richard, it appears to have been as much misrepresented as his actions. Philippe de Commynes, who was very free spoken even on his own masters, and therefore not likely to spare a foreigner, mentions the beauty of Edward the Fourth; but says nothing of the deformity of Richard, though he saw them together. This is merely negative. The old Countess of Desmond, who had danced with Richard, declared he was the handsomest man in the room except his brother Edward, and was very well made. But what shall we say to Dr Shaa, who in his sermon appealed to the people, whether Richard was not the express image of his father's person, who was neither ugly nor deformed? Not all the protector's power could have kept the muscles of the mob in awe, and prevented their laughing at so ridiculous an apostrophe, had Richard been a little, crooked, withered, humpback'd monster, as later historians would have us believe—and very idly. Cannot a foul soul inhabit a fair body?

The truth I take to have been this. Richard, who was slender and not tall, had one shoulder a little higher than the other: a defect by the magnifying glasses of party, by distance of time, and by the amplification of tradition, easily swelled to shocking deformity; for falsehood itself generally pays so much respect to truth as to make it the basis of its superstructures.

I have two reasons for believing Richard was not well made about the shoulders. Among the drawings which I purchased at

Vertue's sale was one of Richard and his queen, of which nothing is expressed but the out-lines. There is no intimation from whence the drawing was taken; but by a collateral direction for the colour of the robe, if not copied from a picture, it certainly was from some painted window; where existing I do not pretend to say: in this whole work I have not gone beyond my vouchers. Richard's face is very comely, and corresponds singularly with the portrait of him in the preface to the Royal and Noble Authors. He has a sort of tippet of ermine doubled about his neck, which seems calculated to disguise some want of symmetry thereabouts . . .*

My other authority is John Rous, the antiquary of Warwick-shire, who saw Richard at Warwick in the interval of his two coronations, and who describes him thus: '*Parvæ staturæ erat, curtam habens faciem, inæquales humeros, dexter superior, sinisterque inferior.*'† What feature in this portrait gives any idea of a monster? Or who can believe that an eye-witness, and so minute a painter, would have mentioned nothing but the inequality of shoulders, if Richard's form had been a compound of ugliness? Could a Yorkist have drawn a less disgusting representation? And yet Rous was a vehement Lancastrian; and the moment he ceased to have truth before his eyes, gave into all the virulence and forgeries of his party, telling us in another place, 'that Richard remained two years in his mother's womb, and came forth at last with teeth, and hair on his shoulders.' I leave it to the learned in the profession to decide whether women can go two years with their burden, and produce a living infant; but that his long pregnancy did not prevent the duchess, his mother, from bearing afterwards, I can prove; and could we recover the register of the births of her children, I should not be surprised to find, that, as she was a very fruitful woman, there was not above a year between the birth of

* Two prints of this very crude drawing were included in the first edition of Walpole's *Historic Doubts*, but are here omitted.
† 'He was of mean stature; he had a harsh face; his right shoulder was higher than his left.'

Richard and his preceding brother Thomas. However, an ancient bard, who wrote after Richard was born and during the life of his father, tells us,

> Richard liveth yet, but the last of all
> Was Ursula, to him whom God list call.

Be it as it will, this foolish tale, with the circumstances of his being born with hair and teeth, was coined to intimate how careful Providence was, when it formed a tyrant, to give due warning of what was to be expected. And yet these portents were far from prognosticating a tyrant; for this plain reason, that all other tyrants have been born without these prognostics. Does it require more time to ripen a foetus, that is, to prove a destroyer, than it takes to form an Aristides? Are there outward and visible signs of a bloody nature? Who was handsomer than Alexander, Augustus, or Louis the Fourteenth? and yet who ever commanded the spilling of more human blood?

Having mentioned John Rous, it is necessary I should say something more of him, as he lived in Richard's time, and even wrote his reign; and yet I have omitted him in the list of contemporary writers. The truth is, he was pointed out to me after the preceding sheets were finished; and upon inspection I found him too despicable and lying an author, even amongst monkish authors, to venture to quote him, but for two facts; for the one of which as he was an eye-witness, and for the other, as it was of public notoriety, he is competent authority.

The first is his description of the person of Richard; the second, relating to the young Earl of Warwick, I have recorded in its place.

This John Rous, so early as in the reign of Edward the Fourth, had retired to the hermitage of Guy's Cliff, where he was a chantry priest, and where he spent the remaining part of his life in what he called studying and writing antiquities. Amongst other works, most of which are *not* unfortunately lost, he composed a history of the kings of England. It begins with the creation, and is compiled indiscriminately from the Bible and from monastic writers. Moses, he tells us, does not mention all the cities founded before the deluge, but Barnard de Breydenback, Dean of Mayence, does. With the same taste he acquaints us, that, though the Book of Genesis says nothing of the matter, Giraldus Cambrensis writes, that Caphera or Cesara, Noah's niece, being apprehensive of the deluge, set out for Ireland, where, with three men and fifty women, she arrived safe with one ship, the rest perishing in the general destruction.

A history, so happily begun, never falls off: prophesies, omens, judgments, and religious foundations compose the bulk of the book. The lives and actions of our monarchs, and the great events of their reigns, seemed to the author to deserve little place in a history of England. The lives of Henry the Sixth and Edward the Fourth, though the author lived under both, take up but two pages in octavo, and that of Richard the Third, three. We may judge how qualified such an author was to clear up a period so obscure, or what secrets could come to his knowledge at Guy's Cliff: accordingly he retails all the vulgar reports of the times; as that Richard poisoned his wife, and put his nephews to death, though he owns few knew in what manner; but as he lays the scene of their deaths *before* Richard's assumption of the crown, it is plain he was the worst informed of all. To Richard he ascribes the death of Henry the Sixth; and adds, that many persons believed he executed the murder with his own hands: but he records another circumstance that alone must weaken all suspicion of Richard's guilt in that transaction. Richard not only caused the body to be removed from Chertsey, and solemnly interred at Windsor, but it was publicly exposed, and, if we will believe the monk, was found almost entire, and emitted a gracious perfume, though no care had been taken to embalm it. Is it credible that Richard, if the murderer, would have exhibited this unnecessary mummery, only to revive the memory of his own guilt? Was it not rather intended to recall the cruelty of his brother Edward, whose children he had set aside, and whom by the comparison of this act of piety, he hoped to depreciate in the eyes of the people? The very example had been pointed out to him by Henry the Fifth, who bestowed a pompous funeral on Richard the Second, murdered by order of his father.

Indeed the devotion of Rous to that Lancastrian saint, Henry the Sixth, seems chiefly to engross his attention, and yet it draws him into a contradiction; for having said that the murder of Henry the Sixth had made Richard detested by all nations who heard of it, he adds, two pages afterwards, that an embassy arrived at Warwick (while Richard kept his court there) from the King of Spain, to propose a marriage between their children. Of this embassy Rous is a proper witness: Guy's Cliff, I think, is but four miles from Warwick; and he is too circumstantial on what passed there not to have been on the spot. In other respects he seems inclined to be impartial, recording several good and generous acts of Richard.

But there is one circumstance, which, besides the weakness and credulity of the man, renders his testimony exceedingly suspicious. After having said, that, *if he may speak truth in* Richard's *favour*, he must own that, though small in stature and strength, Richard was a noble knight, and defended himself to the last breath with eminent valour, the monk suddenly turns, and apostrophizes Henry the Seventh, to whom he had dedicated his work, and whom he flatters to the best of his poor abilities; but, above all things, for having bestowed the name of Arthur on his eldest son, who, this injudicious and over-hasty prophet foresees, will restore the glory of his great ancestor of the same name. Had Henry christened his second son Merlin, I do not doubt but poor Rous would have had still more divine visions about Henry the Eighth, though born to shake half the pillars of credulity.

In short, no reliance can be had on an author of such a frame of mind, so removed from the scene of action, and so devoted to the Welsh intruder on the throne. Super-added to this incapacity and defects, he had prejudices or attachments of a private nature: he had singular affection for the Beauchamps, Earls of Warwick, zealous Lancastrians, and had written their lives. One capital crime that he imputes to Richard is the imprisonment of his mother-in-law, Ann Beauchamp, Countess of Warwick, mother of his queen. It does seem that this great lady was very hardly treated; but I have shown from the Chronicle of Croyland, that it was Edward the Fourth, not Richard, that stripped her of her possessions. She was widow too of that turbulent Warwick, the king-maker; and Henry the Seventh bore witness that she was faithfully loyal to Henry the Sixth. Still it seems extraordinary that the queen did not or could not obtain the enlargement of her mother. When Henry the Seventh attained the crown, she recovered her liberty and vast estates: yet young as his majesty was both in years and avarice, for this munificence took place in his third year, still he gave evidence of the falsehood and rapacity of his nature; for though by act of parliament he cancelled the former act that had deprived her, *as against all reason, conscience, and course of nature, and contrary to the laws of God and man*, and restored her possessions to her, this was but a farce, and like his wonted hypocrisy; for the very same year he obliged her to convey the whole estate to him, leaving her nothing but the manor of Sutton for her maintenance. Richard had married her daughter; but what claim had Henry to her inheritance? This attachment of Rous to the house of Beauchamp, and the dedication of his work to Henry, would make his testimony most suspicious, even if he had guarded his work within the rules of probability, and not rendered it a contemptible legend.

Every part of Richard's story is involved in obscurity: we neither know what natural children he had, nor what became of them. Sandford says, he had a daughter called Katherine, whom William Herbert, Earl of Huntingdon, covenanted to marry, and to make her a fair and sufficient estate of certain of his manors to the yearly value of £200 over and above all charges. As this lord received a confirmation of his title from Henry the Seventh, no doubt the poor young lady would have been sacrificed to that interest. But Dugdale seems to think she died before the nuptials were consummated: 'whether this marriage took effect or not I cannot say; for sure it is that she died in her tender years.' Drake affirms, that Richard knighted at York a natural son called Richard of Gloucester, and supposes it to be the same person of whom Peck has preserved so extraordinary an account. But never was a supposition worse grounded. The relation given by the latter of himself, was, that he never saw the king till the night before the battle of Bosworth; and that the king had not then acknowledged, but intended to acknowledge him, if victorious. The deep privacy in which this person had lived, demonstrates how severely the persecution had raged against all that were connected with Richard, and how little truth was to be expected from the writers on the other side. Nor could Peck's Richard Plantagenet be the same person with Richard of Gloucester, for the former was never known till he discovered himself to Sir Thomas Moyle; and Hall says that King Richard's natural son was in the hands of Henry the Seventh. Buc says, that Richard made his son Richard of Gloucester, Captain of Calais; but it appears from Rymer's *Foedera*, that Richard's natural son, who was Captain of Calais, was called John. None of these accounts accord with Peck's; nor, for want of knowing his mother, can we guess why King Richard was more secret on the birth of this son (if Peck's Richard Plantagenet was truly so) than on those of his other natural children.* Perhaps the truest remark that can be made on this whole story is, that the avidity with which our historians swallowed one gross ill-concocted legend,

* In this passage Walpole refers to the following writers and their works: Francis Sandford (1630–94), herald and genealogist, *A Genealogical History of the Kings of England*, 1677; Sir William Dugdale (1605–86), Garter King of Arms, *The Baronage of England*, 3 vols, 1675–6; Francis Drake (1696–1771), a surgeon of York, *Eboracum, or the History and Antiquities of the City of York*, 1736.

prevented them from desiring or daring to sift a single part of it. If crumbs of truth are mingled with it, at least they are now undistinguishable in such a mass of error and improbability.

It is evident from the conduct of Shakespeare, that the house of Tudor retained all their Lancastrian prejudices, even in the reign of Queen Elizabeth. In his play of Richard the Third, he seems to deduce the woes of the house of York from the curses which Queen Margaret had vented against them; and he could not give that weight to her curses, without supposing a right in her to utter them. This indeed is the authority which I do not pretend to combat. Shakespeare's immortal scenes will exist, when such poor arguments as mine are forgotten. Richard at least will be tried and executed on the stage, when his defence remains on some obscure shelf of a library. But while these pages may excite the curiosity of a day, it may not be unentertaining to observe, that there is another of Shakespeare's plays, that may be ranked among the historic, though not one of his numerous critics and commentators have discovered the drift of it; I mean *The Winter Evening's Tale*, which was certainly intended (in compliment to Queen Elizabeth) as an indirect apology for her mother Anne Boleyn. The address of the poet appears no where to more advantage. The subject was too delicate to be exhibited on the stage without a veil; and it was too recent, and touched the queen too nearly, for the bard to have ventured so home an allusion on any other ground than compliment. The unreasonable jealousy of Leontes, and his violent conduct in consequence, form a true portrait of Henry the Eighth, who generally made the law the engine of his boisterous passions. Not only the general plan of the story is most applicable, but several passages are so marked, that they touch the real history nearer than the fable. Hermione on her trial says,

— for honour,
'Tis a derivative from me to mine,
And only that I stand for.

This seems to be taken from the very letter of Anne Boleyn to the king before her execution, where she pleads for the infant princess his daughter. Mamillius, the young prince, an unnecessary character, dies in his infancy; but it confirms the allusion, as Queen Anne, before Elizabeth, bore a still-born son. But the most striking passage, and which had nothing to do in the tragedy, but as it pictured Elizabeth, is, where Paulina, describing the new-born princess, and her likeness to her father, says, *she has the very trick of his frown.* There is one sentence indeed so applicable, both to Elizabeth and her father, that I should suspect the poet inserted it after her death. Paulina, speaking of the child, tells the king,

— 'Tis yours;
And might we lay the old proverb to your charge,
So like you, 'tis the worse.—

The Winter Evening's Tale was therefore in reality a second part of *Henry the Eighth.*

With regard to Jane Shore, I have already shown that it was her connection with the Marquess Dorset, not with Lord Hastings, which drew on her the resentment of Richard. When an event is thus wrested to serve the purpose of a party, we ought to be very cautious how we trust an historian, who is capable of employing truth only as cement in a fabric of fiction. Sir Thomas More tells us, that Richard pretended Jane 'was of counsel with the Lord Chamberlain to destroy him, and when, in conclusion, no plausibility could he fasten upon these matters, then he laid heinously to her charge the thing that herself could not deny,' namely her adultery; 'And for this cause (as a godly continent prince, clean and faultless of himself, sent out of heaven into this vicious world for the amendment of men's manners) he caused the Bishop of London to put her to open penance.'

This sarcasm on Richard's morals would have had more weight, if the author had before confined himself to deliver nothing but the precise truth. He does not seem to be more exact in what relates to the penance itself. Richard, by his proclamation, taxed

Mistress Shore with plotting treason in confederacy with the Marquess Dorset. Consequently, it was not from detect of proof of her being accomplice with Lord Hastings that she was put to open penance. If Richard had any hand in that sentence, it was, because he *had* proof of her plotting with the marquess. But I doubt, and with some reason, whether her penance was inflicted by Richard. We have seen that he acknowledged at least two natural children; and Sir Thomas More hints that Richard was far from being remarkable for his chastity. Is it therefore probable, that he acted so silly a farce as to make his brother's mistress do penance? Most of the charges on Richard are so idle, that instead of being an able and artful usurper, as his antagonists allow, he must have been a weaker hypocrite than ever attempted to wrest a sceptre out of the hands of a legal possessor.

It is more likely that the churchmen were the authors of Jane's penance; and that Richard, interested to manage that body, and provoked by her connection with so capital an enemy as Dorset, might give her up, and permit the clergy (who probably had burned incense to her in her prosperity) to revenge his quarrel. My reason for this opinion is grounded on a letter of Richard extant in the Museum, by which it appears that the fair, unfortunate, and amiable Jane (for her virtues far outweighed her frailty) being a prisoner, by Richard's order, in Ludgate, had captivated the king's solicitor, who contracted to marry her. Here follows the letter:

Harl. MSS, No. 2378.

By the KING.

'Right reverend father in God, etc. Signifying unto you, that it is showed unto us, that our servant and solicitor, Thomas Lynom, marvellously blinded and abused with the late (wife) of William Shore, now being in Ludgate by oure commandment, hath made contract of matrimony with her (as it is said) and intendeth, to our full great marvel, to procede to the effect of the same. We for many causes would be sorry that he so should be disposed. Pray you

[229]

therefore to send for him, and in that you goodly may, exhort and stir him to the contrary. And if you find him utterly set for to marry her, and none otherwise will be advertised, then (if it may stand with the law of the church) We be content (the time of marriage deferred to our coming next to London) that upon sufficient surety found of her good conduct, you do send for her keeper, and discharge him of our said commandment by warrant of these, committing her to the rule and guiding of her father, or any other by your discretion in the mean season. Given, etc.

To the right reverend father in God, etc.

the Bishop of Lincoln, our Chancellor.'

It appears from this letter, that Richard thought it indecent for his solicitor to marry a woman who had suffered public punishment for adultery, and who was confined by his command—but where is the tyrant to be found in this paper? Or, what prince ever spoke of such a scandal, and what is stronger, of such contempt of his authority, with so much lenity and temper? He enjoins his chancellor to dissuade the solicitor from the match—but should he persist—a tyrant would have ordered the solicitor to prison too—but Richard—Richard, if his servant will not be dissuaded, allows the match; and in the mean time commits Jane—to whose custody?—Her own father's. I cannot help thinking that some holy person had been her persecutor, and not so patient and gentle a king. And I believe so, because of the salvo for the church: 'Let them be married,' says Richard, 'if it may stand with the law of the church.'

From the proposed marriage, one should at first conclude that Shore, the former husband of Jane, was dead; but by the king's query, whether the marriage would be lawful? and by her being called in the letter *the late wife of William Shore*, not *of the late William Shore*, I should suppose that her husband was living, and that the penance itself was the consequence of a suit preferred by him to the ecclesiastic court for divorce. If the injured husband ventured, on the death of Edward the Fourth, to petition to be separated from his wife, it was natural enough for the church to proceed farther, and enjoin her to perform penance, especially when they fell in with the king's resentment to her. Richard's proclamation and the letter above-recited seem to point out this account of Jane's misfortunes; the letter implying, that Richard doubted whether her divorce was so complete as to leave her at liberty to take another husband. As we hear no more of the marriage, and as Jane to her death retained the name of Shore, my solution is corroborated; the chancellor-bishop, no doubt, going more roundly to work than the king had done. Nor, however Sir Thomas More reviles Richard for his cruel usage of Mistress Shore, did either of the succeeding kings redress her wrongs, though she lived to the eighteenth year of Henry the Eighth. She had sown her good deeds, her good offices, her alms, her charities, in a court. Not one took root; nor did the ungrateful soil repay her a grain of relief in her penury and comfortless old age.

I have thus gone through the several accusations against Richard; and have shown that they rest on the slightest and most suspicious ground, if they rest on any at all. I have proved that they ought to be reduced to the sole authorities of Sir Thomas More and Henry the Seventh; the latter interested to blacken and misrepresent every action of Richard; and perhaps driven to father on him even his own crimes. I have proved that More's account cannot be true. I have shown that the writers, contemporary with Richard, either do not accuse him, or give their accusations as mere vague and uncertain reports: and what is as strong, the writers next in date, and who wrote the earliest after the events are said to have happened, assert little or nothing from their own information, but adopt the very words of Sir Thomas More, who was absolutely mistaken or misinformed.

For the sake of those who have a mind to canvass this subject, I will recapitulate the most material arguments that tend to disprove what has been asserted; but as I attempt not to affirm what *did* happen in a period that will still remain very obscure, I flatter myself that I shall not be thought either fantastic or paradoxical, for not blindly adopting an improbable tale, which our historians have never given themselves the trouble to examine.

What mistakes I may have made myself, I shall be willing to acknowledge; what weak reasoning, to give up: but I shall not think that a long chain of arguments, of proofs and probabilities, is confuted at once, because some single fact may be found erroneous. Much less shall I be disposed to take notice of detached or trifling cavils. The work itself is but an inquiry into a short portion of our annals. I shall be content, if I have informed or amused my readers, or thrown any light on so clouded a scene; but I cannot be of opinion that a period thus distant deserves to take up more time than I have already bestowed upon it.

It seems then to me to appear,

THAT Fabyan and the authors of the Chronicle of Croyland, who were contemporaries with Richard, charge him directly with none of the crimes, since imputed to him, and disculpate him of others.

THAT John Rous, the third contemporary, could know the facts he alledges but by hearsay, confounds the dates of them, dedicated his work to Henry the Seventh, and is an author to whom no credit is due, from the lies and fables with which his work is stuffed.

THAT we have no authors, who lived near the time, but Lancastrian authors, who wrote to flatter Henry the Seventh, or who spread the tales which he invented.

THAT the murder of Prince Edward, son of Henry the Sixth, was committed by King Edward's servants, and is imputed to Richard by no contemporary.

THAT Henry the Sixth was found dead in the Tower; that it

was not known how he came by his death; and that it was against Richard's interest to murder him.

THAT the Duke of Clarence was defended by Richard; that the parliament petitioned for his execution; that no author of the time is so absurd as to charge Richard with being the executioner; and that King Edward took the deed wholly on himself.

THAT Richard's stay at York on his brother's death had no appearance of a design to make himself king.

THAT the ambition of the queen, who attempted to usurp the government, contrary to the then established custom of the realm, gave the first provocation to Richard and the princes of the blood to assert their rights; and that Richard was solicited by the Duke of Buckingham to vindicate those rights.

THAT the preparation of an armed force under Earl Rivers, the seizure of the Tower and treasure, and the equipment of a fleet, by the Marquess Dorset, gave occasion to the princes to imprison the relations of the queen; and that, though they were put to death without trial (the only cruelty which is *proved* on Richard) it was consonant to the manners of that barbarous and turbulent age, and not till after the queen's party had taken up arms.

THAT the execution of Lord Hastings, who had first engaged with Richard against the queen, and whom Sir Thomas More confesses Richard was *loth to lose*, can be accounted for by nothing but absolute necessity, and the law of self-defence.

THAT Richard's assumption of the protectorate was in every respect agreeable to the laws and usage; was probably bestowed on him by the universal consent of the council and peers, and was a strong indication that he had then no thought of questioning the right of his nephew.

THAT the tale of Richard aspersing the chastity of his own

mother is incredible; it appearing that he lived with her in perfect harmony, and lodged with her in her palace at that very time.

THAT it is as little credible that Richard gained the crown by a sermon of Dr Shaa, and a speech of the Duke of Buckingham, if the people only laughed at those orators.

THAT there had been a precontract or marriage between Edward the Fourth and Lady Eleanor Talbot; and that Richard's claim to the crown was founded on the illegitimacy of Edward's children.

THAT a convention of the nobility, clergy, and people invited him to accept the crown on that title.

THAT the ensuing parliament ratified the act of the convention, and confirmed the bastardy of Edward's children.

THAT nothing can be more improbable than Richard's having taken no measures before he left London, to have his nephews murdered, if he had had any such intention.

THAT the story of Sir James Tyrell, as related by Sir Thomas More, is a notorious falsehood; Sir James Tyrell being at that time master of the horse, in which capacity he had walked at Richard's coronation.

THAT Tyrell's jealousy of Sir Richard Ratcliffe is another palpable falsehood; Tyrell being already preferred, and Ratcliffe absent.

THAT all that relates to Sir Robert Brakenbury is no less false: Brakenbury either being too good a man to die for a tyrant or murderer, or too bad a man to have refused being his accomplice.

THAT Sir Thomas More and Lord Bacon both confess that many doubted, whether the two princes were murdered in

Richard's days or not; and it certainly never was proved that they were murdered by Richard's order.

THAT Sir Thomas More relied on nameless and uncertain authority; that it appears by dates and facts that his authorities were bad and false; that if Sir James Tyrell and Dighton had really committed the murder and confessed it, and if Perkin Warbeck had made a voluntary, clear, and probable confession of his imposture, there could have remained no doubt of the murder.

THAT Green, the nameless page, and Will Slaughter, having never been questioned about the murder, there is no reason to believe what is related of them in the supposed tragedy.

THAT Sir James Tyrell not being attainted on the death of Richard, but having, on the contrary, been employed in great services by Henry the Seventh, it is not probable that he was one of the murderers. That Lord Bacon owning that Tyrell's confession did not please the king so well as Dighton's; that Tyrell's imprisonment and execution some years afterwards for a new treason, of which we have no evidence, and which appears to have been mere suspicion, destroy all probability of his guilt in the supposed murder of the children.

THAT the impunity of Dighton, if really guilty, was scandalous; and can only be accounted for on the supposition of his being a false witness to serve Henry's cause against Perkin Warbeck.

THAT the silence of the two archbishops, and Henry's not daring to specify the murder of the princes in the act of attainder against Richard, wears all the appearance of their not having been murdered.

THAT Richard's tenderness and kindness to the Earl of Warwick, proceeding so far as to proclaim him his successor, betrays no symptom of that cruel nature, which would not stick at assassinating any competitor.

THAT it is indubitable that Richard's first idea was to keep the crown but till Edward the Fifth should attain the age of twenty-four.

THAT with this view he did *not* create his own son Prince of Wales till after he had proved the bastardy of his brother's children.

THAT there is no proof that those children were murdered.

THAT Richard made, or intended to make, his nephew Edward the Fifth walk at his coronation.

THAT there is strong presumption from the parliament-roll and from the Chronicle of Croyland, that both princes were living some time after Sir Thomas More fixes the date of their deaths.

THAT when his own son was dead, Richard was so far from intending to get rid of his wife, that he proclaimed his nephews, first the Earl of Warwick, and then the Earl of Lincoln, his heirs apparent.

THAT there is not the least probability of his having poisoned his wife, who died of a languishing distemper: that no proof was ever pretended to be given of it; that a bare supposition of such a crime, without proofs or very strong presumptions, is scarce ever to be credited.

THAT he seems to have had no intention of marrying his niece, but to have amused her with the hopes of that match, to prevent her marrying Richmond.

THAT Buc would not have dared to quote her letter as extant in the Earl of Arundel's library, if it had not been there: that others of Buc's assertions having been corroborated by subsequent discoveries, leave no doubt of his veracity on this; and that that letter disculpates Richard from poisoning his wife; and only shows the impatience of his niece to be queen.

THAT it is probable the queen-dowager knew her second son was living, and connived at the appearance of Lambert Simnel, to feel the temper of the nation.

THAT Henry the Seventh certainly thought that she and the Earl of Lincoln were privy to the existence of Richard, Duke of York, and that Henry lived in terror of his appearance.

THAT the different conduct of Henry with regard to Lambert Simnel and Perkin Warbeck, implies how different an opinion he had of them; that, in the first case, he used the most natural and most rational methods to prove him an impostor; whereas his whole behaviour in Perkin's case was mysterious, and betrayed his belief or doubt that Warbeck was the true Duke of York.

THAT it was morally impossible for the Duchess of Burgundy at the distance of twenty-seven years to instruct a Flemish lad so perfectly in all that had passed in the court of England, that he would not have been detected in few hours.

THAT she could not inform him, nor could he know, what had passed in the Tower, unless he was the true Duke of York.

THAT if he was not the true Duke of York, Henry had nothing to do but to confront him with Tyrell and Dighton, and the imposture must have been discovered.

THAT Perkin, never being confronted with the queen-dowager, and the princesses her daughters, proves that Henry did not dare to trust to their acknowledging him.

THAT if he was not the true Duke of York, he might have been detected by not knowing the queens and princesses, if shown to him without his being told who they were.

THAT it is not pretended that Perkin ever failed in language, accent, or circumstances; and that his likeness to Edward the Fourth is allowed.

THAT there are gross and manifest blunders in his pretended confession.

THAT Henry was so afraid of not ascertaining a good account of the purity of his English accent, that he makes him learn English twice over.

THAT Lord Bacon did not dare to adhere to this ridiculous account; but forges another, though in reality, not much more credible.

THAT a number of Henry's best friends, as the lord chamberlain, who placed the crown on his head, knights of the garter, and men of the fairest characters, being persuaded that Perkin was the true Duke of York, and dying for that belief, without recanting, makes it very rash to deny that he was so.

THAT the proclamation in Rymer's *Foedera* against Jane Shore, for plotting with the Marquess Dorset, not with Lord Hastings, destroys all the credit of Sir Thomas More, as to what relates to the latter peer.

In short, that Henry's character, as we have received it from his own apologists, is so much worse and more hateful than Richard's, that we may well believe Henry invented and propagated by far the greater part of the slanders against Richard: that Henry, not Richard, probably put to death the true Duke of York, as he did the Earl of Warwick: and that we are not certain whether Edward the Fifth was murdered; nor, if he was, by whose order he was murdered.

After all that has been said, it is scarce necessary to add a word on the supposed discovery that was made of the skeletons of the two young princes, in the reign of Charles the Second. Two skeletons found in that dark abyss of so many secret transactions, with no marks to ascertain the time, the age of their interment, can certainly verify nothing. We must believe both princes died there, before we can believe that their bones were found there: and upon what that belief can be founded, or how we shall cease to doubt whether Perkin Warbeck was not one of those children, I am at a loss to guess.

As little is it requisite to argue on the grants made by Richard the Third to his supposed accomplices in that murder, because the argument will serve either way. It was very natural that they, who had tasted most of Richard's bounty, should be suspected as the instruments of his crimes. But till it can be proved that those crimes were committed, it is in vain to bring evidence to show who assisted him in perpetrating them. For my own part, I know not what to think of the death of Edward the Fifth: I can neither entirely acquit Richard of it, nor condemn him; because there are no proofs on either side; and though a court of justice would, from that defect of evidence, absolve him; opinion may fluctuate backwards and forwards, and at last remain in suspense.

For the younger brother, the balance seems to incline greatly on the side of Perkin Warbeck, as the true Duke of York; and if one was saved, one knows not how nor why to believe that Richard destroyed only the elder.

We must leave this whole story dark, though not near so dark as we found it: and it is perhaps as wise to be uncertain on one portion of our history, as to believe so much as is believed in all histories, though very probably as falsely delivered to us, as the period which we have here been examining.

INDEX